HYMN OF FREEDOM

Freedom has continually to be won, it cannot merely be possessed.
It comes as a gift but can only be kept with a struggle.
Gift and struggle are written into pages, hidden yet open.
You pay for freedom with all your being; therefore call this your
freedom, that paying for it continually you possess yourself anew.
Through this payment we enter history and touch her epochs.
Which way runs the division of generations, the division between those
who did not pay enough and those who had to pay too much?
On which side are we? And exceeding in so many self-determinations,
did we not outgrow our strength in the past? Are we upholding the
burden of history like a pillar with a crack still gaping?

Pope John Paul II[1]

HYMN OF FREEDOM

Celebrating and Living the Eucharist

MICHAEL L. GAUDOIN-PARKER

T&T CLARK
EDINBURGH

T&T CLARK LTD
59 GEORGE STREET
EDINBURGH EH2 2LQ
SCOTLAND

First published 1997

ISBN 0 567 08549 X

British Library Cataloguing-in-Publication Data
A catalogue record for this book is available from the British Library

Typeset by Waverley Typesetters, Galashiels
Printed and bound in Great Britain by Page Bros, Norwich

In gratitude to God
for
Louis Volpe
whose lifelong friendship
has taught me
to appreciate the truth that:

A person's freedom, far from being restricted
by this fidelity,
is secured
against every form of subjectivism
or relativism
and is made a sharer
in creative wisdom.[2]

Contents

Abbreviations   ix

Preface   Cardinal Edouard Gagnon PSS   xiii

A Pretext for Writing?   xv

PART I – QUEST FOR FREEDOM   1
1. *Freedom: A New Language?*   5

PART II – REVELATION AND GIFT OF FREEDOM   31
2. *Hope and Freedom: Evangelisation in View of the*
   Kingdom of God   35
3. *Truth and Freedom: Working for Freedom in the*
   Fourth Gospel   59
4. *Faith and Freedom: Proclamation of Christ's Revelation*
   in the Pauline Tradition   81

PART III – RESPONSE TO THE GIFT OF GOD   105
5. *Liturgy: The Dynamic Rhythm of Freedom in Christ's*
   Paschal Mystery   109
6. *Eucharistic Adoration: Extending the Grace of the Sacrifice*   141

CONCLUSION – FREEDOM: A NEW REALITY?   161
7. *The Spirit of Freedom*   165

Notes   181
Bibliography   223
Index of Names   235

Abbreviations

AAS	*Acta Apostolicae Sedis*
AG	*Ad Gentes* – Vatican II Decree on the Church's Missionary Activity
BT	*Basic Text* – for the 46th International Eucharistic Congress in Wroclaw, Poland (1997)
CA	*Centesimus Annus* – Encyclical Letter of Pope John Paul II
CCC	*The Catechism of the Catholic Church* (1993)
CL	*Christifideles Laici* – Post-synodal Apostolic Exhortation on the Calling and Mission of the Lay Faithful (Pope John Paul II)
CT	*Catechesi Tradendae* – Post-synodal Apostolic Exhortation on Catechesis (Pope John Paul II)
CTS	Catholic Truth Society (London)
CUA	Catholic University of America Press
CUP	Cambridge University Press
DLT	Darton, Longman & Todd
DM	*Dives in Misericordia* – Encyclical Letter (Pope John Paul II)
DO	The Divine Office
DS	Denzinger-Schönmetzer
DV	*Dei Verbum* – Vatican II Constitution on Divine Revelation
DVi	*Dominum et Vivificantem* – Encyclical Letter on the Holy Spirit (Pope John Paul II)
EM	*Eucharisticum Mysterium* – Instruction on the Eucharistic Mystery

EN   *Evangelii Nuntiandi* – Post-synodal Apostolic
          Exhortation on Evangelisation (Pope Paul VI)
EV   *Evangelium Vitae* – Encyclical Letter on the Value
          and Inviolability of Human Life (Pope John
          Paul II)
FC   *Familiaris Consortio* – Post-synodal Apostolic
          Exhortation on the Christian Family in the Modern
          World (Pope John Paul II)
Flannery   Austin Flannery OP (ed.), *Vatican Council II: The
          Conciliar and Post Conciliar Documents,* Dominican
          Publications, Dublin, 1975, cited unless otherwise
          indicated
GIRM   *General Instruction on the Roman Missal*
GS   *Gaudium et Spes* – Vatican II Constitution on the
          Church in the Modern World
ICEL   International Committee for English in the Liturgy
IEC   International Eucharistic Congress(es)
JB   Jerusalem Bible translation
JBC   Jerome Biblical Commentary
LE   *Laborem Exercens* – Encyclical Letter on Human
          Work (Pope John Paul II)
LG   *Lumen Gentium* – Vatican II Constitution on the
          Church
NRSV   New Revised Standard Version Bible translation
OL   *Orientale Lumen* – Apostolic Letter (Pope John
          Paul II)
OUP   Oxford University Press
PDV   *Pastores Dabo Vobis* – Post-synodal Apostolic
          Exhortation on the Formation of Priests in the
          Present   Day (Pope John Paul II)
PG   Patrologia Graeca (Migne)
PL   Patrologia Latina (Migne)
PLS   Patrologia Latina Supplementa
PO   *Presbyterorum Ordinis* – Vatican II Decree on the Life
          and Ministry of Priests
RH   *Redemptor Hominis* – Encyclical Letter (Pope John
          Paul II)
RM   *Redemptoris Mater* – Encyclical Letter (Pope John
          Paul II)

RMi	*Redemptoris Missio* – Encyclical Letter (Pope John Paul II)
RP	*Reconciliatio et Paenitentia* – Post-synodal Apostolic Exhortation on Reconciliation and Penance in the Mission of the Church Today (Pope John Paul II)
RSV	Revised Standard Version Bible translation
SC	*Sacrosanctum Concilium* – Vatican II Constitution on the Sacred Liturgy
S.C.	Sources Chrétiennes
SPCK	Society for Promoting Christian Knowledge
SRS	*Sollicitudo Rei Socialis* – Encyclical Letter (Pope John Paul II)
ST	*Summa Theologica*
TMA	*Tertio Millennio Adveniente* – Apostolic Letter (Pope John Paul II)
UR	*Unitatis Redintegratio* – Vatican II Decree on Ecumenism
UUS	*Ut Unum Sint* – Encyclical Letter on Commitment to Ecumenism (Pope John Paul II)
VS	*Veritatis Splendor* – Encyclical Letter on Certain Fundamental Questions of the Church's Moral Teaching (Pope John Paul II)

NOTE

In transliterating Greek characters into English letters the following practice has been adopted to distinguish certain lengthened vowels from open ones:

eta (long e)   = ē – whereas epsilon (short e) = e;
omega (long o) = ō – whereas omicron (short o) = o;
~ over upsilon   = ū.

Preface

For the International Eucharistic Congress in Wroclaw, Poland (1997), Pope John Paul II chose the theme of 'The Eucharist and Freedom'. An ecclesial event of worldwide interest such as this gives Catholics in Eastern Europe the occasion to show how the Eucharist has given them the strength to persevere in their faith amidst overt or subtle persecution and finally recover freedom. Real herosim was often required to make eucharistic celebrations possible. And it is surely Christ present in the tabernacle who was the source of such strength and perseverance.

But is there an essential connection between the Eucharist and freedom? And can a renewed eucharistic devotion preserve us from the new forms of servitude to which we are exposed in our climate of materialistic ideologies and propaganda?

In his new book Father Michael L. Gaudoin-Parker gives us elements that can lead us towards answers which are not superficial. In his previous writings he has accustomed us to rediscover the richness of the traditional Catholic doctrine of the eucharistic mystery. He leads us now 'towards celebrating and living the Eucharist' as a *Hymn of Freedom*.

Drawing on traditional and modern theology, scripture and literature, this author endeavours to illuminate the human desire for freedom and its relationship to our desire for God in religious experience: a double-edged desire which God initiates and brings to fullness in the Church through Christ's gift of the paschal sacrament of his sacrifice in the Eucharist.

This book consists of three parts: the first deals with the bankruptcy of Western thought resulting in individualism, the outcome of an overreliance on human reason, especially since the Enlightenment; the second turns to the Word of God as revealing and calling humanity to the depth of human freedom in his redemptive covenant relationship with creation; the third considers how the Church realises this relationship of freedom in a communal and personal way in worship of the eucharistic mystery.

The whole book is concerned with bringing out that in the face of a growing 'culture of death' today, the Eucharist offers the key to life, genuine liberation and social transformation.

This book thus offers a valid contribution to the reflection which more people every day deem necessary as we prepare for the third Christian millennium. It is the whole Church which the Holy Father invited to be spiritually present at the International Eucharist Congress in Wroclaw and to benefit from the theological debate this event stimulates. This makes Father Gaudoin-Parker's work more timely.

CARDINAL EDOUARD GAGNON PSS
President of the Pontifical Committee
for International Eucharistic Congresses

A Pretext for Writing?

All the best songs and poems have long ago been composed and sung many times over about freedom. All the best things have already been said and all the best sentences have already been written about it; all the best thoughts regarding this or any subject relating to so deep a yearning for a qualitatively deeper way of living have already been articulated in one way or another. The noble ideals of our heritage of freedom – whatever their origins, whether from tribal codes of behaviour or ancient systems of law, Graeco-Roman philosophy, Christian teaching or the dreams and aspirations of human beings from time immemorial – these ideals, which have given a particular shape to our heritage, are the foundations and supporting girders of the structure called 'civilisation'. Despite all this, however, one has the distinct impression that each successive generation is haunted both by a sense of yearning to experience freedom and also by a sense of anxiousness about what lies ahead of it. The evidence for this impression abounds: the screams and tears of the children and violated women in Bosnia-Herzegovina;[3] the suffering of oppressed peoples in the shanty towns of Brazil; the frustrated anger of the growing masses of the unemployed who are exploited by political and economic forces manipulated by a few . . . In the midst of such yearning and anxiousness there grow the seeds of responsibility for remaking 'that civilisation about which we dream, *the civilisation of love*'.[4]

The *pretext* for beginning this essay arises not only from an awareness of this impression, but also from something more

firm than the flimsiness of an impression: it springs from a
desire. Indeed, it arises out of something even more solid than
the possibilities of either the mistakenness or fluctuation of
human desire: it is suggested by the sense of conviction that
there exists an important need to examine the relationship
between the human desire for freedom and the divinely etched
longing in the human heart for God.

In the course of this essay I have borrowed extensively from
some of the best things written mentioned above. Since these
things form and *inform* almost the entire cluster of ideas,
values, beliefs and convictions which make up our heritage or
Christian cultural tradition, they are the rich *pre-texts* of this
essay in the sense of being both the inspiring motive and also
basis for it.

As the background of this essay consists in reference to and
examination, discussion, and employment of quotations from
many persons' enquiry, insights, reflections, ideas, etc., it is
worthwhile considering at the outset what function is served by
quotation. First of all, it must be recalled that the primary
meaning of idea (*eidos*) in antiquity is to do with a view of how
things appear – that is, how things show, disclose or present
themselves. This is rather different from the inverted sense of
the modern translation and usage of 'idea', which moves the
emphasis from the objective disclosure of the data or 'given' of
sense experience to the subjective notion which we form of
things either from the impact, impression, things make on us
or by the inventive skill of our imagination in imposing on
things our own 'ideas'.[5]

This modern subjective sense of emphasis regarding ideas is
implied in give-away expressions such as: *I think,* and, particularly, *I feel.* This move inwards, as will be considered in the first
part of this essay, is a clear indication of an attempt to achieve a
certain makeshift freedom in the way that we can control,
manipulate and dictate the way we consider and wish reality to
be. But instead of achieving a sense of authentic freedom, this
move only results in becoming checkmated, as it were, by the
dominant force of modern ideologies and every kind of self-
centredness. Ideologies and self-centredness offer nothing to
renew or liberate humanity but only exile us to the fringes of

being barely human in the penal settlement reserved for idolatry of ephemeral ideas and false value-systems. But as recent history has demonstrated, ideologies and self-centredness have introduced the direst consequences for human existence: the suffocation of any personal desire and initiative to be authentic persons and all expression of religious freedom in the gas chambers of Nazi Germany or the concentration camps of the totalitarian Communist régime. But so what's new about this? In every age self-centredness has occasioned terrible wars – even in the name of religion and freedom.

Every quotation is set in the context of a personal history. Behind it, so to speak, stands a person – and indeed the whole tradition of language received from, developed and used by living persons. Every quotation somehow witnesses, at least implicitly, to that personal struggle, which involves taking up the challenge and responsibility of plunging into the stream of human dialogue. Every quotation, indeed, reveals that this struggle is more than a matter of undertaking a tussle with ideas or striving to get the better of words to communicate those obscure depths underlying words, namely, our present emotions, the hopes of our imagination, the joys and pain lurking in our memories – and much more as well! Every quotation points to the great human adventure of penetrating into the depths of endeavouring to experience a freedom of communication, the fullness of which is the intimacy of communion not needing the words of speech. In the intimacy of this communion, our lives become bound paradoxically in the discovery of freedom. This discovery – like its fount and fullness, communion – is not a matter of human speech: it is an experience of that silence too deep for human words – the silence of the beginning in which God's Word called creation to share and enjoy his being, simply *being-in-love*.

The use of quotation and reference leads to the recognition of the value and, indeed, necessity of a sense of belonging to a cultural environment called 'tradition'. This belonging is more than a matter of mere passive submission to certain inherited prevailing ethical patterns of behaviour and ritual customs or of pining for what is past. It is quite different from self-indulgent nostalgia. It entails, rather, a positive discovery of the riches of

all that makes us aware of the religious dimension and quality
of being human – that dimension and quality of living worship
which reveals and makes us capable of realising freedom. The
Judaeo-Christian cultural and religious tradition of freedom is
intrinsically connected with the significance of worship, which
enables us to remember our enormous sense of indebtedness,
gratitude and the expression of praise or wonderment for the
gift and giftedness of life as coming from God through creation
and renewed through the work of redemption of Christ, the
Lord of history. This means nothing other than being in touch
with the Eucharist, the source and summit (*fons et culmen*) of
the deepest and ultimate dimension of freedom – that freedom
from our sinful clinging to ideas and every form of time-bound
condition. Pope John Paul II describes the condition of being
without a sense of continuity with tradition or eschatological
expectation of Christian hope as consisting in keeping us
'prisoners of the present'.[6] On another occasion he spoke of
that kind of spiritual 'amnesia' about one's origins and growth
which always constitutes the risk of cultural alienation.[7] Christ
gives his Spirit of freedom to do the truth, so that we are
enabled to remember with praise and thanksgiving, realise and
look forward at the same time to the kingdom of God. The
Holy Spirit, whom the Father sends, gathers and unites us to
celebrate the 'memorial' of Christ's work of redemption; he
transforms us to become of 'one mind and heart' with Christ
(cf. Acts 4:32; Rom. 12:1–2; Eph. 4:23; Phil. 2:5) with all with
whom we offer and share Christ's sacrifice, with all who have
gone before us 'marked with the sign of faith' and with all whose
faith is known to God alone, so that we may know the lasting joy
of being a 'living sacrifice of praise'.[8]

It is part of the joy of anyone who is aware of being a recipient
of such inherited riches – and especially of anyone who
acknowledges those of the Judaeo-Christian civilisation – to
desire to share them with others freely. The joy of this freedom
in sharing reflects in some feint way the generosity in which
past generations bequeathed their cultural heritage to the
world at large. Indeed, whatever has become common property
cannot be merely appropriated and jealously kept to oneself.
This is particularly the truth revealed, celebrated and lived in

the eucharistic mystery. For the freedom communicated by
Christ in this ultimate gift of generosity – the gift of himself –
both bespeaks and generates the spirit of generosity and the joy
of sharing our lives – that sharing which reflects the divine life
of the communion of saints in the new creation, where we are
called to experience 'the glorious freedom of the children of
God' (Rom. 8:21; cf. 1 Jn 3:1–3). The freedom to acknowledge,
that is, to appreciate the presence of others' words, deeds and
lives with praise and thanksgiving before God – not just to
know facts about them and to be able to cite their words – this
freedom is at the heart of the Church's life in its eucharistic
worship and communion. In so far as it teaches and acclaims
holiness, that is, the worth of being truly human, the Church is
Christ's instrument or means of promoting that depth of
freedom which is salvation.[9]

The *pretext* or motive for this undertaking, thus, consists in
seeking to explore how the human desire for freedom is related
to and, indeed, rooted in our common vocation to see and be
united with God. More precisely still, the focus of this essay is
concerned with discovering how human freedom is quite
uniquely realised through both encountering and responding
to the revelation of God's dynamic presence and action in
Christ's gift of the Eucharist, the mystery of faith. This focus
occupies the second and third parts of the endeavour in this
essay, which concludes with a section on the transformative
grace of contemplating God's love in the sacrament of Christ's
sacrifice.

Recently while preaching on St John's words about being
healed and made whole by looking at Christ crucified, the
source of the true grandeur and dimensions of human freedom
(cf. Jn 3:14f.; 8:28; 12:34), I turned and pointed to a large
crucifix in the sanctuary. It was bedecked by cobwebs which
were clearly visible to all in the shaft of sunlight which streamed
across it. Struck by this fact, I commented that evidently the
crucifix of this church had not been looked upon – or looked
after! – for some time or it would not be in the state it was . . .
Perhaps we avoid gazing at the Crucified, the supreme symbol
of disfigured humanity, because we fear to be confronted with
ourselves or because human suffering is too ghastly or, again,

because we do not want to face a God who freely assumed our suffering and by doing so transformed it through his immense love, which he presents in the gift of his reality in the Holy Eucharist. But, since we shirk facing the burden of reality, as the poet T.S. Eliot remarks on more than one occasion,[10] we seek to evade the stillness of the centre of freedom revealed by the Word of God. The result is only boredom with our sliding easily from one distraction to another.[11] Eliot warns that the facility or skill in employing a multiplicity of expressions, though seeming to express a freedom of thought and speech and though seeming to team with creative versatility, may often indicate no more than merely a compulsive concern for meaning for meaning's sake or an addiction to one's subjective ideas and points of view, rather than a genuine yearning for meeting and entering into the relationship of communion with the mystery of the Other. He emphasises that some depth of encounter with the transcendence of the Other is a necessary requirement for discovering the inner meaning of freedom and, hence, our own interior depths through freely confronting the challenge of facing human suffering.[12]

After seeing photographs of tortured victims of the Nazi concentration camps Graham Sutherland commented on the universal significance of Christ's crucifixion, which he translated into his painting hanging in the Tate Gallery, London: 'It is the most tragic of all themes yet inherent in it is the promise of salvation. It is the symbol of the precarious balanced moment, the hair's breath between black and white.'[13]

G.K. Chesterton saw the distinctive significance of Christ's cross:

> As we have taken the circle as the symbol of reason and madness, we may very well take the cross as the symbol at once of mystery and of health. Buddhism is centripetal, but Christianity is centrifugal: it breaks out. For the circle is perfect and infinite in its nature; but it is fixed for ever in its size; it can never be larger or smaller. But the cross, though it has at its heart a collision and a contradiction, can extend its four arms for ever without altering its shape. Because it has a paradox in its centre it can grow without changing. The circle returns upon itself and is bound. The cross opens its arms to the four winds; it is a signpost for free travellers.[14]

This Christian significance of the crucified Saviour's self-emptying offered Hans Urs von Balthasar a constant focus of meditation. As one of his recent exponents puts it:

> neither the austere, naked cross of Protestantism nor the stylized, glorious cross of Orthodoxy are fully expressive of that body nailed to the Cross which for Balthasar is God's answer to the problem of human suffering, to the ugliness and evil in the world. The answer is love, the Trinitarian love expressed once and for all in the Son and poured out into the world in the Spirit. It is a love that accepts the world as it is and is immersed in the world to the point of sharing the death which is the world's ultimate destiny.[15]

Long ago Pascal realised: 'Jesus will be in agony until the end of the world.'[16]

The title of the essay is inspired by Pope John Paul II's words of encouragement to the National Delegate regarding their work in preparing for the Forty-sixth International Eucharistic Congress in Wroclaw, Poland (1997), the theme of which is *Eucharist and Freedom*: 'The Congress will be an extraordinary hymn of gratitude to Christ for the gift of freedom, which from central Europe has benefitted the whole Church and brought blessings on the entire world.'[17]

Not only the title, but the entire approach in this essay is focused by Pope John Paul II's call for a new evangelisation, which is nothing other the proclamation of Christ's gift of freedom – that proclamation which corresponds to the needs of humanity today.[18] Pope John Paul II, who writes as a poet, pastor and man of exquisite sensitivity, has repeatedly expressed his deep fascination to penetrate the mystery of human freedom. In his Encyclical Letter on Social Concern, for instance, he stated:

> The freedom with which Christ has set us free (cf. Gal. 5:1) encourages us to become the *servants* of all. Thus the process of *development* and *liberation* takes concrete shape in the exercise of *solidarity*, that is to say in the love and service of neighbour, especially of the poorest: 'For where truth and love are missing, the process of liberation results in the death of a freedom which will have lost all support.'[19]

The same Pope likewise referred to the freedom of dialogue as marking a new stage of relationship between Catholics and

Orthodox – a stage that reflects the new situation which has arisen as a result of the collapse of Communism dramatically symbolised by the fall of the Berlin wall dividing East and West at the end of 1989:

> Being faithful witnesses to *Jesus Christ who has set us free* should be the main concern in our time of cultural, social and political changes, so that we can preach together and with credibility the one Gospel of salvation, and be builders of peace and reconciliation in a world always threatened by conflicts and wars.[20]

This Pope, a man from a country in the Communist East, who has personally experienced the Christian truth of freedom put on trial and vindicated, could not be better qualified to emphasise the perennial validity of the supreme sacrifice of martyrdom. For the life of every martyr coherently witnesses to the search for truth – the truth of freedom and the freedom of truth. Every Christian martyr is one whose witness accords with the truth of freedom celebrated in the eucharistic mystery, that truth of Christ's presence and action in his freedom-giving dedication and sacrifice of himself for the life of the world. Because of the materialistic atmosphere of decadence, particularly in the West, Pope John Paul II has often highlighted the urgent need for such inspiring witnesses and examples of persons who have drawn their energy from and imitated the passover mystery of Christ, the primary witness to freedom. As he stated at the above-mentioned meeting of the National Delegates:

> The Eucharist in this century – no less than in the first ages of the Church – has been the bread of freedom, the viaticum of courage and martyrdom. Its celebration in the catacombs of the twentieth century has brought about the dimension of faith and hope, in which new martyrs have been tested and borne glorious witness by their lives and often deaths to the high dignity of conscience and the value of obeying God's law.[21]

Christian iconography powerfully communicates the light of divine truth contained in the mysteries of faith. Religious imagination, which inspired the icon painters of the East, frees us from our habitual attachment to words and the heart-wearying enterprise of rational explanations. Imagery forms the environment of beauty, which is the *pretext* for praising the Lord, whose Word comes to illumine the darkness of our minds in the grace and truth of his Spirit-filled presence. We readily respond to the sacramentality of religious imagery because of the spark of divine light in us, who have been created in the image and likeness of God. Thus, the icon of the *Harrowing of Hades* (School of Novgorod, fifteenth century), which appears on the cover of this book, depicts the cosmic effects of Christ Jesus' resurrection, which is the dawn of the ultimate freedom – his triumphant smashing down the doors of death to lead humanity to share the freedom of all who await his glorious coming with the hope of the prophets, kings and poor in spirit (the *anawim*) and in the Blessed Virgin Mary's 'love beyond all telling'. This ancient teaching of the Apostles' Creed is implicit in one of the Easter hymns:

> Hell's gloomy gates yield up their key,
> paradise door thrown wide we see;
> never-tiring be our choiring,
> alleluia.[22]

It is impossible to acknowledge by name the many persons to whom my appreciation is due in the research and writing of this essay – apart from my parents, teachers, friends . . . It would be appropriate, however, to take this opportunity to give public expression of my gratitude to certain persons besides Louis Volpe, to whom I have dedicated this work, because of their direct interest in and influence on the shape and content of what appears here: Leslie and Kathleen Parker, whose example, advice and support I have constantly valued for many years regarding fidelity to the Catholic Church's truth of the eucharistic mystery; Stratford and Léonie Caldecott, for their encouragement from the beginning to the completion of the endeavour; the community of the three Franciscan Sisters of the Eucharist in Assisi, who, apart from the witness of their dedication to the Eucharist, have not only enriched my understanding of the task undertaken in this project by pointing out important references, but also provided most stimulating comments and suggestions in our discussion on the final draft. Lastly, I would wish especially to thank a priest-friend, who must remain anonymous, for the particularly inspiring and courageous manner in which he continues to strive to discover and communicate to others the significance of the Eucharist as the unique source, motivating energy and focus of authentic freedom. As he expressed it in a recent letter to me:

> In my own life I would like to act more out of love and less out of fear, hurt, and the human desire for achievement. Freedom from these is something that I am seeking. It occurs to me that many of the things I do are influenced by such motivations working somewhat quietly but nonetheless powerfully within me. Of course only Christ will be able to free me from this at the deepest levels within me, and my experience has been that this freeing comes most powerfully through His presence in the Eucharist. . . . I am coming to appreciate that Christ in the Eucharist is total giving, and that I receive the ability to live that way through the Eucharist. This really is the freedom and the life I am seeking. I see that Christ in the Eucharist needs to be not isolated from the rest of my life but gradually acting as a leaven for the rest of my life. This seems to be where I am in my spiritual life.

St Augustine recognised the truth of freedom in speaking of the whole life of a praise-singer becoming a song. The joy of a Christian's graced-life ultimately cannot be held bound in the prison of words; it bursts forth in living praise to God as a hymn of freedom – the most fitting hymn for celebrating the jubilee of humanity's redemption:

> We are a new humanity, we have a new alliance with God; so let our song be new; a new song is not for the old man. Only the new mankind can learn it, mankind renewed by grace out of the ancient stuff [*renovati per gratiam ex vetustate*]. . . . Our whole heart yearns for it as it sings the new song. Let it sing the new song, not with voices, but with its life. . . .
>
> You ask in what way you are to sing, each one of you, the praises of God. Sing to him, but not out of tune. God does not want his ears assaulted by discords. So, sing in harmony, brothers. . . .
>
> This is the way of singing God gives you; do not search for words. You cannot express in words the sentiments which please God: so, praise him with your jubilant singing. This is fine praise of God, when you sing with jubilation.
>
> You ask, what is singing in jubilation? Understand this: one cannot express what the heart is singing. At the harvest, in the

vineyard, whenever men must labour hard, they begin with songs whose words express their joy. But when their joy brims over and words are not enough, they abandon the syllables of words and give themselves up to the sheer sound of jubilation. Jubilant sound means that the heart brings forth what cannot be said. And to whom does this jubilation most belong? Surely to God who is unutterable. And does not unutterable mean what cannot be uttered? If words will not come and you may not remain silent, what else can you do but be exultant? What else, when the rejoicing heart has no words and the immensity of your joys will not be imprisoned in speech? What else but 'sing out with jubilation'?[23]

MICHAEL L. GAUDOIN-PARKER
Assisi, Italy
15 August 1996
Assumption of the Blessed Virgin Mary

PART I

QUEST FOR FREEDOM

One of the indispensable foods of the human soul is liberty. Liberty, taking the word in its concrete sense, consists in the ability to choose. We must understand by that, of course, a real ability. Wherever men are living in community, rules imposed in the common interest must necessarily limit the possibilities of choice. . . . When the possibilities of choice are so wide as to injure the commonweal, men cease to enjoy liberty. . . . As regards freedom of thought, it is very nearly true to say that without freedom there *is* no thought. But it is truer still to say that when thought is non-existent, it is non-free into the bargain. There has been a lot of freedom of thought over the past few years, but no thought. Rather like the case of a child who, not having any meat, asks for salt with which to season it.

Simone Weil, 'The needs of the soul'[1]

However rational, however compelling, however logical the arguments for Western unity may be, however obvious the benefits of economic co-operation, however hopeful the promise of amity between the nations, one may still question whether reason or logic, of themselves, are enough to change the direction of Western development.

Barbara Ward, *Faith and Freedom*[2]

We are inmates, not begetters or masters, of our lives. Yet the indistinct intimation of a lost freedom or of a freedom to be regained – Arcadia behind us, Utopia before – hammers at the far threshold of the human psyche. This shadowy pulse-beat lies at the heart of our mythologies and of our politics. We are creatures at once vexed and consoled by summons of a freedom just out of reach . . . to be is to be at liberty.

George Steiner, *Real Presences*[3]

1

Freedom: a new language?

The language of modern anxiety

Despite the countless beneficial achievements and positive improvements of the material quality of human life through science and technology, and despite the growth in a conscientious understanding of and endeavour to assure national, social and personal freedom, the twentieth century has also undeniably witnessed the dawn of a reign of terror which is possibly more ghastly than any other humanity has ever known. The crimes against humanity's right to freedom have formed a chapter of recent history which may be entitled in letters of blood: 'the culture of death'.[4] This description is a shameful indictment against modern civilisation which boasts of having reached a position of intellectual superiority and moral freedom so that it not only can choose the means to achieve certain objectives, but also attempts to set for itself its ultimate goals.

'A culture of death', however, seems not inappropriate considering the evidence of recent history and the manifold threats to life today. Human memory has been scarred by the terrible wounds inflicted on countless persons: the killings of thousands of human beings not only during the two World Wars but also in various other conflicts during the last half-century of 'peace'; the torture and mass murder of people in concentration camps; the use of chemical weapons that exterminate defenceless civilian people; the accelerated rise of incidents of organised international terrorism and urban violence; the increase of starvation, homelessness and poverty, which – though perhaps not the immediate cause of death – signify that countless deprived persons are as good as dead socially in so far as they experience alienation not only in the so-called 'Third' or even 'Fourth' worlds within our one world, but also, as Mother Teresa has often remarked, along the pavements, in the subways, under the bridges of the world's great cities, such as London, New York, Chicago, etc.

To this shameful litany of human alienation must be added two other atrocities which are evidence of an even more callous dimension of the killing speed of the 'culture of death' through which humanity struggles for survival: the legalisation of abortion and discretionary use of euthanasia. Without wishing or attempting here to assess the moral, social, political or legal aspects of these highly complex issues, the fact remains that – in the name of being reasonable, humane and civilised and in the interest of affirming personal liberty of choice and individual rights – our nations ('welfare states'!) permit, sanction and would seem to promote death.

This phenomenon of a 'culture of death' now threatening the world at large presents a bizarre paradox: the rightful claim of intellectual freedom and honesty as an exercise of rational existence has resulted in the discovery of becoming capable of destroying the freedom of human life and also, as ecologists alarmingly remind us, every form of life on this planet.[5] The quasi-apocalyptic event of mass extermination caused by the explosion of the atomic bomb in the middle of this century in Japan may be seen as a symbol of the unforeseen catastrophic effects which may result from use put to the legitimate scientific exploration for morally questionable political expediency. Although this event remains a most terrifying lesson that has deterred nations from engaging in nuclear warfare, it has not been powerful enough to prevent them from continuing to pursue nuclear experimentation and stockpiling, or from engaging in the highly profitable business of the arms trade.[6] The politics or economics of taking calculated risks with death has now become a way of life and a profitable means of livelihood for some people.

The multiple hazards of modern existence together with the heightened sense of the precarious and fragile condition of human relationships restrict the freedom of people who are subjugated to a situation of anxiety and, as the psychiatrist Erich Fromm brought out superbly, are forced to live in *The Fear of Freedom*. The fact is that the disease of anxiety has insidiously crept into and consumes the very marrow of modern consciousness. This disease of anxiety and fear has only grown with the spread of the HIV virus(es) of AIDS in our confused times which are riddled with infidelity and suspicion, uncertainty and fear. All the talk of freedom today is like whistling in the dark. Such an unhealthy climate can hardly be expected to nurture the seeds of genuine freedom, much less bear witness to the mature fruition of communities of free persons. Fromm's book examines the condition of enslavement into which people allow themselves to be allured so that they surrender their freedom to leaders or fall under the sway of the dominant ideas, pervasive ideologies and prevalent patterns of behaviour of the day, just as in the days of Fascism and Nazism whole nations were beguiled by dark tyrannical forces.[7] In his analysis of the complex struggle for autonomy spurred on by the ethos of individualism, Fromm pointed to the increase in a sense of insignificance, alienation, impotence, guilt, fear and anxiety, which modern writers such as Kafka, Sartre, Julien Green, have also dramatically portrayed through the haunting *persona* of their novels, characters who not atypically are burdened with the neuroses of a growing number of people even, or rather, especially in democratic countries.[8] According to Fromm, these neuroses are evaded in different ways: on the one hand some people may disguise their neuroses more or less successfully by masks of self-assertiveness, routine of work and roles played out in society; on the other hand other people – perhaps the majority – are lulled into a false sense of security by the distractions of material well-being. People are cheated of genuine freedom by the vast scope of multiple choices opened to them by multi-national monopolies, whose owners or executive directors deftly manipulate competitive market forces and control the media to determine the popular fads and fashions, tastes and materialistic 'needs' of the vast majority in our consumer societies. Through being seduced by a climate of intense pressure to conform to social expectations regarding becoming successful and productive, the capacity of many people to be authentically free and whole as persons becomes threatened, distorted and greatly diminished. The 'freedom' featuring at least implicitly in the language of every advertise-ment in the mass media is notoriously delusory. The truth of this is a joke as old as time: for from the beginning golden apples, with or without the advertiser's promotional description of 'delicious', were held out as promising the freedom of divine immortality.

As a result of a disproportionate emphasis placed on merely acquiring and managing facts in an atmosphere conditioned by the priority given to Information Technology (IT), human freedom and relationships themselves have greatly deteriorated and become subject to arrangement by instruments of information-sorting and data-processing organisations.[9] This is evidenced not only in 'computer dating' schemes, but also in the more sinister, widening spectrum of social and political fields, where gravely immoral techniques, such as genetic typing and engineering, invitro-fertilising, etc. pass unquestioned as 'progress' and even risk becoming commercialised.[10] But the material advances in science and technology, for all their potential contribution to human well-being, cannot be equated with progress of the spiritual dimension of being human in the discovery of authentic freedom.[11]

George Orwell's predictions in his satirical novel *Nineteen Eighty-four* have long ago been realised in ways more frightening than what he described in 1949 about how totalitarian systems of a police state can deprive people of their rights to privacy and freedom. In such a scenario there is little or no place for realising the interior human drama of freedom in becoming acting persons.[12] Thus, the language of modern anxiety and uncertainty is nervously preoccupied with *having* rather than *being*.[13] It cannot be otherwise in an environment characterised by materialism and hedonistic self-centredness. Since the value of human beings becomes increasingly measured by economic efficiency and subjected to political interests, their lives are held cheap, dispensable, and replaced by the ever more sophis-ticated instruments of 'hi-tech', against which they run in a highly competitive race against time: for, 'time is money!' Thus in his autobiography Stephen Spender notes that as long ago as the 1930s writers were driven in a race against time by an impatient urge to churn out some new literary work; he laments the lack of 'stillness' essential for artistic quality and severely denounces the tortured obsession with the temporal and ephemeral concerns.[14]

The modern crisis of Western culture is closely connected with the crisis of faith. What is at issue is the tendency of our civilisation to break up because of its loss of a unifying faith-vision, which gave former ages a sense of identity and worth oriented to an ultimate purpose. The phenomenon of fragmentation and alienation, especially evident in Western civilisation, was perhaps prophetically announced earlier this century by the poet W.B. Yeats in his insight about things falling apart without a centre of interiority, that is, lacking in spirituality, the soul of authentic freedom.[15]

From a vision of wisdom to loss of perspective

In order to get some idea of how interiority has become threatened it is useful to review briefly the history of discussion about human freedom. Western thought has taken many turns and appears like a winding stair issuing in many levels of meaning, each level having introduced new dimensions to understanding of what constitutes or contributes to well-being. The pursuit of promoting a just state in Athens of the fourth century BC led philosophers such as Plato and Aristotle to regard freedom as directly related to understanding the nature of the good as constituting the quality of life in a just society.[16] The purpose of education was to free a person for engaging in those things that mattered, for quality in life.[17] In contrast to the tendency in recent centuries to accumulate information and to categorise it into various specialised branches of knowledge,[18] people in the ancient world were content to seek above all else a general understanding in interpreting common experience. They called this manner of understanding, which provided them with an overall vision of human life, wisdom, which for them was the 'science of freedom'.[19]

The ancients considered wisdom as descending from heaven. This view became commonplace among the Fathers of the

Church, who baptised and married the Jewish doctrine of divine
revelation with the teaching of the Greek philosophers,
especially the Neoplatonists, who held that in the course of time
human life went into progressive decline morally and religiously
from its pure idea of the truth and beauty of God.[20]

St Augustine's approach may be taken as a fine example of
the further development of this attitude of giving priority to the
'love of wisdom', the philosophy of living. The story of his
conversion is more than merely fascinating; it offers a wealth of
encouragement for it relates the beginning of his lifelong
search to discover the intrinsic link between freedom and the
sense of Christian vocation. It would betray a serious misreading
(and also reveal our own preoccupations and moralistic hang-
ups!) to regard Augustine's struggle for freedom in his early
life as directed solely against the hold of his passionate
temperament. For there was much more to his make-up – as in
that of every human person – than the dimensions of sensuality
and pleasure-seeking, deeply rooted as these are in the life-
instinct of sexuality. He realised that the deep passion of the
human mind and heart for the value of truth was a love that
could not be satisfied by the various ethical and intellectual
systems of his day – systems with which he thoroughly
acquainted himself: Manichaeanism, which not only denigrated
the body and the material world, but also insulted the power of
human intelligence; Neoplatonism, which proposed so
idealistic and abstract a programme of intellectualism that
proved unrealistic in practical living. Augustine himself recalls
how from the time he came across Cicero's *Hortensius* at the age
of eighteen he experienced an incredible fire in his heart for
wisdom.[21] His conversion gradually began to take shape after
years of honestly seeking to be freed not only from the snares of
the weakness of flesh, but also to know the beauty of the truth
and goodness of being free. It ripened to maturity only when
he discovered the truth of God's beauty in the Christian community's hymns, songs of praise, and joyous spiritual canticles
celebrated especially at the Eucharist.[22] Some years after
reflecting on his conversion experience Augustine announced
the major theme of all his writings in the famous opening lines
of his great work the *Confessions*, namely, that the human heart

is restless until it experiences its true identity and worth in worshipping God.[23] In a word, to acknowledge God with praise and thanksgiving was for him the deepest meaning and purpose of communication and the primary significance of *confession*.[24] He interpreted the maxim in the Roman world: *otium est negotium* ('leisure is a duty'), as expressing the importance of employing 'free time' for pursuing the truth of religious wisdom.[25] He even goes on to identify wisdom with worship, *pietas*, the heart of worship of God (*Dei cultus*), which he was at pains to point out is the meaning of the Greek word *theosebeia*.[26]

For Augustine the distinction between acknowledging and knowing God was crucial: the acknowledging of God with praise and thanksgiving is the highest wisdom; it is superior to every kind of mere knowing of facts, for it is the most integrating of all human activities. In showing that the pursuit of wisdom in a spirit of worship leads to true freedom and personal wholeness,[27] Augustine introduced the world of antiquity to the yet deeper and integrating vision of Christian faith, which freed thought to enjoy the freedom of truth in the light of Christ, whose mystery contains the treasures of wisdom and knowledge (cf. Col. 2:3).[28] As one scholar put it: 'whereas in classical culture man reached an understanding of the power and value of thought, through Christianity there is added a new dimension, that of freedom, and out of the fusion of thought and freedom has come a higher and more potent form of intellectuality'.[29]

In the Middle Ages Augustine's approach was highly influential in shaping the Church's understanding of its providential role in the disclosure of divine revelation. St Thomas Aquinas speaks of the incarnation – the definitive descent and disclosure of the fullness of divine wisdom – as being of greater importance than the ascent of humanity's endeavours towards God.[30] These endeavours of human reason's enquiry, however, were considered legitimate and encouraged provided that they remained in conformity with the *sacra doctrina* as expressed by the Church's Magisterium, the faithful's sole guardian of truth in matters of faith and morals. Theology was called the 'queen of the sciences', to which all other disciplines (especially

philosophy) were regarded as being the 'handmaids'. It was
developed in the centres of mediaeval learning, the monasteries
and newly founded universities, which were subject to the
discipline of ecclesiastic authority. The function or *modus
operandi* of theology was described as: faith seeking understanding.[31] St Anselm of Canterbury expressed the whole thrust
of theological enquiry in the form of a prayer: 'I make no
attempt, Lord, to reach to your heights, since in no way do I
consider my mind adequate for this, but in some measure I
desire to understand your truth which my heart believes and
loves.'[32] This approach derived largely from St Augustine, who
took as axiomatic a phrase in the prophet Isaiah: 'believe in
order to understand'.[33] Faith was regarded as the crucial, inter-
pretative key, as it were, to all knowledge and wisdom.

Thus, discussion about freedom became focused (though
not exclusively by any means) on the aptitude for making
responsible choices in accordance with the guiding principles
taught by the Church. Anselm and many mediaeval thinkers
treated the question of free will in their endeavour to do justice
to a special problem which since Augustine became a vexed
and somewhat embarrassing question for theologians, namely,
the need to reconcile freedom with God's pre-knowledge, since
according to Augustine (particularly as emphasised in his
later works) God's pre-knowledge predestines human beings
to salvation or its opposite, damnation.[34] The two questions of
God's freedom and the necessary motive of the incarnation
were considered to be intrinsically related. They presented to
the mediaeval scholastics a problem whose parameters cannot
be properly grasped unless seen according to their perspective
in relation to the mystery of the Trinity. Only the mysterious
reality of the relations of the three divine Persons – that reality
which the incarnation uniquely reveals – enables us to penetrate
into the depths of God's motive for loving the world to such an
extent and in such an extravagant way as to give up his own Son
to save it (cf. Jn 3:16f.). The mediaeval theologians regarded
this offer of salvation as disclosing the true depth of human
freedom. Only the communication of the grace of Christ assures
the transformation of human understanding and exercise of
freedom.

This transformation, it seems, is suggested by the imagery of Michelangelo's magnificent *Creation of Adam* on the ceiling of the Sistine chapel. Here the great artist seems to present the integrating vision of the Middle Ages of faith rather than the Renaissance's ideal regarding confidence in human reason's attainment of freedom. While he depicts God reaching out and down to draw Adam into his life, he respects the infinite ontological difference between Creator and creature, however, by the gap barely discernable between both of their almost touching outstretched forefingers. This difference does in no way separate the two, for, as Michelangelo superbly shows, it is overcome and transformed by the freedom in God's dynamic descending movement towards Adam, whose response consists in allowing himself to be drawn up into the indescribable arc or embrace of divine life.

At another level, that of the relationships between people in society, it would be quite mistaken to interpret the mediaeval concept of human freedom as shaped in terms of its view of a functional society in which everyone had his or her proper place according to the tasks and responsibilities apportioned to or performed by them. Rather, it was the other way round: the social order was seen as being called to reflect or 'imitate' the theological order of God's design to realise a harmony of relationships in the whole of cosmic creation, of which humanity was the highest part because endowed with the divine powers of intelligence and self-determination, that is, a dynamic capacity towards recognising and realising ultimate values. It must be, nevertheless, admitted that this magnificent concept was open to misinterpretation and manipulation, consciously or unconsciously, by those with an eye to seizing, maintaining or increasing their own power and control over the masses. But it must be also recognised that all too often this concept led to a distortion of Christian spirituality. This kind of distortion and abuse is what Jean-Jacques Rousseau took for the true face of Christianity which he described in terms of servitude and dependence.[35]

The roots of the franchise of human reason to go its own way or, at least, to seek independence from the constraints of authority, whether of religious faith or of secular conformity,

can in a sense be traced back to scholasticism in the thirteenth
and fourteenth centuries. A critical stance of the mediaeval
theologians' method was taken by the historian Christopher
Dawson, who observed that St Thomas Aquinas' whole system
was hinged on the principle that Christ's incarnation which
does not destroy or supersede nature, but is analogous and
complementary to it.[36] In developing this line of approach,
Aquinas and the scholastics followed Boethius in faithfulness to
the common tradition of all the Fathers, who in their commentaries on the words of Genesis 1:26f. understood the image
of God as referring to humanity's power of reason, which they
took as the basis of human freedom.[37]

In recent times the same criticism of mediaeval scholasticism
as Dawson's has been levelled by the Greek theologian John
Zizioulas, whose rich approach and magnificent vision Paul
McPartlan has provided the valuable service of introducing to
the West.[38] Zizioulas shows how freedom is realised by his
explanation that Christ restored God's image in humanity
through revealing humanity's corporate identity in him – that
revelation which calls for and draws human beings to affirm
their freedom in their response of faith to Christ, the Word
(*logos*) of life.[39]

It should not be forgotten, however, that if subsequent
theology had given due recognition to St Bonaventure's more
integrating symbolic and mystical approach as complementary
to the scholastic method, a greater balance might have been
achieved to off-set the later challenge of rationalism.[40] This
more integrating Franciscan line of approach may be discerned
in Gerard Manley Hopkins' profound perception of the unique
quality of every human life and of each creature – a perception
which owes much to the teaching of Duns Scotus regarding the
value of the 'thisness' (*haeccietas*) of each individual.

Various factors, however, prepared the way for the dissolu-
tion of the unifying faith-vision and the sense of perspective of
mediaeval society. These factors are more complex than simply
a growing dissatisfaction with the feudal system of authority
exercised in the Middle Ages. Apart from the long struggle
between Church and State, which resulted in the eventual
breakdown of relations and separation between the two, it is

important to take into account many other things, among which the following are significant: the emergence and promotion of personal piety, a sanctification of nature and the emphasis placed on the humanity of Christ and human emotions, particularly through the rapid spread of the Franciscan spirit, which Dawson says 'marks a turning point in the religious history of the West';[41] the fall of Constantinople shortly after the collapse of relations between Rome and the East at the Council of Florence; the beginning of the flowering of humanism in letters and art; the rise of democratic movements and the spread of the spirit of secularism and nationalism, on the one hand, and that of independence of thought and way of life, on the other. Such factors among many others put in place those milestones along the road to the modern notion (and religion) of freedom and the 'creed' proclaiming the rights of the individual: the Renaissance, the Protestant Reformation, the birth of modern times in the 'new age' of the Enlightenment's celebration of the autonomy of reason.

One of the leading figures in the period of the Enlightenment was the German philosopher Immanuel Kant, who clearly described the characteristic features of this new approach to philosophy and the subsequent rationalist tradition in the following way:

> Enlightenment is man's emergence from self-incurred immaturity. Immaturity is the inability to use one's own understanding without the guidance of another. This immaturity is self-incurred if its cause is not lack of understanding, but lack of resolution and courage to use it without the guidance of another. The motto of enlightenment is therefore: *Sapere aude!* Have courage to use your own understanding.[42]

Whereas Descartes separated philosophy from theology, which he considered unscientific in both its methodology and also object, Kant went even a stage further in separating science from metaphysics. The philosophers of the eighteenth century substituted for faith in divine revelation an unbounded confidence in the power of reason – a confidence that may be even called faith or a religion of social and political progress.[43]

Furthermore, since the Renaissance – and especially after the impetus given to philosophy by the method of doubt introduced by Descartes – ample signs may be detected in the lively interest directed towards the thinking subject. One recalls Pascal's description of a human being as nothing but 'a thinking reed'.[44] It was the Enlightenment, however, which definitively brought about a radical shift of focus in Western culture from the level of common faith to that of subjective *meaning*, which undermines a sense of the basis of a community of freedom.[45] The characteristic of the modern, post-Enlightenment method of critical thinking posits the primacy of meaning unshackled from responsibility to seek truth.[46] In the last few decades this process has been acclaimed by some thinkers and philosophical theologians as more interesting than the attainment of truth itself, which with the rejection of metaphysics is judged as irrelevant or impossible.[47]

The radical challenges of Modernity

Since Bishop J.A.T. Robinson's controversial *Honest to God*, not only traditional expressions of Christian faith in doctrine and morality, but the very object of worship, the 'Otherness' of a personal God, have attracted theological debate and have added to the general confusion of opinion. However, the free 'God-talk' did not finish in the halcyon days of the 1960s; it has continued – evidently without 'God' becoming a dead issue, but rather one of increasingly lively concern. This concern expressed in certain quarters, however, is not with God's reality, but with our language about 'God'. For instance, Don Cupitt describes the task confronting Christians today as having to reject all that has gone before: 'To put it brutally, there *is* no ready-ordered objective reality any more: there is only the flux of becoming, and the continuing ever-changing human attempt to imagine and impose order. We have to *make* sense; *we* have to turn chaos into cosmos.'[48]

Cupitt does not merely present a brilliant account of the history of the last few centuries of Western thought and how the currents of the Renaissance, Reformation and Enlightenment have thoroughly disturbed the quiet waters of mediaeval piety, so that Christians, like the fishermen of Galilee, have been forced once again to confront a stormy 'sea of faith', as his book is aptly entitled; he also clearly pitches in his lot with those who see the need to face up to the radical challenge of discovering a new interpretation regarding the evangelical significance of believing today. In what amounts to a personal testimony, Cupitt makes an appeal for a new kind of approach to faith:

> After centuries of being lazy and cosmological, faith becomes more demanding again, more a matter of the will, less a matter of serving a pre-established order and more a pilgrimage towards a new one. It becomes more eschatological, in that it is directed towards a new world and a new human nature which this present era thinks impossible. It no longer sees (or rather, fancies that it sees) its objects. They become invisible, things unseen, ideals and things hoped-for. Do not tell me that this complete loss of objectivity is hard, for nobody knows that better than I do. It is hardest of all to give up the last slivers and shreds of objectivity, but only by doing so can faith finally free itself from all that is outworn and become as fully voluntary, creative and courageous as it is required to be today.[49]

It is interesting to recall these words since they illustrate how Cupitt regards the terrible leap that must be made into the unknowns of the present age. These sentences seem to echo the tones of certain prophetic passages in the scriptures and may have a similar ring to what is heard in the preaching of the greatest evangelists – from Paul to Wesley, Augustine to Pope John Paul II. However, these sentences (read in their whole context) really introduce quite an utterly new language about the freedom of faith, an understanding which is radically different from that of the tradition of the Christian Church, as Cupitt himself would readily admit.

This radical departure from Christian tradition consists in the claim that language is all that matters: the endeavour to master and manipulate the language of faith is the major preoccupation. Reflection on the language of Christian tradition becomes the 'heart' of this modern religion of a highly intellectualised kind. On the one hand, Anselm's description of the work of theology becomes reversed: instead of faith seeking to deepen its understanding of the mystery of God's revelation, theological enquiry focuses its attention on human thought-processes and language. Mind and its expression, rather than the mystery of God, become the centre of human-kind's faith in this approach. On the other hand, a further stage of Descartes' famous premise is attained: God exists merely because of the freedom and courage of human thought to express and uncover his meaning in language.

This radically qualitative shift of direction away from what has been held by Christian tradition ought to present cause for concern to believers especially because one is hard put to find the nucleus of the essential Christian *kerygma* – that is, the Church's sacramental proclamation of the freedom that comes as the gift of Jesus Christ's paschal mystery of death and resurrection. The emphasis as well as the entire content of this approach is focused on human meaning which is realised through the force of intelligence and will. What happens here is that the meaning of freedom becomes reduced to the exercise of individual ingenuity, inventiveness, skill – an exercise which has come to be called since the end of the eighteenth-century Romantics by the dubious name of 'creativity'.[50] Since the vital centre-piece of faith receives scant recognition, this endeavour at renewal by speaking the language of modernity is seriously flawed. For this kind of endeavour to reinterpret Christianity gives ample evidence of subjectivism.

Renewal means much more than being up to date – *aggiornamento*! The prestige attached to 'renewal' has perhaps a lot to do with what C.S. Lewis calls 'chronological snobbery', which disparages the past and regards only the 'new' as of any value.[51] As long ago as 1942 Lewis showed up the shallowness of trendiness in faith. Novelty is the devil's age-old trump card, as Screwtape points out to his apprentice, whom he instructs in the cunning of diverting people from focusing on simple questions of ultimate concern, such as asking whether something is right or wrong.[52] His *Christian Reflections* appeared in 1967 when it was becoming fashionable to stir up restlessness for a 'new morality' of 'situation ethics', and to discard not merely 'traditional values', but also the very quest for truth and goodness. In one of the essays in this little book Lewis strongly reacted against what he called 'The Poison of Subjectivism', which he saw as a dangerous tendency pervading literature and distorting the deepest levels of life, namely, the arduous responsibility to search for truth and to affirm the possibility of its existence. This responsibility is exercised through entering into that patient dialogue with others which, despite many failures, is at the very heart of the rich heritage of the Western tradition of freedom and underlies our meaning of democracy. Lewis sought in this essay to expose the falsity of that brand of enchantment with worldliness which sought to jettison one of the most basic truths about being human, namely the quest for truth and reality.[53] This essay has a particular relevance today when people badly need to be freed from their obsessive passion for instant sensation and their short (and selective) memory regarding the values of tradition, against which they hold a definite prejudice.

Hans Urs von Balthasar has frequently pointed out that as a result of Western thought having come to a large extent under the prevalent sway of the philosophy of subjectivism, which has accentuated and glorified the individual in isolation from the common good of society, many persons have lost their fundamental sense of direction to the transcendent quality of existence as well as their orientation to a transcendent 'Thou'.[54] This transcendent quality and orientation is deeply religious since it is directed to the 'Holy'. Only a transcendent 'Thou' can guarantee an authentic significance of identity and freedom for the privatised 'I', particularly when this 'Thou' is encountered in the communion of the Church.[55]

Whether in the 'rugged individualism' of Anglo-Saxon pragmatism about ethics (as in John Stuart Mill's utilitarian approach to liberty) or in the emphasis placed on the dramatic lonely ordeal of an individual in becoming *authentic*, as elaborated by some European existentialist thinkers (such as Jean-Paul Sartre, or Albert Camus), all approaches fostering individualism somehow imply a justification of human violence which compromises and even jeopardises the very notion and expression of freedom in human society at large. For these approaches to freedom, in one way or another, regard it as something to be decisively chosen by sheer determination of 'will-power', struggled for, wrested by force and seized by individuals or classes. The irony is that what is meant to express strength of character and freedom of choice ends sadly in the self-alienating state of becoming entrapped by voluntarism or imprisoned by the whim of the present moment.[56]

Furthermore, because the Aristotelian notion of 'final cause' was long ago abandoned as empirically unverifiable, there follow dire consequences regarding the significance of freedom. In the post-Enlightenment era many moral philosophers no longer assess the right purpose of human actions in relation to or as having to be consistent with the final or ultimate purpose of human nature. Without this criterion of object-oriented finality, which was closely aligned and based on divine revelation transmitted and guaranteed through the Church's authority – that basis which was both rejected by the rationalist and empirical currents of the Enlightenment – the result is that personal choice becomes 'liberated' to run riot. Rather than enlarging human capability, however, such 'liberation' delimits both the understanding of true value and dignity of human life and the scope of human vision and hope. The result of modern atheistic humanism's choice against any divine design in creation and for deciding how to re-create the world has been not only the rejection of God, but also the denial of the deepest value of the human person, which the Fathers of Christian culture recognised as the grace-given capacity to reflect the divine splendour – divinisation. Writing at a time of great turmoil in the aftermath of the Second World War, when the ideology of atheistic Communism in Stalinist Russia was about to succeed the fascist régimes of Hitler's and Mussolini's idolatries of race and nation, the great theologian Henri de Lubac pointed out that: 'Atheist humanism was bound to end in bankruptcy. Man is himself only because his face is illumined by a divine ray ... If the fire disappears, the reflected gleam immediately dies out.'[57]

In a careful examination of the various phases of 'modernity' – logical positivism, linguistic analysis, existential nihilism and deconstructionism, etc. – George Steiner contends that they all lead to a dead end. For in essence modernity is a denial and emptying of the objective power of the divine Word to communicate a sense of reality. Steiner argues that modernity's withdrawal from encountering the presence of the Ground of Being can be traced back through the various attempts of rationalism, which itself is the sterile outcome of the tendency of the rabbinic and kabbalist schools and also of mediaeval scholasticism to generate commentaries upon commentaries on the living Word of God.[58] Nevertheless, he pays tribute to Thomas Aquinas' endeavour to determine the precise sense of the Word ('*this* and *this*, but not *that*'); and he also points out the value of the Roman Catholic Church's warning that unless interpretation is kept within recognisable finite bounds by some divinely revealed authoritative Magisterium, freedom of thought and expression in interpreting the Word of God only becomes schismatic.[59] While modernity usefully insists on the importance of the word, it contradicts itself by denying the primacy of the personal truth of the 'Thou' of God's presence addressing us in the mystery of the Word incarnate.

An overemphasis on meaning and exaggeration of the importance of reason lead to a distortion of the rich vitality and multiple resonances of the word, to which Paul Ricoeur has pointed in his profound phenomenological analysis of the relation between human work and the word of poetry and worship:

> Thus the word develops self-awareness and self-expression in multiple directions which we have only outlined in passing: the imperative word by which I come to a decision, bringing judgment upon my affective confusion; the dubitative word by which I question myself and bring myself into question; the indicative word by which I consider, deem, and declare myself to be such; but also the lyrical word by which I chant the fundamental feelings of mankind and of solitude.[60]

The various manoeuvres of modernity have highlighted merely one or other of these rich dimensions of the word. Even though analysis and description may have been made by philosophers of all these functions of human language, what has been glaringly neglected is the act of actually entering into the liberating dynamism and spirit of the lyrical word – the soul-realising and freedom-expressing word of praise of God.

Recognition of the individual and the politics of liberation

It would be a quite serious mistake not to recognise the important distinction between the self-enclosed introversion of subjectivism and the value of subjectivity. Bishop Christopher Butler points out that after centuries of emphasising the objectivity of the Christian religion – following the Counter-Reformation reaction to the subjective tendency of the Reformers – the Second Vatican Council 'gave evidence of a shift of emphasis from the objective to the subjective aspect of human and Christian experience'.[61] The significance of this shift is particularly important, not only as regards deeper personal participation in the Church's liturgical worship, but also as regards the whole range of the Church's teaching – from sacramental theology to the relation of worship to the most knotty moral questions of human worth and freedom in education, involvement and commitment to human development, politics, etc.

Among the questions concerning – and indeed requiring – a shift, or rather, development of approach in the Church's Magisterium to the recognition of the responsibilities of conscience of individual human persons (and groups of persons), there are those which come under the general name of 'liberation theology', which in the last thirty years has claimed much attention.[62] These questions have, on occasion, sadly become a matter of embittered debates which have been given wide coverage due to the claim of the right to freedom of expression on the part of the indiscreet and irresponsible elements in the media. It is true that certain currents of liberation theology have taken freedom of thought and speech to exaggerated lengths. However, exaggerations, especially when made with strident emphasis, have unfortunately brought ridicule and disrepute upon the genuine attempts at theological coherence in the field of liberation theology and the legitimate demands of the feminist movement. For the theologies of human liberation have also in general more serious concerns than those of the 'fringe front' just indicated. Underlying their various genuine concerns, liberation theologians have sought in one way and another to answer the age-old questions: How can human beings today know/see God? How can humankind be free and possess fullness of life? How can this fullness of life reflect the fundamental purpose for which Christ came to save humanity and to divinise it? How can Christ's life and death be the source of discovering human freedom and fulfilment in situations of poverty due to oppression and injustice? The thrust of a genuine liberation theology is focused by a love of the Church as the instrument of salvation of all people; it aims at provoking a serious and urgent reappraisal of the burning, practical question: How can the Church make the truth of God's love for the world a liberating reality? This question is none other than a call to all Christians to be consistent with the demands of the Christ's gospel of freedom and the sacrament of his immense charity, the Eucharist. The practical issue goes back to the beginning of the Church, at which, as the Second Instruction on Liberation Theology recalls the teaching of saints John and Paul,

> Fraternal love is the touchstone of [the] love of God: 'He who does not love his brother whom he has seen cannot love God whom he has not seen' (1 Jn 4:20). Saint Paul strongly emphasises the link between sharing in the Sacrament of the Body and Blood of Christ and sharing with one's neighbour who is in need.[63]

In regard to the particular branch of liberation theology concerned with women's rights and their role in the Church[64] – a branch which in some places has unfortunately tended to eclipse other important issues of life and death, such as poverty or the rights of the unborn – one may legitimately ask if the driving energy is really concerned about discovering the truth about God's revelation and doing his will today or about 'winning an argument' and dominating the opponents. If the latter is the case, then the issues become not those of freedom, but of a power-struggle, which is unworthy of human persons called to the freedom of Christ's gospel.

For, the deepest significance of freedom, which certainly involves striving for human liberation and for not only the doing of justice but also for ensuring that justice is seen to be done, cannot be detached from the question of seeking truth. As Pope John Paul II has stated: 'only the freedom which submits to the Truth leads the human person to his true good. The good of the person is to be in the Truth and to *do* the Truth.'[65] Truth must not be reduced to or confused with merely the passing on of information, which is often called 'the facts', which in turn are no more than the presentation of a selection of newsworthy items, that is, sensational items which are considered to arouse the public interest and which are coloured according to the ideological position of journalists and determined by editorial policy and economic interests of media agencies. Thus, for instance, in the case of the crisis of Latin American liberation theology, the central issue of the relation of human justice to the gospel of love has become all too often clouded by a polarisation of viewpoints and of the issues themselves around personalities. These personalities are depicted, on the one hand, as representing an ideological position favouring human development in conflict with 'the institution', and, on the other hand, as authority figures merely concerned about maintaining power and the status quo irrespective of the urgent questions of justice and freedom.

What is often forgotten in this kind of grotesque caricature of the dialectic forces of liberation is that the challenge to face the truth of freedom is what Jesus Christ's whole life witnessed. This challenge was focused by him at that critical moment of his trial before the judgement seat of Pilate, who was unfree to do justice, because, being unable to face the candour of his prisoner's majestic presence, he turned his back on his responsibility to the truth of Jesus and succumbed to public opinion, which was manipulated by the religious leaders of the populace (cf. Jn 18:28ff.). The haunting mystery of that dramatic night requires deep reflection and honest heart-searching on the part of all.

The splendour of the gospel of truth and life in a culture of death

The situation of alienation resulting from an ambiguous approach to human freedom has not been passed unnoticed by the pastoral solicitude of the Church, especially since the Second Vatican Council.[66] It would be no exaggeration to say, however, that up to this momentous turning point in history the Church's official position regarding the exercise of the 'rights of conscience' and religious freedom had been somewhat estranged from the notion of democracy developing during the last two centuries in Western nations. Without assuming an attitude of moral superiority or imposing our criteria of civil rights and democratic freedom in passing judgement on the past, it must be acknowledged, moreover, that until relatively recent times the Magisterium of the Church was regrettably slow and hesitant about encouraging Catholics to become committed to the development of the material conditions of this world; its anti-rationalist and anti-modernist warnings are well-known about engaging in the major thrusts of secular society towards discovery of human responsibility. It must be remembered, however, that the crucial issue in the last two centuries was the Church's deep concern to safeguard the religious truth of its unique salvific role against the growing tide of indifferentism. It is in the light of this concern that one must regard some of the Church's guarded and severe statements on freedom of conscience in the last century.[67] While these statements bear witness to an attitude of melancholic intransigence, the effect was a widening of the rift between Church and State and, also, between 'conservatives' and 'liberals' within the Church itself.

Thus it was timely that the Second Vatican Council reviewed the positive and negative sides of modern society's achievements, among which must be acknowledged a deepened appreciation of the values of the inalienable dignity of the human person, personal responsibility and freedom of conscience. This attempt marked a decisively new step in the history of the official position of the Catholic Church's relationship to 'the world'. In Bishop Butler's words, 'The outcome was not only an invitation to dialogue but a result of dialogue.'[68] This climate of dialogue had been prepared not only by the theologians of the decades preceding the Council, but also by popes who followed Leo XIII. Pope Paul VI played no small part in fostering that process of openness to genuine human values which his predecessor John XXIII had envisaged in calling the Second Vatican Council. In his great Encyclical

Letter, *Ecclesiam Suam*, which was written and published while the Council debated the thorny issues of the relation of the Church to the modern world and the inculturation of the values of the gospel in secular society, he devoted a lengthy section to examining the proper attitude required of the Church in regard to contemporary problems. The entire Encyclical – and especially this section, entitled 'Dialogue' – marked a fresh and positive approach on the part of the Church in calling all people to take seriously the challenge and duty of dialogue. Since the responsibility of dialogue flows directly from the drive of the gift of charity, it entails a profound reverence for all people, an attentiveness to their complex needs, and respectful listening to their questions and sincerely held convictions, even when these differ from our own. The programme and attitude of dialogue, as described by Paul VI, is not only the path leading to a discovery of genuine freedom; it is also the fruit of realising Christ's proclamation that by fidelity to his word – his command to love all as he has loved us – we come to know the truth, and the truth will make us free (cf. Jn 8:32; 14:23; 15:12). There is no doubt that Pope Paul VI promoted a deeper understanding of human freedom by truly living out his own moving commitment to the Christian truth of dialogue:

> We will strive, so far as our weakness permits and God gives us the grace, to approach the world in which God has destined us to live. We will approach it with reverence, persistence and love, in an effort to get to know it and to offer it the gifts of truth and grace of which God has made us the custodian. We will strive to enable the world to experience divine redemption and the hope which inspires us. Engraved on our heart are Christ's words which we would humbly but resolutely make our own: 'For God sent his Son into the world, not to condemn the world, but that the world might be saved by him' (Jn 3:17).[69]

Although the Church's emphasis on dialogue with contemporary culture and social questions is fresh, it would be churlish and, indeed, a falsification of the abundant evidence to the contrary to accuse the Church's Magisterium of directing the gaze of Christ's faithful away from the welfare of the majority of humanity embroiled in the cauldron of the world's problems. For, this accusation would neglect to recognise the Church's century-long social teaching about living the gospel of freedom in the modern world. This consistent teaching can be traced particularly to the famous and most important pronouncement from the Magisterium on 15 May 1891, the Encyclical Letter *Rerum novarum* of Pope Leo XIII, who for more than thirty years had been Archbishop of Perugia in Umbria, where he learned much about the arduous working conditions of the peasant community.[70] Pope John Paul II, as his predecessors had likewise done, not only paid due tribute to the contribution of this great pope of social reform,[71] but he has also developed the Church's social teaching on the various issues related to justice, the dignity of human life, and the fundamental right to freedom. He has magnificently brought out that these issues cannot be left unconsidered or in any way divorced from the values of Christian morality enshrined in the splendid truth of Christ's gospel of life. Furthermore, he has set the Church's social doctrine as an important part of the positive spiritual programme proposed in preparations for the forthcoming celebration of the Jubilee of the Redeemer's birth in the year 2000.[72]

In drawing up its great document on the Church in the modern world, *Gaudium et Spes*, the Second Vatican Council paid careful attention to the question of the Church's relation to culture and thoroughly examined the most pressing problematic conditions of present-day human life with its insatiable craving for every form of social equality and 'liberty'. The meaning of the latter issues has been the focus of the Church's pastoral vigilance, reflected particularly in the statements of Pope John Paul II, who has quite deliberately assumed a 'high profile' in proclaiming the splendour of Jesus Christ, who is the gospel of truth, life and freedom. In his tireless pastoral journeys to many countries and meetings with world leaders, this pastor has played a significant part in raising the moral conscience of the world regarding the fundamental responsibility to recognise, cherish and promote in all spheres of human life God's gift of freedom.

Furthermore, Pope John Paul II, who comes from a country whose spirit was all but crushed under the oppressive totalitarian system of Communism, repeatedly draws attention to the fact that the Church's moral teaching on freedom is gloriously confirmed and exemplified in the lives of countless Christians across the centuries.[73] These Christian witnesses – laity as well as ecclesiastical personages – would be undistinguished and pass into the shadows of oblivion except for the fact that they not only strove to live in solidarity with those in need, but that they also drew their inspiration and energy to serve others from the liberating gospel of Jesus' charity and the sacraments, especially his great Passover to freedom celebrated in the eucharistic mystery. The Church has never failed at any time in history to proclaim and celebrate this gospel in the Eucharist, the sacrament *par excellence* of God's love for the world (cf. Jn 3:16f.; 6:51). In this perspective of pastoral solicitude the saints remind us of the transcendent dimension of human existence, which is sustained by the sacramental life of the Church. Without recognition of this transcendent dimension of freedom, human life itself would have no sense or purpose. For only the energy of God's love, which is manifest and communicated in the Christian sacraments and especially in the eucharistic mystery, can transform, sustain and empower human beings to discover and attain that adequate and authentic freedom and sense of wholeness which the holiness of the saints' lives manifests. The lives of the saints – not only those officially canonised, but also the martyrs of our times such as Bonhoeffer, Gandhi, Martin Luther King, Romero – bear witness to the light of the truth of human freedom. This light cannot be extinguished by the will of dictators or by whatever destructive force of régimes of oppression, because this light is enkindled from the purifying fire of love which Christ came to cast on the earth in his supreme and unique sacrifice of himself for freedom (cf. Lk 12:49).

Theories, philosophies, ideologies, systems and programmes of indoctrination have all had their day: they pass in and out of fashion. What brings grace to human life and transforms it into an art, what counts ultimately in the realisation of human freedom is the divinely infused reality of love – this is the real gift of being responsive to the concrete details of our situation in the world, for which we know how to experience and demonstrate the *praxis* or practical wisdom of responsibility.[74]

The eternal quest: the relation of culture and religion

In this century especially much attention has been focused on the relationship between the concept of the development of culture and religion. With the birth of the history of religions and its recognition as a distinct scientific discipline in the latter part of the nineteenth century, many studies have been published from various perspectives – historical, cultural, psychological, sociological, phenomenological – regarding the connection, interaction and relatively recent tendency to separate what has been called the secular or profane from the sacred spheres of human existence.[75] In confronting the present cultural crisis of faith with its loss of confidence, it would be well to reconsider with the seriousness it deserves the category of the sacred or 'the holy' as the deepest dimension of human experience. To recover a sense of cultural regeneration, it is necessary to rediscover that the key lies in a sense of the sacred. For only this sense of the sacred can open the way to the central dimension of human life and the transforming power and dynamic influence in the formation of what is worthy of the name 'culture'. It must be one of those curious facts of history, that a century which has nearly lost its sense of the sacred, a century that has emphasised the meaning of humankind and the importance of this world, a century that has quarrelled about the use of the word 'God', this same period of history began with *The Idea of the Holy*.[76]

In two articles Stratford Caldecott has recently argued for the need to find and construct a new approach to the crisis which confronts the world today. He demonstrates that the roots of this crisis go deeper than economic and social, cultural and psychological factors since they are ultimately religious. Without a recognition or heeding of God's revelation about the purpose of human life and his design for creation, the pursuit of freedom only becomes frustrated and ends in sterility. Following Pope John Paul II's analysis of the current critical situation – especially as expounded in his Encyclical Letter on social problems, *Centesimus Annus* (1991) – Caldecott states that sound theological thinking rather than merely philosophical reflection is required. Discussion of freedom, however, must be moved beyond the level of merely a reactionary and moralistic stance against liberal positions or tendencies, and also, beyond the polarities of 'Left and Right', of 'liberals' and 'conservatives'. In an attempt to bridge the false dichotomies that have divided people for centuries – dichotomies stemming from Western society's deep-rooted dualistic tendency – there is need for setting a new kind of agenda which grapples with the secular assumptions of people today. He concludes that the problem and challenge starkly facing contemporary society turn upon the fulcrum of choosing between giving priority to freedom or love.[77]

But, in order to know the meaning and purpose of the 'love' spoken of here – as distinct from its common equation with sex, pleasure, or sentimentality – it is necessary to turn to what has been revealed about it by God, who is its vital source, substance and summit (cf. 1 Jn 4:16ff.). In the next section, we shall consider the teaching of the New Testament where God's love is made manifest in Jesus Christ, who reveals the fullness and ultimate expression of this love in the Passover mystery of the Eucharist, which Christians celebrate as the supreme gift and *hymn of freedom*. The renewal of an understanding and appreciation of living the eucharistic mystery as the sacred sign or sacrament of love and unity is the key to the transformation of our endeavours to achieve that quality of personal liberation and to build a society of justice, peace and brotherhood beyond national boundaries – a society which Pope Paul VI often called most appropriately the *'civilisation of love'*.

PART II

REVELATION AND
GIFT OF FREEDOM

The Gospel is not a statement of general truths of religion, but an interpretation of that which once happened. The Creeds are anchored in history by the clause 'under Pontius Pilate'. Above all, in the Sacrament of the Eucharist the Church recapitulates the historic crisis in which Christ came, lived, died and rose again, and finds in it the 'efficacious sign' of eternal life in the Kingdom of God. In its origin and in its governing ideas it may be described as a sacrament of realized eschatology. The Church prays, 'Thy kingdom come'; 'Come, Lord Jesus.' As it prays, it remembers that the Lord did come, and with Him came the Kingdom of God. Uniting memory with aspiration, it discovers that He comes. He comes in His Cross and Passion; He comes in the glory of His Father with the holy angels. Each Communion is not a stage in a process by which His coming draws gradually nearer, or a milestone on the road by which we slowly approach the distant goal of the Kingdom of God on earth. It is a re-living of the decisive moment at which He came.

C.H. Dodd, *The Parables of the Kingdom*[1]

Gradually the kingdom reveals itself to me, not so much as an institution or anything of that sort, but as a person summoning me, trying to establish a more and more intimate, friendly, living relationship with me.
The kingdom is the home of the King: his divine essence of peace, justice, mercy and truth. . . .
The Promised Land was an objective appropriate to people needing a country where they could enjoy their freedom.
The kingdom responds to the need we all have, to see, to hear, to serve the King who is God himself. . . .
We were orphans? Now we have a Father.
We were only children? Now we have brothers and sisters.
We had no friends? Now we have a Friend.
We were sterile? Now we are fruitful.
We were inadequate? See, the victory of freedom.
But above all, were we lonely? Behold the bridegroom.

Carlo Carretto, *Journey Without End*[2]

Hope and Freedom: Evangelisation in View of the Kingdom of God

'The Spirit of the Lord . . . to set prisoners free' (Lk 4:18f.)

The deepest meaning or personal truth of history which the Gospels portray in revealing Christ is finely caught in a poem by the literary critic C.S. Lewis, who may be better known for his superb children's stories. In this poem Lewis says that Christ focuses and frees the human mind, imagination and heart from its anxious eternal quest, which meanders through nature, philosophy, the arts, for he leads directly to the object of all yearning by revealing the presence of the God who saves in the simple forms of bread and wine.[3]

The freedom proclaimed on every page of the Gospels is good news precisely because the Gospels witness to God's fulfilment of his promise to remain with his people. The fulfilment of this promise in Jesus Christ is the well-spring of authentic human freedom; it is the realisation of something utterly new in human history – the 'new and eternal covenant'. God's faithfulness consists in his fidelity of love which discloses how close he is and wishes to remain with human beings in their darkest hour and situation of greatest need, namely, in the hour of their anxiety over death which results from the common situation of sinfulness. Redemption is the name for the fullness of freedom;[4] it implies 'liberation in the strongest sense of the word'.[5]

The Gospels are consistent with the Old Testament scriptures regarding the notion of redemption or freedom being closely connected with Israel's awareness of God's special relationship to it.[6] Redemption signifies something quite similar to

that of salvation: both notions refer to the same reality considered from different angles – rescue from slavery in the
former case, preservation and restoration of life in the latter.[7]
Usually when we think or speak of redemption, we tend to refer
to what has happened to us through God sending his Son into
the world to save it by redeeming or 'buying it back' from the
power of evil, that is, from all that sets limits to or restricts
human beings from being free to realise their fullest potential.
The language of tradition from the time of the Fathers, thus,
frequently employs the biblically based imagery of Christ paying
the 'price of our redemption'.[8] The language of this imagery is
familiar to us in the prayers of the liturgy. While this is true,
there is, however, another, deeper meaning of redemption than
that referring to what happens *to us* – wonderful as this truth is.
Redemption applies in the first place and in the fullest sense to
the objective truth of faith which focuses on *God's act* of
proclaiming and realising his desire to free human beings from
their circumstances of every kind of bondage, particularly from
sinfulness.

Furthermore, the deepest dimension of redemption, that
is, of the objective truth of God's saving action, is the reality of
the revelation of the personal mystery of Jesus Christ, 'the
Redeemer of humanity'. It is to him that the notion of redemption applies most fully. We can, therefore, say that he himself is
redemption. Pope John Paul II states that he makes God's
mercy *incarnate* and personifies it: '*He himself, in a certain sense, is
mercy.*'[9]

The Gospels enable us to see most clearly how redemption
or freedom is intrinsically related to God's faithful presence to
all humanity through his liberating involvement in human
history. In virtue of revealing and realising his presence in all
the circumstances of human life, history is seen as having a
design and purpose. Human history signifies, thus, not merely
the succession or a turning around of human events or the
interaction of socio-political, economic and cultural factors and
natural causes and effects. Nor is it merely determined by what
is considered 'progress' in the conditions of human life and
work,[10] but in the relationship of all human endeavour to God's
saving work of our redemption.[11] The perspective of the Old

Testament scriptures shows that history has a meaning and purpose when all events and human experiences are related to the saving presence of God, who gradually shapes in the human heart – particularly the attentive heart of the people of Israel – the hope that a Redeemer would come, a Messiah or 'Christ' whom God would send to proclaim and bring about the definitive deliverance of humankind. In the light of this perspective of hope, history takes on its true meaning, a sacred meaning and sense of direction; it becomes the history of salvation or redemptive freedom when understood as related to Jesus Christ. In a very profound sense, thus, the Gospels reveal how history becomes intrinsically part of the story of Jesus Christ when he entered the conditions of our flesh and blood experience. In the most profound sense, that is, the personal and communal dimension of the struggle of human existence for freedom, the Gospels are the good news of our history inseparably merged with *his* story.[12] God's design and purpose are intrinsically related to his freedom-giving presence which is revealed by and in Jesus Christ, whom the Church faithfully acknowledges as one and the same person, the Redeemer of humanity and Lord of history.[13] Since he not only proclaims, but *is* the living gospel, it is to his saving presence that Christians turn their loving gaze in seeking the source and fulfilment of their hope for human freedom.

Freedom to encounter the living God

The Gospels may be read or listened to in different ways. One way is to hear in them the proclamation of various stories which relate the significant moments of Jesus' meetings with different kinds of people. During the last half-century this way of understanding and presenting the data of the Gospels, which was employed by the great Fathers of the Church, has been developed and emphasised by theologians who have fruitfully adapted and pastorally applied the phenomenological and existential approach to the service of the gospel as the living Word of God. It is a particularly appropriate way of presenting Jesus' good news in our times which are marked by a situation of alienation and anxiety, as seen in the first part of this essay.[14] Furthermore, this manner of approaching Jesus Christ's gospel of life introduces all people of good will and especially the community of his faithful to those contemplative depths of relating to him, the Splendour of Truth, which cannot be attained or perceived by any other methods available to human reason. For Jesus Christ, who surpasses all human knowledge and understanding, discloses the hidden wisdom of the Father's loving design of redemption and reveals that the deepest truth about being human is love.[15]

Jesus reveals God encountering human persons in every circumstance of life: fishermen and tax collectors; a bewildered student, zealous about following God's law more fully; a Pharisee seeking a new interpretation of religion, but who dared to approach him only under the cover of darkness; a handful of persons genuinely seeking answers to their intellectual or religious dilemmas or others merely curious about the kind of reply he would give them; people forced to become street beggars because of their physical handicap, such as blindness or lameness; countless persons in various situations of personal grief or in dire need of physical or moral or spiritual assistance and guidance; a dying thief stealing his way to heaven's reward by a 'death-bed' conversion. There is the description even of Pilate, a man of some education and culture, who could ask the crucial question: What is truth? – but, who lacked the freedom enough to recognise or acknowledge it staring him in the face in the presence of Jesus, his prisoner. The moment of encounter in each case is shown as being a crucial point on which everything depended in the lives of these people. Their lives would never again be the same: they were introduced to something utterly new; they were presented with the choice of a new way of life; they were provoked into the situation of making a conscious decision – a fundamental option – to follow or turn away/against Jesus. The moment of encountering Jesus occasioned people to plead for his intervention in their situations of human anguish or to thank him for his care and assistance or to be struck with a sense of wonderment about his extraordinary and awesome authority and power.

The deeper, dynamic quality of the gospel of Jesus, as the living and effective Word of God, is that every one of these encounters – which are representative of any at life's crossroads – confronts us with the mysterious and wonderful presence of him who is the unique source and summit of freedom. Freedom is that quality of life directly related to entering his presence; it is the gift offered by him, who is the Word made flesh (as in John), the kingdom amongst/within/in our midst (as in Luke), the Son of God (as in Mark), Emmanuel, God-with-us (as in Matthew). This gift of freedom, moreover, draws us ever deeper into the mystery of faith where we – like the first of Christ's faithful – become worshippers of the Father in spirit and truth (cf. Jn 4:24).

In other words, the key theme underlying and running through all the descriptions of Jesus' meetings with people in the Gospels is that he frees the human awareness of individuals from being preoccupied about fleeting things and time-bound concerns and transforms their whole perspective so that they may become persons focused on the 'one thing necessary'. His gift of freedom unites individuals into the community of his disciples, whose life is characterised by the new quality of his love (*agapē*). This love unites them with him as 'a eucharistic hearted' people in the worship of God in praise and thanksgiving and the service of all humankind. In this sense we might rightly say that the freedom revealed and communicated by Jesus Christ is a 'theological' reality in so far as we understand clearly that theology involves experience *of* the Word of God, a response *to* the Word of God in worship and service, and an attempt to express or communicate something *about* the Word of God.[16]

St Augustine characteristically brings out the existential dynamic quality of the Christian faith-experience of 'being of one mind and heart' (Acts 4:32) by adding the words 'on the way to God'.[17] This phrase: 'on the way to God', captures Augustine's fine appreciation of the Passover nature of the whole theological or God-oriented life of the Church's faith, hope and love. As a pilgrim community, the Church's unanimity is not a cosy complacency, but is focused on the source and goal of the self-transcending vitality of Jesus' proclamation in the gospel: 'Blessed are the pure of heart [that is, single-mindedness], they shall see God' (Mt 5:8). Augustine saw these two features of unanimity and movement towards God as intrinsically related to the evangelical nature of the Christian vocation of all members of the Church: the calling to follow Christ applies to all, not only to monks or those who are the 'professionals' of religion. Thus, in a sermon to the people he succinctly states his understanding of oneness of life in the Christian community: 'Together one, in the one Christ, on the way to the one Father.'[18] Christian freedom is founded and realised in this Passover movement to oneness – or, *at-onement*, which strengthens Christ's faithful in their unslackening attention to the gospel and in their constant tending towards the Father in the freedom of the Spirit of the Lord Jesus Christ.

There is no transformation as great or long-lasting as that which comes about through encountering and becoming aware of another person's presence – especially that of another person lovingly turned towards one. The sheer transforming beauty of this mystery of encounter is the constant focus of mysticism as well as of the greatest love poetry and literature.[19] One recalls Anne Frank's account of the transformation that took place on a certain day when, while hiding in fear from the Nazi terror, she discovered that a boy, Peter, began looking at her in a new way, that of a loving gaze. Indeed, the familiar human experience of personal encounter ('falling in love') becomes enriched by the central truth of divine *revelation*, which means that the veil of sadness which separates human beings from the face of the living God is drawn back. The Fathers of the Church delighted to look on Christ as the light communicating God. Thus, for instance, Clement of Alexandria says: 'Christ is the face [*prosōpon*] of God'.[20]

Since Matthew's Gospel shows us, so to speak, the human face of God turned towards us – *Emmanuel*, 'God-with-us' – perhaps this is why this evangelist is represented by the symbol of an angel or messenger with a human countenance.

The Gospels are 'good news' in so far as they proclaim that Jesus Christ uniquely makes freedom possible because he reveals the presence of God to humanity. In presenting a selection of his words and deeds according to the theological perspective of the different evangelists, the Gospels show that his identity and mission are one and the same, namely God's declaration to invite human beings to live in his presence wherein they may know the joy of their real worth in freedom. Thus, Jesus' very name means 'the Lord saves' (Mt 1:11; cf. Lk 2:11). This invitation implies, moreover, the vocation or calling of all human beings; it calls all to welcome as good news God's presence in Jesus Christ. He not only calls, but also enables or empowers them to respond to his divine gift of freedom by sacrificing the alienation of *self*dom to enter the new reality of communion in the kingdom of God, that is, to become related to God and humankind and the whole world. This gift is offered through the continued working of his Spirit in the new covenantal community of the Church.

Discovery of freedom and renewal through celebrating the Church's origin

An attentive listening to the Gospels makes it clear that the truth of freedom, for which humanity always yearns, is a dynamic reality which grows and develops to fulfilment in so far as Christ's faithful receive and respond to the good news of his life. This receptiveness to the freedom of Jesus Christ's life implies that the Christian community is held in a constant creative tension of discovering in the midst of their temporal condition of history the progressive revelation of the reality of God's presence and kingdom – that kingdom which *was* uniquely revealed by and in Jesus Christ and which *is* being made ever clearer in the course of the ages by the Holy Spirit *until* it *shall* become fully realised according to the Father's wonderful salvific design to draw all creation into the embrace of his redemptive love, which signifies the fullness of freedom. The Gospels witness to the early Christian community's growth in awareness of this creative tension through its proclamation that the freedom of God's kingdom, which was definitively communicated by and in Christ, was becoming part of its experience.[21] In so far as these same Gospels continue to be proclaimed in the celebration of this reality of Christ's freedom,

they generate anew the energy to realise the creativity of the
gift of freedom at every new stage of history and through every
cultural setting. As in the early Christian communities, so too
in every successive age the Gospels' proclamation commits
Christians to pray and strive for an ever deeper realisation of
this redemptive gift and reality of freedom.

Following closely this perspective of the New Testament,
particularly in the teaching of the Synoptic Gospels about the
kingdom of God, the Fathers of the Second Vatican Council
adopted the language of the patristic tradition in describing
the Church in the sacramental terms of 'mystery':

> The mystery of the holy Church is already brought to light in the
> way it was founded. For the Lord Jesus inaugurated his Church by
> preaching the Good News, that is, the coming of the kingdom of
> God, promised over the ages in the scriptures: 'The time is fulfilled,
> and the kingdom of God is at hand' (Mk 1:15; Mt 4:17). This
> kingdom shone out before humanity in the word, in the works and
> in the presence of Christ. The word of the Lord is compared to a
> seed which is sown in a field (Mk 4:14); those who hear it with faith
> and are numbered among the little flock of Christ (Lk 12:32) have
> truly received the kingdom. Then, by its own power the seed
> sprouts and grows until the harvest (cf. Mk 4:26–9). The miracles
> of Jesus also demonstrate that the kingdom has already come on
> earth: 'If I cast out devils by the finger of God, then the kingdom of
> God has come upon you' (Lk 11:20; cf. Mt 12:28). But principally
> the kingdom is revealed in the person of Christ himself, Son of
> God and Son of Man, who came 'to serve and give his life as a
> ransom for many' (Mk 10:45).[22]

Developing the Council's teaching on the continuity of Jesus'
revelation of the kingdom in the mystery or sacrament of the
Church, Cardinal Ratzinger exposes the shortcomings of an
overly 'this-worldly' and materialistic interpretation of the
gospel, such as given by certain liberation theologians who
uncritically adopt a Marxist viewpoint of 'kingdom' as identified
solely with the ideological objective or goal of forming a classless
society in this world – a 'utopia' for which people ('the
proletariat') are urged to strive might and main. Rather, the
immanence of God's kingdom is all inclusive of this world and
the world to come in accordance with the teaching of the Lord's

Prayer: 'Thy kingdom come'. This prayer plunges us into the creative tension of freedom. St Teresa of Avila says that the request for God's kingdom is linked with that for God's name to be hallowed, because we need to realise that God's reign in this world signifies that God is praised and honoured by those around us as well.[23] The whole purpose of the proclamation of the gospel is to lead people to be able to pray the Lord's Prayer[24] – that is, to have the inner dispositions and attitude implied in this 'summary of the whole gospel'.[25] At the heart of this pattern of prayer which he gave his disciples, Jesus teaches that the grace of God's presence is indispensable: this is a need as basic for realising the fullness of life in freedom, as that of food is to material well-being. Human endeavour and work take on their truest significance and become most deeply worthwhile only when orientated by a sense of hunger for this food. This profound hunger is both revealed by God's Spirit and satisfied in Christian prayer and worship. Ratzinger goes on to point out that what John the Baptist and the Qumran community heralded as coming 'soon', Jesus fulfilled in the 'now' of Christology, that is, his real presence through the Church in the world. He sums up this new reality of the powerful 'now' of Christ's presence that frees in the following words:

> Jesus himself is God's action, his coming, his reigning. In Jesus' mouth, 'Kingdom of God' does not mean some thing or place but the present action of God. One may therefore translate the programmatic declaration of Mark 1:15, 'the Kingdom of God is near at hand', as 'God is near'. We perceive once more the connection with Jesus, with his person; he himself is God's nearness. Wherever he is, is the Kingdom. In this respect we must recast Loisy's statement: Thy Kingdom was promised, what came was Jesus. Only in this way can we understand aright the paradox of promise and fulfilment.[26]

What Ratzinger states about the origin of the Church is of particular relevance to the deepest dimensions of the question of human freedom. Christ reveals human freedom in all its amplitude in relating and making accessible his freedom-giving sacrifice to his new community or Church by instituting the Eucharist. Since all the institution accounts are presented as linked with Christ's new sacrifice of the covenant,[27] they have direct bearing on the founding of the Church, the community of Christ's body given for the life of the world. By the time the Gospels were written down, the community of Christ's followers had already been gathering for a number of years to celebrate the Eucharist, which they had come to realise in one way or other constituted them as a new people of freedom and from which they drew their inspiration and energy. In the light of the Eucharist, the early Christian community had learnt, as Dom Gregory Dix truly says, to 'read' the life of Jesus Christ; they discovered 'in the eucharist an entire epitome of "the Gospel"'.[28] The eucharistic sacrifice is 'the permanent origin and centre of the Church' in so far as the people of the new covenant are formed from the body and blood of Christ and united closely 'to the one Lord and to his one and only Body'.[29]

Freedom accompanies and is an integral part of the gift of the Lord Jesus' revelation of his kingdom through founding the Church in the institution of the Eucharist. In this freedom, as the Council put it, 'the Church, or the kingdom of God already present in mystery, becomes evident in the world through the power of God'.[30] Towards the end of his Encyclical Letter on Social Concern, Pope John Paul II develops the thought expressed in an enlightened passage of the Pastoral Constitution of the Church in the World concerning the kingdom already present in mystery in relation to the Eucharist. He sees human development of the world as intrinsically linked to the Eucharist, the privileged atmosphere of grace in which are fostered the characteristic qualities of the Christian life: human dignity, fraternal communion and freedom.[31]

The gift of redemption or freedom of humanity and the whole of creation becomes realised through the power of Jesus Christ's Word and the Father's Holy Spirit – that power which is especially operative in the 'making' and building up of the body of Christ at the celebration of the Eucharist. Freedom, which is the gift of the risen Lord's Spirit, is realised through his community's faithful and loving obedience to Jesus Christ's command: 'Do this in memory of me.' In the words of one scholar, 'it is scarcely too much to say that, wherever Christianity has found a home, these few verses have helped to change the world'.[32]

The Church's constant tradition in understanding its identity and mission in relation to the Eucharist, the sign of the kingdom of God,[33] is firmly based on the New Testament evidence of a perspective which has been called 'realised eschatology'.[34] In the Synoptic Gospels especially, it is abundantly clear that, whereas Jesus' chief concern or intention was undoubtedly focused on preparing for the kingdom of God, the notion of Church is by no means alien to his intentions, as a sort of afterthought. Jesus was no impractical dreamer, unconcerned about the realities of human existence. In all his activity of calling together, purifying and uniting people, Jesus included the idea of a community of those who would be free to form a new worshipping communion with him. That is, far from abolishing the law of worship, he brings out its deepest significance as leading beyond a servitude or servility of ritual and legalism to the intimacy and freedom appropriate to all who belong to the household or family of God. Jesus transforms worship into something entirely new and beautiful: it is no longer a tax extracted and paid reluctantly, a duty sullenly fulfilled, an obligation of ritual carried out perfunctorily or as if it were bestowing some favour or honour on God, but a gift to be received with gratitude. Jesus' whole teaching and especially his own example in prayer show the heart of worship: the loving turning of a child towards its parent, or rather, the return of a wayward child to the welcoming embrace of its father who has all along, as if by an invisible energy of tenderness and mercy, been drawing his child back from the bankruptcy of headstrong or impetuous selfishness to the intimacy of the familiar hearth. In the Gospels Jesus is repeatedly shown calling people from their habitual condition of infidelity, weakness and pride to respond in the freedom of gratitude to praise his Father's wonderful design to give them a share in his banquet of life, as the kingdom of God or heaven is often depicted in the parables, such as, for example, in the parable of the Prodigal Son (cf. Lk 15). The relationship of the many references to meals to the Eucharist is summed up by the ecumenical theologian Jean-Marie Tillard:

The Gospel narratives attach great importance to the meals of Jesus.[35] And this throws light on the significance of the Last Supper. ... But the eucharistic meal is not only rooted in the basic symbolism of the meals of the people of God on its journey and the meals of the first Christian community gathered around its Risen Lord, it also reminds us of the prophetic image of the eschatological banquet. It is not simply the announcement of that banquet but the mysterious 'anticipation of the Supper of the Lamb' (I, 1 [Lima Statement]). Every time it is celebrated, there is not only a meeting with the Lord in his 'sacramental meal', 'as the continuing people of God, until his return' (I, 1), but we are also nourished with hope. According to the interpretation proposed by J. Jeremias,[36] the words 'until he come' (*achri hou elthēi*) in 1 Cor. 11:26 denote far more than waiting for the final moment of history; they imply an active reaching out towards it, a sighing, a prayer, a *marana tha*.[37]

The end of evangelisation: to proclaim hope in the God who frees

The Gospels – especially in the parables about the kingdom of God – present much more than moral lessons. They present morality in a new light, not as a moralism of 'must' and 'ought' as regards the fulfilling of external laws, but as response to Jesus' person. They raise human responsibility to the level of dialogue with God's Word who discloses the inner values and truth of human actions. The way of life which the Gospels point out is first and foremost Christ's. Christian morality becomes, thus, something more than the study of human ethics; it is the expression of the implications of Christology. The Gospels give us Jesus not as, in H.G. Wells' description of him, 'some terrible moral huntsman digging mankind out of the snug burrows in which they had lived hitherto'.[38] Rather, they relate something far more exciting: namely, the theological story of that 'brief and tremendous crisis', in which Jesus is the principal figure. The 'crisis' pertains both to Jesus and his hearers: they involve the hearers of the parables – both those of Jesus' day and of every generation – to take a stand for or against him.[39]

The underlying New Testament notion of crisis implies more than what our modern sense of the word suggests – viz. a state of psychological discomfort or unease or disorder. It bears the biblical, theological sense of judgement unto salvation, which provokes a response of discernment and decisiveness. It is in this sense that we should understand the profound significance of what Christian freedom implies: as Christ's gift to respond in the responsibility of his Spirit's love to the mystery of God's presence. This teaching is expounded everywhere in the writings of St Augustine, who insists that the grace of Christ's Spirit in no way restricts the capacity to use human freedom, but rather enlarges and enriches it as the crowning of God's gifts.[40]

The gift of freedom accompanies Jesus' revelation of his kingdom at the important moment of inaugurating the 'new and eternal covenant' – the moment, that is, when he instituted the Eucharist and at the same time founded a new community which would realise the intentions for which he prayed to his Father at the Last Supper. The gift of Christian freedom is directly connected with the Eucharist as the Eucharist is with the Church, that is, that community which is called to be a sacrament of God's unity, the communion of the Father, Son and Holy Spirit. The theme of the kingdom of God is thus typically eucharistic.[41]

To deepen our understanding of the all-pervading theme of the Gospels one might compare the end of Matthew's account with parallel sections presented by the other evangelists. Here one has a resumé of the essential proclamation of the journey of faith to freedom which the Christian community is called to undertake. The last verses of the Gospels, particularly in Matthew, provide, as it were, a map of both the path of faith and also of its scope, namely, to bring believers to the goal of human life which consists in entering the kingdom of God. These verses record the risen Lord Jesus' clear revelation of the new relationship of the community of his disciples to the presence of the Father, Son and Holy Spirit. In the light of this revelation the post-resurrection community of disciples or the Church is enabled to read all Jesus Christ's deeds and words, in which the parables hold pride of place, as signs pointing to the coming of the kingdom of God, in which the human hope for freedom becomes fulfilled according to God's design.

In considering the passages in the Gospels dealing with the risen Lord Jesus' definitive commissioning of his disciples,[42] which for convenience are presented below, we can also appreciate the continuity of Jesus' proclamation of the kingdom of freedom in the Church, and especially of how this continuity is realised through the Church's central act of proclamation in the Eucharist. These passages contain the Church's crucial mission statement and provide the key to understanding the intrinsic connection between the purpose of Jesus' whole life and the Church as the sacramental community of the presence of the risen Lord.

Although the accounts in the Synoptics of Jesus' final encounter with his disciples after the resurrection before ascending to his Father differ in their descriptions of the details of the circumstances, certain important similarities are worth noticing: Jesus addresses 'the eleven' disciples – Judas having fallen from their number (Matthew and Mark); despite the hesitation of disbelief of some, the disciples worship or adore him (Matthew and Luke use the same word meaning profound prostration – *prosekúnēsan*/*proskunēsantes*; cf. also Mt 14:33); the risen Lord Jesus commissions them with his own divine authority (most explicit in Matthew, where the strong word *exousia* is used and the place of assembly is intended as a symbol recalling the giving of the new law on the mountain of the Beatitudes by Jesus, the new Moses); he commands his disciples to go and preach his good news of God's kingdom to all people and to make disciples of them; he authorises them to baptise 'in the name' (Matthew and Mark, though Matthew alone specifies the trinitarian formula in use in the Church); he instructs his disciples to teach others obedience to his saving teaching (Luke specifies the call to conversion [*metánoian*] and its freedom-giving effect, namely, forgiveness [*áphesin*] of sins). The Church has thus been entrusted with the fundamental task of evangelisation by representing Jesus' own missionary work of bringing people to the deepest sense of hope for freedom or redemption through his Holy Spirit's gift of forgiveness, as John particularly emphasises.

The most important point in these accounts of the risen Lord Jesus' final address to his disciples as a group consists in his assurance of remaining with them. Matthew alone quotes Jesus' statement verbatim. However, Mark implies it in speaking of the Lord's working with the disciples, who are confirmed or strengthened in proclaiming his message; and Luke likewise implies the continuity of Jesus' presence through his gift of the Father's 'promise'. Jesus' remarkable assurance about being with his disciples is fulfilled in the fact that the tradition of the gospel of Jesus Christ was passed on and that it continues to be proclaimed and also effective in building up the Church in all parts of the world today. These narratives bring out clearly that the risen Lord continues to be present and who communicates the power of the Father's Spirit to the Church, the community of believers. The risen Lord's assurance of his presence is the basis of his community's whole life and mission. His last words to his community of disciples reiterate what was announced at the beginning of Matthew in fulfilment of the prophecy of Isaiah: ' "Behold, a virgin shall conceive and bear a son, and his name shall be called Emmanuel" (which means, God with us)' (Mt 1:23; cf. Is. 7:14). In view of the fulfilment of this prophecy through the co-operation in the Virgin Mary's obedience in faith to God's design, we might truly see the relationship of the community of the risen Lord's disciples to her, 'the handmaid of the Lord' (cf. Lk 1:38, 48), who is the prototype, exemplar and model of the Church, the new Israel.[43] The Blessed Virgin Mary's graced response in freedom to God's Word provides the pattern of the Church's and every disciple's response to the presence of God among us.[44] Thus, the Holy Virgin Mother, whom the Greeks call the God-bearer (*Theotokos*), is both the Mother of Christ the unique Redeemer, who brings us freedom, and also, in Pope Paul VI's memorable declaration during the Second Vatican Council: 'the Mother of the Church',[45] the privileged environment in which the risen Lord's grace and truth of freedom are communicated and realised. For from the beginning the Blessed Virgin responded to the good news of God's presence and taught the disciples, by her presence among them in the Cenacle, to overcome all natural disappointment and fear through awaiting prayerfully for the outpouring of the risen Lord's Spirit of freedom, as Luke records (cf. Acts 1:14).

The revelation of the event of the resurrection was necessary for the realisation of the deep truth of 'God with us'. For this event was the culminating point of Jesus Christ's whole life and his Passover mystery. The heart of the Church's whole life and mission is focused on the proclamation of this reconciliation in freedom of the kingdom of God in the celebration of the Eucharist, which contains and communicates the full richness of the gospel and which is the good news in deed – evangelisation *par excellence.*[46]

Mt 28:16–20

Now the eleven disciples went to Galilee, to the mountain to which Jesus had directed them. And when they saw him they worshipped him; but some doubted.

And Jesus came and said to them, 'All authority in heaven and on earth has been given to me.

Go therefore and make disciples of all nations, baptizing them in the name of the Father and of the Son and of the Holy Spirit, teaching them to observe all that I have commanded you; and behold, I am with you always, to the close of the age.'

Mk 16:14–20

Afterward he appeared to the eleven themselves as they sat at table; and he upbraided them for their unbelief and hardness of heart, because they had not believed those who saw him after he had risen.

And he said to them,

'Go into all the world and preach the gospel to the whole creation. He who believes and is baptized will be saved; but he who does not believe will be condemned . . . .' So then the Lord Jesus, after he had spoken to them, was taken up into heaven, and sat down at the right hand of God. And they went forth and preached everywhere, while the Lord worked with them and confirmed the message by the signs that attended it. Amen.

Lk 24:44–53

Then he said to them,

'These are my words which I spoke to you, while I was still with you, that everything written about me in the law of Moses and the prophets and the psalms must be fulfilled.' Then he opened their minds to understand the scriptures, and said to them, 'Thus it is written, that the Christ should suffer and on the third day rise from the dead, and that repentance and forgiveness of sins should be preached in his name to all nations, beginning from Jerusalem. You are witnesses of these things. And behold, I send the promise of my Father upon you; . . .' While he blessed them, he parted from them, and was carried up into heaven. And they worshipped him. . . .

Jn 14:23

'If a man loves me, he will keep my word, and my Father will love him, and we will come to him and make our home with him.'

Jn 20:21–3

Jesus said to them again, 'Peace be with you. As the Father has sent me, even so I send you.' And when he had said this, he breathed on them, and said to them, 'Receive the Holy Spirit. If you forgive the sins of any, they are forgiven; if you retain the sins of any, they are retained.'

The rich depths of the statement in the last verse of Matthew, 'Behold, *I am with you* always, to the close of the age', must be appreciated. Literally the statement is: 'I with you am' (*ego meth' humōn eimi*). The community of disciples are as it were within the embrace of Christ's being. Throughout this Gospel the idea of the mysterious divine reality revealed through Christ's presence is expressed on different occasions – as, for instance, when Jesus reassures his disciples' sinking hearts of being at hand to support (cf. 14:27), or when he speaks of being with two or three who gather in his name (cf. 18:20), or when he identifies himself at the last judgement with the poor, prisoners, etc. (cf. 25:31ff.). It is implied certainly in the disciples' and others' confessions of faith in him, such as at the important moment at Caesarea Philippi when under divine inspiration Peter acknowledges that he is the Son of the living God, the Messiah (cf. 16:16; cf. also Mt 14:33; Mk 15:39; Jn 11:27; 19:35; 20:28).

The background of Matthew's idea of God's nearness with his people goes back to the very roots of religious consciousness. In the beginning God walked with Adam in the garden in the cool of the evening (cf. Gen. 3:8). Later, Israel became aware of God's mysterious life-giving presence through the law which he revealed to Moses, to whom he spoke face to face (cf. Ex. 33:11). In fact, so strong was Israel's sense of God that its boast was: 'No other people has its gods as near to it as our God is to us' (Deut. 4:7). From the beginning human worth was intrinsically related to worship of God – as is evident even in the Anglo-Saxon etymology of 'worth' and 'worship'. In examining one of the most challenging problems of our present situation – namely, how, in a technological age of materialistic values, we can recover a sense of God's presence as Creator, and hence of creation as an order of love freely given by God – Ratzinger observes:

> The creation accounts for all civilisations point to the fact that the universe exists for worship and for the glorification of God . . . the danger that confronts us today in our technological civilisation . . . is that increasing scientific know-how is preventing us from being aware of the fact of creation.[47]

This sense of awareness of the presence of the divine was sharpened by the prophets into the finest point of hope for the

actual coming of God in history as the Saviour-Messiah. This is
particularly accentuated in the famous prophecy of Isaiah
(7:14), which, as seen above, Matthew quotes verbatim right at
the beginning of his proclamation of the 'good news'.

The specific revelation which shaped Israel's consciousness
as the holy people of God was encompassed in the Lord's
disclosure of his sacred Name *Yahweh* – I AM! (Ex. 3:14). This
revelation not only authenticated Moses' mission, but also
welded the disordered Hebrew tribes into a single people sealed
with an identity by the covenant God made with them. This is
the background of Jesus' words in commissioning his disciples
with his own authority and mission to preach the good news to
the whole world and to bring others under the power of the
divine Name, baptising them into the communion with the holy
Trinity whose inner mystery of life he himself had witnessed
among them.[48] Jesus' words became the baptismal formula used
by the Church. Their significance as plunging believers *into* the
ocean of mystery of the relationships of the holy Trinity, so to
speak, is best conveyed in the liturgy carried out in the Eastern
Churches. For, the dynamic nature of movement into God's
life is symbolically expressed not only by the meaning of the
verb *baptizein*, which means to plunge or immerse, but also by
the preposition *eis*, which is followed by the accusative case in
Greek and hence would be more faithfully translated as: '*into*
the Name', instead of the rather static phrase in our formula:
'in the Name'. Jesus' words in commissioning his disciples to
baptise imply the ongoing, dynamic discovery of the mystery of
God in the freeing movement of continual conversion, that is,
the total immersion into his newness of life. This movement
entails uniting with Jesus in his Passover. The Lord Jesus
himself, who was worshipped at the Mountain of Galilee (cf. Mt
28:17), guarantees the realisation of this Passover by giving his
covenantal assurance to all who become members of his
Christian community: '*Behold, I am with you*'. This proclamation
is the explicit basis for the Church's realisation of its identity as
being the instrument and sacrament of God's promise to bring
freedom to his people.[49] For the risen Lord's assurance of being
near his people announces and guarantees the continuity of his
effective redemptive power through the Church's proclamation

of the Word, its liturgical celebrations of the sacraments, and also in its fidelity in seeking to discover and realise the reality of his presence in various other ways and circumstances of human experience, especially among the poor.[50] In all these situations Christ's proclamation resounds: '*Behold, I am with you*', not as a dead letter of his last will and testament, but as his poignant invitation to living dialogue.

Resonances of the deep meaning of this proclamation are heard in different ways through the Gospels. For instance, the biblical image of God visiting his people with salvation is the theme of the canticle of Zechariah on recovering his speech at the birth of John the Baptist: 'Blessed be the Lord God of Israel for he has *visited* and redeemed his people . . . the tender mercy of our God . . . will bring the rising Sun to *visit* us from on high (Lk 1:68, 78; cf. also Lk 7:16; 19:44; Acts 15:14).'[51] The whole of Luke's Gospel may be seen as a commentary on the theme of the kingdom of God which has already come, and is already present.[52] Four times Luke describes Jesus' ministry in terms of a divine visit: 1:68; 1:78; 7:16; 19:44. In the words of one commentator on Luke:

> God is not merely the playwright who has devised the plot for the drama of redemption; he is an actor who makes a personal appearance on the stage and whose presence brings the whole action to its denouement. The same idea is conveyed by Luke's frequent use of the verb *euangelisesthai* (to 'bring good news'), which he uses in preference to the noun *euangelion*, because in his mind it carried definite associations from its use in the Old Testament [Is. 40:9–10; 52:7]. As to the prophet, so to Luke, 'the gospel of the kingdom' meant the news that God had arrived among his people to assume his sovereign power. The coming of the Saviour was the coming of God.[53]

This theme of God's saving and freeing visitation is closely linked to another, which is described everywhere in the Gospels – namely, the important theme of Jesus' *coming* and *entry*, which implies the opening of God's presence to human beings.[54] He comes as God's anointed one – that is, the 'Messiah' or Christ – at the most opportune moment of history, in the fullness of time.[55] The dawning of the recognition of faith in his coming is presented by Luke at the solemn inauguration of his public ministry at the synagogue of Nazareth; here Jesus proclaims and applies to himself the prophecy of the third book of Isaiah about God's plan to free people from every kind of enslavement:

> 'The Spirit of the Lord is upon me, because he has anointed me to preach good news to the poor. He has sent me to proclaim release to the captives and recovering of sight to the blind, to set at liberty those who are oppressed, to proclaim the acceptable year of the Lord.' And he closed the book, and gave it back to the attendant, and sat down; and the eyes of all in the synagogue were fixed on him. And he began to say to them, 'Today this scripture has been fulfilled in your hearing' (Lk 4:18–21; cf. Is. 61:1–2).[56]

It is highly significant that Luke mentions the fact that Jesus commanded the attention of all in the synagogue.[57] It is indeed extraordinary that on hearing Jesus' application of the prophet Isaiah's words about the freedom brought by the Messiah the people should exclaim their amazement in the precincts of the temple where it is customary to remain silent. The atmosphere buzzed with their comments, questions, exclamations.[58] The significance of this comment is much more than that of recording the psychological interest which he aroused in his audience – as though, for example, the people's curiosity was attracted by his eloquence or by his unusual and even magnetic personality. Luke's remark holds a deeper, theological significance which accords with the perspectives of all the evangelists' central proclamation that this person, Jesus of Nazareth, speaks with the authority of God, whose presence he uniquely reveals as near to humanity's need of freedom. Again and again, this significant theological theme is illustrated by the evangelists: Jesus' attitude of compassion for the multitudes; his miracles of healing; his moving parables of God seeking what is lost and oppressed – for instance, those of the Good Samaritan, the Prodigal Son or Patient Father, the Good Shepherd. In revealing God's presence in deed and word, Jesus was inviting and preparing ordinary people to appreciate and accept the ultimate good news of God's new and eternal covenant, which he himself fulfilled by remaining present to his disciples in accordance with his longing to share everything of himself with them in love unto the end (cf. Lk 22:15; Jn 13:1).

All the evangelists record the coming of the expected Messiah at the climactic moment of his entry into the city of Jerusalem – that entry which they emphasise was joyously welcomed by the simple people and especially by children. Thus, Luke's description richly alludes to the angelic announcement to the shepherds of the coming of the messianic reign of peace and freedom, an earthly reflection of God's glory (cf. Lk 2:8–14):

> he went on ahead, going up to Jerusalem. . . . As he was now drawing near, at the descent of the Mount of Olives, the whole multitude of the disciples began to rejoice and praise God with a loud voice for all the mighty works that they had seen, saying, 'Blessed is the King who comes in the name of the Lord! Peace in heaven and glory in the highest!' And some of the Pharisees in the multitude said to him, 'Teacher, rebuke your disciples.' He answered, 'I tell you, if these were silent, the very stones would cry out.' (Lk 19:28, 37–40; cf. Mt 21:1ff.; Mk 11:1ff.; Jn 12:12ff.)

The context of this account is important. Luke places it shortly after relating Jesus' entry into the house – and into the life – of a tax collector, Zacchaeus, to whom he proclaims: 'Today salvation has come to this house . . . For the Son of man came to seek and save the lost' (19:9–10). He goes on to describe Jesus' lament over the city which would be destroyed because it failed to discern the hour of God's visitation to bring about its true liberation (cf. 19:41–4). At this point Luke recalls the incident of Jesus' entry into the temple, from which he drives out those who profane God's house of prayer (cf. 19:45–6).

The phrase 'he who comes' (*ho erchomēnos*) was a very important title for the Messiah in early Christology.[59] The other Gospels include the word 'Hosanna!' with the people's welcome to Jesus' entry into Jerusalem. The original meaning of this word referred to freedom. For in Hebrew/Aramaic it expressed an urgent cry to God for deliverance or liberation: 'Save, now!'[60] In the course of time this meaning modulated in the usage of popular language to signify respectful acclaim and greeting: 'Hail!' Thus we could say that 'Hosanna' came to express an acclamation or shout of joy to welcome the freedom experienced at the coming of the Lord Jesus at his solemn entry into

Jerusalem, the city of David, on the eve of his passion (Mt 21:9,
15; cf. Mk 11:9–10; Jn 12:13). This important hour definitively
reveals the mystery of the kingdom of God, of which Jesus had
often spoken in the parables. Those who recognised and hailed
Jesus in the freedom of faith as the true 'King of Israel', the
Messiah anointed by God's Spirit, shared in his blessedness. The
Gospels cite Jesus' declaration that they are not merely 'happy'
or fortunate, but 'blessed', using the same word (*makārioi*) of
the Beatitudes: 'Blessed are your eyes, for they see, and your
ears, for they hear. Truly, I say to you, many prophets and
righteous men longed to see what you see, and did not see it,
and to hear what you hear, and did not hear it' (Mt 13:16–17;
Lk 10:23–4). Elsewhere in the Gospels, especially in the 'hymn
of jubilation', Jesus praises the Father for granting to mere
children the simplicity and freedom of heart to acknowledge
his presence (cf. Mt 11:25–7; Lk 10:21–2). These children are
all those people described in the Old Testament as 'the poor of
Yahweh' (*anawim Yahweh*); they know a most wonderful
freedom, which springs from their complete abandonment and
trust in God. They know something which is hidden from
people who are bound by the limitations of human systems of
thought and the restrictive vision of rationalism, on which they
solely rely. Furthermore, these 'little ones' recognise him whose
coming is the personal focal point of many righteous people's
and prophets' longing (cf. Mt 13:16–17; Lk 10:23–4).

We have been considering here a few of the different ways
and images in which the Gospels frequently present Jesus Christ
as the personal focus of this longing, expressed in the law and
the prophets. For he is the bearer and revealer of the divine
name, 'I AM', who has come and who remains present with his
community to communicate the fullness of the truth of being
free. In the following section we shall consider this fundamental
theme of God-with-us in the Fourth Gospel's presentation of
Jesus Christ, the Word made flesh, whose truth sets us free (Jn
8:32) because he alone most truly can say: 'Before Abraham
was, I am' (Jn 8:58). The Word passes over into that manner of
being with us in the Eucharist as our Emmanuel: God-with-us. In
a splendid passage from Pope St Leo the Great's second sermon
for the Ascension the rich significance of the mystery of Christ's

Passover is lucidly expressed in the following fine summary of sacramental communication of our new, graced state of freedom, which consists of *being in love*. 'The visible presence of the Redeemer has passed over into the sacraments [*transivit in sacramentis*].'[61] This statement recalls St Ambrose's words: 'You have shown yourself to me, Christ, face to face. I find you in your sacraments.'[62] Yet, only Jesus, Son of Man, reveals that God is close to the poor and naked, the hungry and thirsty, the prisoner and beggar, the refugee, outcast, battered wife and abused child . . . Each and all of these persons imply that God is there in and with them: he is their deepest *I AM*. Only he who is the Word of life can transform the prosaic grammar of human existence into the greatest poetry, God's life-giving mystery. He alone, the Creator-Word, remakes language and all existence with the reality of God's presence, freely giving up himself as the answer to the deepest prayer of every person and the human community: '*I am the bread of life come down from heaven . . . This is my body given for you . . . This is the cup of my blood . . . for the forgiveness of sins . . .*'. This proclamation is the greatest good news the world has ever heard. It is the annunciation of the beginning of something utterly new. It is evangelisation at its very fountainhead. It is the very source of all truth and freedom. It is the Christian community's most treasured gift, its eloquent word of renewal and encouragement, its focal point of faith, hope and love, its mystery of faith and *hymn of freedom*.

3

Truth and Freedom: Working for Freedom in the Fourth Gospel

The truth will make you free (Jn 8:32)

It might seem facile, and almost trite, to say that the reason that Jesus never wrote a Gospel was because he himself was the living Word of God.[1] The Fourth Gospel demonstrates that his whole life leads beyond the literal sense of words to the spiritual perception, understanding and living out of the design and work of God's revelation, which is disclosed in the covenantal grace and truth of his Word made flesh (1:14). One is tempted here to apply Shakespeare's plea for the deeper understanding of love which sees what words cannot express:

> O! learn to read what silent love hath writ:
> To hear with eyes belongs to love's fine wit.[2]

The task of interpretation always entails a risk. With regard to John's Gospel this risk concerns daring to confront the 'terrible freedom' of Jesus' truth, as Bonhoeffer has well described Jesus' freedom, which is truly *disturbing* with every nuance that this word may possibly imply:

> Jesus often seems not to understand at all what men are asking Him. He seems to be answering quite another question from that which has been put to Him. He seems to be missing the point of the question, not answering the question but addressing Himself directly to the questioner. He speaks with a complete freedom which is not bound by the law of logical alternatives. In this freedom Jesus leaves all laws beneath Him; and to the Pharisees this freedom necessarily appears as the negation of all order, all piety and all belief.[3]

Particularly in the Fourth Gospel we obtain such a glimpse of Jesus. While we may attribute this manner of interpretation of Jesus' character to what is called 'Johannine irony', there seems to lurk something else, something far more subtle than an author's figure of speech: the presence of some mysterious person behind, below or beyond the levels and scope of the Gospel's texture. The 'Word' – John's brilliant epithet for his and the world's teacher of truth – is much more than the idiom of Hebrew religious experience of divine revelation (*dabar Yahweh*) translated or transposed, without losing any of its dynamic vitality, into and made accessible to the Hellenistic thought patterns in terms of the *Logos* or 'Idea'. John's *Word* is too rich to be restricted to or contained in a message or philosophical concept. It bespeaks a freedom far grander, far more awesome and noble than that yearned for, aspired to, or claimed by any human being, while at the same time expressing all that any human being or the whole of humanity has ever dreamt of or dared to hope for. The *Word* is more than truth personified; it is the Truth *in persona*, the personal 'grace and truth', or better, 'the grace of the Truth' made flesh. Why does John use this phrase, if not to express the majestic, indeed, divine freedom of Jesus, the only-begotten Son of God? It is this Word who is misunderstood and whose freedom is easily misinterpreted – both in his own day and in every age. He is misunderstood and his freedom misinterpreted because he himself has allowed this to happen. Why? Simply because he respects human freedom – he challenges human beings to become his disciples in the freedom of the faith-response of love and obedience to him, the Word of life.

It is virtually impossible to say where the literal sense ends and the spiritual sense begins in this Gospel according to John, 'the beloved disciple'.[4] At the crucial moment of revealing how his grace and truth would be communicated in the sign of his flesh for the life of the world (6:51), this disciple records that Jesus insisted that the gift of this new manner of communication required the intervention of his Spirit: 'It is the spirit that gives life, the flesh is of no avail; the words that I have spoken to you are spirit and life' (6:63). Later, at the Last Supper, the same disciple recalls that Jesus promised the Spirit who would be sent by the Father after his glorification as the interpreter and guide to teach and remind his disciples of the significance of his teaching and gift of life and to lead them into the whole truth (cf. 14:26ff.; 16:12–14; cf. also 7:39).

This Gospel, therefore, has been aptly called the 'spiritual Gospel' by Clement of Alexandria, since it richly points to depths of the meaning of the mystery of the incarnation, that is, the truth of the historical reality and mystery of Jesus. This truth dominates the whole perspective of this Gospel: Jesus himself is the truth.[5] 'Truth' (*alētheia*) in John is applied only to Jesus, incarnate Son of God – not to God himself – for the Father expresses himself uniquely in his Word/Verb; he communicates his life/truth only in the Word-made-flesh.[6] The key which enables us to understand the purpose of this Gospel and to penetrate the mystery of the Word-made-flesh as the revelation of the Father is expressed in John's thematic statement: 'No one has ever seen God; the only Son, who is in the bosom of the Father, he has made him known' (1:18). This statement, which alludes to Exodus 33:20, is echoed everywhere. For instance, in the revelation made at Capernaum to the Jews during the discourse on the bread of life, Jesus says: 'For this is the will of my Father, that everyone who sees the Son and believes in him should have eternal life; and I will raise him up at the last day. . . . Not that any one has seen the Father except him who is from God; he has seen the Father' (6:40, 46).

Or, again at the Last Supper, Jesus replies to Thomas' question about where Jesus was going: 'I am the way, and the truth, and the life; no one comes to the Father, but by me. If you had known me, you would have known my Father also; henceforth you know him and have seen him' (14:6–7).

And he gently rebukes Philip for a lack of discernment of his divine transparency: 'Have I been with you so long, and yet you do not know me, Philip? He who has seen me has seen the Father; how can you say, "Show us the Father?" Do you not believe that I am in the Father and the Father in me?' (14:9–10a).

John's is a 'spiritual Gospel' in so far as it provokes reflection on the intrinsic connection between the depths of the mystery of the incarnation and the quality of the spiritual life of the community of Jesus' disciples, that is, the Church.

This connection, which undeniably was intended by John, has been perceived, interpreted and understood in various ways by Christians in the course of the centuries: those whom the Gospel addressed at the time of proclamation and composition; the generations of Christians who subsequently read, proclaimed, explained or heard it proclaimed and explained in the liturgy; the countless saints who meditated on it and drew from it nourishment for their lives and who mined in its depths the treasures of mysticism; those who study and interpret it as professional scholars of the scriptures and theologians.[7] Moreover, due consideration must also be given to its doctrinal use by the Church's Magisterium – such as Pope Paul VI's eucharistic interpretation of the phrase 'Word made flesh' in relation to the notion of 'Emmanuel', God-with-us.[8]

In our reading, listening to and reflecting on this Gospel, we are invited by John 'the divine' or 'the theologian' to respond to John's Word.[9] This is always the eternal Word, the only begotten Son of the Father. Since he is uniquely qualified, he alone reveals the Father: he 'made him known', a phrase which literally means: *exegeted (exēgēsato)* [him].[10] We may go on to suggest that the fundamental proclamation in John, *the Word has become flesh*, is also the principle of ecclesiology and sacramentality. This proclamation concerns a twofold significance: 1) the revelation *of* the Word become flesh; and, 2) the revelation *through* the enfleshed Word, so to speak, in the sacrament of the Church. Since the Word made flesh already is the principle of interpretation of the mystery of the Church, the same Word *informs* and reveals the significance of those actions in which the Church is most or best itself – namely, in the sacraments and especially in celebrating the paschal mystery of the Eucharist. Here the *work of our redemption is realised and made manifest*. It has been pointed out that John

> is God-intoxicated, God-possessed, God-articulate. He insists that God is more than a blur of longing, and other than a monosyllabic curse (or blessing), but capable of *logos*, that is, of intelligent discourse. John is full of exclamations in relation to God, quite overwhelmed with the experience of God, but through it all there

is *logos*: God revealed is God known. He is not so completely known that he can be predicted. He is not known so thoroughly that there is no more to be known, so that we can go on now to the next subject. Still, he is known and not unknown, rational and not irrational, orderly and not disorderly, hierarchical and not anarchic.[11]

Saturated with the Word-revealed in the flesh and blood experience of being human, John is a poet in the strongest sense of the word, that is, one who employs the art of communication not primarily to provide information or to teach what he has learnt to understand or to describe what he perceives of reality, nor to seek to convince by the use of discursive reason, but essentially to make something in such a way that it invites and draws others towards participating in being. For a poet's revitalising vocation is to 'make', as the original significance of *poesis* indicates.

'Signs' of God's work for the freedom of humanity

The whole of Jesus' life manifested and bore witness to the purpose of the Father's work, which was to communicate the freedom-giving truth of his life of love. John chooses certain events of Jesus' life and calls them 'signs' (*sēmeia*), which he situates in the context of Jewish liturgical festivals. In this way the Gospel celebrates that these events (*sēmeia*) themselves are not only 'the wonderful works of God', but also and especially the culmination of all God's saving deeds: Jesus' life witnesses to nothing other than the glory of God's work. The evangelist points out that these signs, though their meaning was hidden at first, would be remembered and understood by Jesus' disciples after his glorification in virtue of the Holy Spirit's guidance, as mentioned above; these signs are given to lead to faith in Jesus' claim to do the work of the Father (cf. 2:22; 12:16; also 13:7; 20:30f.). While the frequent use of words for 'work' (either as a noun or in the verbal forms of working or doing) may be contrasted with the Synoptics' use of the same words, one may ask whether the same perspective as the Fourth Gospel is shared by the other Gospels and Paul regarding the Sabbath controversy of law (works) verses love and regarding the question of the priority of faith over good works (or vice versa). If John's emphasis was different, one may further ask why it was so different and what was the particular pastoral situation addressed by the Fourth Gospel. John's intriguing omission of the account of the institution of the Eucharist may offer a clue, as some scholars have suggested,[12] to his desire to relate every-thing to Jesus' central revelation that he came to communicate his abundant life of communion with the Father (cf. Jn 10:10; 17:3). Lest this focus became lost or dimmed by the danger of ritualising the new eucharistic Passover, which may have been happening in certain Johannine communities,[13] John highlights Jesus' insistence on the need of members of the Christian community to grow in the sense of spiritual worship, that is, to become more deeply imbued with his inner attitude as worshippers in 'spirit and truth', whom the Father seeks (cf. Jn 4:24). If this is the perspective of the Fourth Gospel, as it seems quite likely, then we can recognise in John's presentation of Jesus as the Word of life made flesh a profound mystagogical catechesis of the Eucharist which opens the way to penetrate the truth of freedom in the Christian life.

It is still a debated question among scholars whether John's intention was to present these 'signs' as indicating the sacra-ments of the Christian community, or rather, the deeper meaning of these sacraments in extending the incarnate Word's mission of carrying out the work of the Father.[14] However, we may discern this intention from the various clues in the important themes of the Gospel, among which mention must be made of the following themes: the relation of the Holy Spirit to the Church's remembering Christ's command to celebrate his *memorial*; the reciprocal glorification of the Father and the Son in the communion of the Holy Spirit; participation in this communion through Christian worship in spirit and truth.

The new commandment of love

The whole of the Fourth Gospel presents a eucharistic catechesis, the first in the Church, which enables Jesus' com-munity of disciples to distinguish clearly between the deadening effect of being bound to human observances of ritual worship as *our works*, and the life-giving freedom of love which flows from Jesus continuing *the work* of the Father through the Spirit in his sacramental gift.

John does not in any way deny the historical truth, validity or importance of Jesus' command in the other Gospels: 'do this in memory of me', which certainly becomes realised in the Church's faith-obedience of the eucharistic celebration. He records only Jesus' new commandment to his disciples after washing their feet at the Last Supper. This new commandment proclaims the world-transforming order of freedom: to love one another *as* he loved them (cf. Jn 13:34). Understood in the context of the Last Supper, this means to follow the example he had set, namely, to express the humility, of loving service – that is, the down-to-earthness of the Word's incarnation. The significance of the word 'as', which occurs both in this commandment and also in Jesus' recommendation of brotherly service (13:15), cannot be missed.[15] For this little word focuses explicitly on the full density of the reality of Jesus' own seeking in loving obedience to do the work of the Father, which is evident everywhere in the Fourth Gospel. From this all else flows, namely, the work of our redemption in which Jesus involves his disciples. Through them he would extend his redemptive incarnation which reveals to the world both his filial love of the one Father and his spirit of fraternal service after his example at the Last Supper. In this regard it is worth recalling Gerald Vann's comments on the profound significance of Jesus' act of laying aside his garments to wash the disciples' feet:

> It is 'the eve of the pasch'. They have sat down to supper. Jesus lays aside his clothes, and washes their feet. In biblical usage the literal sense of 'naked' is often 'without one's outer garments'; symbolically the term refers us back to the figure of the *puer aeternus*;[16] here, as also later in the Passion when Jesus is 'stripped of his garments', what the symbol conveys to us is the recovery of the youthful vitality, the freedom, the joy of the child *through* the *kenosis* – the standing before God in poverty and nakedness – of the man; and this idea of the humble reversal of the original arrogant falsehood is carried forward in the maundy, the washing.[17]

The characteristic feature of the Christian community of disciples, thus, is their love for one another. This must be seen,

however, as more than a high ideal or moral discipline, as is
implied in what is heard often enough: all that matters is to love
others. This characteristic feature is the fruit of being united
with the Christian community of Jesus' disciples in its believing
and acknowledging with praise and gratitude that he himself is
the revelation of the Father's love of the world (cf. Jn 3:16).
Through their living out of Jesus' example of humble service
all people are drawn, as it were, into the intimate circle of God's
neighbourhood, 'the radius of the fatherhood of God'.[18]
Commenting on Jesus' new command and covenant of love, St
Augustine says: 'You do not yet see God, but by loving your
neighbour you gain the sight of God; by loving your neighbour
you purify your eye for seeing God, as John says clearly: "If you
do not love the brother whom you see, how will you be able to
love God whom you do not see?" (1 Jn 4:20).'[19] The discourse of
human yearning to be liberated from all limiting factors of
existence becomes transformed by Jesus, the Word made flesh,
into a dialogue for freedom.

Without mentioning the institution of the Eucharist, the
sacred sign of Jesus' freely giving his life for the world, John's
Gospel, thus, lays emphasis on the depths of what it implies.
John's insistence on obedience to Jesus' new commandment of
love, the keeping of which is the sign by which disciples would
be recognised as his (cf. 13:34f.; 14:15, 21ff.; 15:10ff.), must be
seen against the background of what is expressed elsewhere
in the Gospels as the significance of the two interconnected
vital questions: 'What is the greatest commandment' and 'Who
is my neighbour?'. In his fine analysis of the parable of true
neighbourliness Paul Ricoeur brings out that the failure of the
two who passed the unfortunate man beaten and robbed by
brigands has its roots in their self-consciousness about their
role and definition by social category. They are more preoccupied with their function as priest or levite than with the
one in need so that they become 'unavailable for the surprise
of an encounter. In them, the institution (the ecclesiastical
institution, to be precise) bars their access to the event'.[20] It
has not infrequently come about that people have regarded
the Church's institutions and rites as quasi ends in themselves. Ricoeur's analysis, however, does not lead to the rash

conclusion about the rejection of social or religious institutions, but points to the primordial truth of their *raison d'être* – namely, that their ultimate meaning consists in 'the service which they render to persons'. (The *raison d'être* or *logos* of all institutions, which are means to hold society together and to promote its well-being, may be thus seen as disciplines of the *Logos*.) Ricoeur states that it would be shortsighted not to recognise that personal charitable benefits have also come about through the institutions of the Church. However, it is as well to admit that even the expression of charity can become exhibitionism; worse, it may also lose its transcendent orientation and vital dynamism by becoming attachment to the laws of ritual, rather than express the inner focus of the revealed law of worship.[21]

This transcendent orientation of the living worship which the Word made flesh reveals is clearly proclaimed in the poetic Prologue of the Fourth Gospel, which many scholars regard as an early Christian hymn to Christ, sung possibly at the eucharistic celebration. The entire Prologue is enclosed between two statements regarding the personal eternal identity of Jesus, Word of God. These statements show that Jesus' identity consists of his intimate relationship to the Father, whom John refers to as '[the] God'. Thus:

vv. 1–2	v. 18
. . . the Word was *with God* . . . He was in the beginning *with God*.	. . . God the only Son, who is *close to the Father's heart* . . .

This translation of the NRSV in the italicised phrases does not bring out sufficiently the sense of the original Greek – a sense which in both instances indicates dynamic movement. For in these verses the prepositions (*pròs* and *eis*) followed by the accusative case (*tòn theón* and *tòn kólpon*) would be better translated as 'towards' or 'in communion with' rather than in the somewhat static English versions which we are used to.[22] John describes in this way Jesus' deep intimate, personal relationship to the Father and brings out the dynamic, transcendent orientation of Jesus' whole being, which is always an attitude of perfect filial love. This orientation of Jesus' attitude, which is expressed in the little phrase 'towards the Father', has the profound implications for human beings in their most fundamental relationship to God, namely, in prayer. These implications are summed up by Cardinal Ratzinger:

> The basic reason why man can speak with God arises from the fact that God himself is speech, word. His nature is to speak, to hear, to reply, as we see particularly in Johannine theology, where Son and Spirit are described in terms of pure 'hearing'; they speak in response to what they have first heard. Only because there is already speech, 'Logos', in God can there be speech, 'Logos', to God. Philosophically we could put it like this: the Logos in God is the ontological foundation for prayer. The Prologue of John's Gospel speaks of this connection in its very first sentences: 'In the beginning was the Word, and the Word was in communication with God' (1:1) – as a more precise translation of the Greek *prós* suggests, rather than the usual 'with God'. It expresses the act of turning to God, of relationship. Since there is relationship within God himself, there can also be a participation in this relationship. Thus we can relate to God in a way which does not contradict his nature.[23]

John describes his posture close to Jesus' breast or heart (*en tōi kólpōi*; cf. 13:23) at the Last Supper in a phrase which recalls Jesus' own relationship to the Father at the end of the Prologue. The evangelist seems to go on to suggest that just as Jesus is turned towards the Father's heart from which he draws all that he *is* as the Word, so too, in leaning back on Jesus' breast (*anapesōn . . . epì to stēthos*'; cf. 13:25), the beloved disciple draws from Jesus, the Word of life, understanding of his mystery, whose depths are revealed through participating in the morsel and the cup. In recounting his privileged place of reclining on Jesus' breast, John provides, thus, more than merely a description of the Graeco-Roman manner of eating that the Jews had adopted, which would have been quite familiar to people of John's day. In stating this detail he was, moreover, not explaining how the arrangement of places at table conveniently enabled him to whisper to Jesus, at Simon Peter's prodding, the terrible question which in the intense atmosphere of that evening was on all the disciples' minds: 'Lord, who is it?' Rather, he seems to be making a point about the significance of not only of his proximity to the heart of Christ as 'the disciple whom Jesus loved', but of any true disciple of the Lord.

This is quite a different kind of privilege to that which he and his brother, James, once claimed to have, namely, to sit on his right and left and reign with him in his kingdom as they imagined or mistook his kingdom to be; their privilege-seeking on that occasion earned them Jesus' brusque rebuke that they did not know what they were asking (cf. Mk 10:35–40; Mt 20:20–8).[24] Jesus' prophetic challenge on that occasion, however, about drinking of his cup was now being realised. For, at this strangely disturbed banquet, without knowing it they were being given a taste of the cup of his passion. Without fully realising it they were drinking a toast to the new Passover, which the Eucharist is. Although they were unaware of it, Jesus was drawing them into his sacrificial giving: through sharing in what he himself was doing, they were being involved in his work of redemption. But, years later, after he had much time to savour the implications of the paschal banquet of the Eucharist, after he had been led by the Spirit of Truth to realise that Jesus' unique Eucharist communicated the central truth of Christian experience, John recalled every vivid detail of that unforgettable farewell repast. By the time he came to dictate his reminiscences in the Gospel, he had come to perceive the theological significance of his reclining on his beloved Master's breast. For these recollections – or better, reminiscences – were prompted by the Holy Spirit of Truth who enabled him to discern the spiritual truth of the Eucharist through the years of having experienced the community of Christ's faithful celebrating it as the continuation and most intimate extension of the incarnation – the Word made *flesh*. So, the theological point John makes about his privileged position of intimacy in reclining on Christ's heart is this: just as Christ, the beloved Son, was nearest to the Father's heart (Jn 1:18), so was he intimate with Christ as the beloved disciple at the banquet of love. But, lest this be taken as a slight to others, in whom it might have provoked competitive envy and hostility, his experience of such intimacy and accessibility to Christ in confidence was itself meant to be a sign and model of true discipleship. To put the same thing slightly differently: as a witness of the Father's eternal Word and beloved Son, John would hardly have been credible if his own life was not consistent with and

modelled on Christ's life – that life of the Word made visible
which he proclaimed and celebrated in the sacrament of his
flesh and blood as eternal communication and communion
with the Father. This is precisely how in his first letter John sees
Christ's faithful, though, here again, our translations do not do
full justice to the dynamic sense of the Greek:

> Little children, let us not love in word or speech but in deed and in
> truth. . . . Beloved, if our hearts do not condemn us, we have
> confidence [*parrēsían*] before God [*pròs tón theón* – literally:
> 'towards the Father']; and we receive from him whatever we ask,
> because we keep his commandments and do what pleases him (1
> Jn 3:18, 21, 22).

Abiding or living in Christ means keeping his commandments, which in turn give the joyous assurance of knowing God
as friends. This is the *raison d'être* of Christ's choice of his
disciples (cf. Jn 15:12–17). As friends recognise and live in constant gratitude for the gratuitous gift of their friendship, so
Christ's faithful abide in his loving utterly gratuitous choice of
them. Because of this ever-deepening sense of gratitude for the
intimacy of knowing the Father, which Christ's gift of friendship brings to their lives, the quality of life of Christ's faithful is
ennobled (cf. 15:15). Only friends, not slaves, can know the joy
of freedom which comes in keeping his commandments and
doing his truth in humble service of one another after the
pattern he set at the Last Supper on the eve of his sacrifice. This
teaching in John's Gospel is ultimately no less demanding than
in Matthew's parable of the Last Judgement.[25] It is also, perhaps,
far more attractive and easily carried out for, unlike the motive
of fear to avoid that terrible curse: 'Depart from me . . .', the
motivating energy in John's teaching from beginning to end is
always the invitation of Jesus' love and example to 'Come and
see' where he abides (cf. 1:38f., etc.). To become Christ's faithful means to abide in him, as he lives or abides in the Father.
This entails becoming, in St Irenaeus' phrase, 'disciples of
the Truth', or, as Tertullian calls Christians, 'worshippers of
the Truth'.[26] For only such as these are capable of expressing
and bearing witness to the full rich tradition of his living
memory.[27]

Disciples of the Truth, who makes them free (Jn 8:32)

We must consider in some detail how John presents Jesus' gift of the Eucharist as the way which leads his disciples to the freedom of abiding or being in communion with his truth of eternal life (cf. 14:6). In his masterly treatment of the theme of truth in John's Gospel, Ignace de la Potterie examines the significance of Jesus' important statement about being disciples of his own word of truth, which is the deepest source of their truth:[28]

> Then Jesus said to the Jews who had believed in him. 'If you continue [*meinēte*] in my word [*en tōi lógōi tōi emōi*], you are truly [*alēthōs*] my disciples [*mathētaí moú*]; and you will know [*gnōsesthe*] the truth, and the truth [*hē alētheia*] will make you free [*eleutherōsei*].' (8:31–2 NRSV)

Although certain similarities may be sought to this statement in the rest of the literature up to his time – whether in biblical, Judaic, Hellenistic or Gnostic writings – John presents quite a unique teaching in his Gospel on the theme of freedom in its inner connection with the truth. Because of its mysterious and enigmatic character, this statement has exercised a fascination that has lead to it becoming a sort of slogan or catch-phrase for different kinds of ideologies and holds a special interest to various, at times contradictory, approaches regarding freedom in modern times. The truth in question here is not philosophical, abstract, scientific or political, but primarily religious. For John, Jesus reveals the fullness of freedom because he, the living Word of God, is the Truth.[29]

Any statement of this kind is dangerously seductive to all kinds of misinterpretation if one does not clarify its precise meaning. This statement of Jesus is particularly dangerous if taken out of context. Hence, any attempt to understand it must situate it in the context in which Jesus made this declaration. The immediate context of Jn 8:31–2 is the section of the Gospel that spans the four chapters (7:1—10:42) focused by the Jewish feast of Tabernacles or Tents.[30] This section can be seen as comprising three important parts:

1. 'the middle of the feast' (7:14–36);
2. 'the last day, the great day' (7:37—10:21);

3. 'the festival of the dedication of the temple' (10:22–39), which
seems to form part of the feast of Tabernacles.

The verses (8:31–2) come at the central part (2), which is long
and doctrinally dense, for it is here that Jesus makes the great
messianic revelation in three stages:

> a) he openly discloses his eternal identity as equal to God (7:37—
> 8:59);
> b) he confirms this revelation by the symbolic gesture of
> enlightening the man born blind – a gesture which is so pregnant
> with meaning that it, as it were, speaks for itself (9:1–41);
> c) he describes the implications of being sent by God in the
> 'parable' of the Good Shepherd (10:1–21).

This whole section (7:1—10:39) may be seen as providing an
elaborate catechesis both of all that has preceded it in the
Gospel, and particularly of the previous section regarding Jesus'
promise of the bread of life (chapter 6), and also a preparation
for what follows – in the description of the raising of Lazarus
(chapter 11) and especially in the account of the great reality
of the Passover (chapters 13 to the end of the Gospel), to which
all the 'signs' of Jesus' deeds and words point.

The section begins with a description of Jesus avoiding public
attention because of the threat to his life on the part of those
who did not believe in him. This disbelief in him had been
provoked by his promise, which John records in the previous
section in chapter 6,[31] to provide bread from heaven and
especially by his claim to be this bread, which must be eaten as
the condition of knowing the freedom of his eternal life: 'I AM
the living bread that came down from heaven. Whoever eats of
this bread will live forever; and the bread that I will give for the
life of the world is my flesh [*hē sárx moú*]' (6:51, NRSV). As if
this was not enough to stir up dispute, Jesus went on to state
even more emphatically the following words which must not
only have sounded grossly outrageous, but even been quite
repulsive to any pious Jew:

> 'Truly, truly [*amēn, amēn*],[32] I say to you, unless you eat the flesh of
> the Son of man and drink his blood, you have no life in you; he
> who eats my flesh and drinks my blood has eternal life, and I
> will raise him up at the last day. For my flesh is food indeed, and

my blood is drink indeed (lit. my flesh is true [*alēthēs*] food and my blood is true [*alēthēs*] drink). He who eats my flesh and drinks my blood abides [*menei*] in me, and I in him. As the living Father sent me, and I live because of the Father, so he who eats me will live because of me.' (6:53–7)

These last words underline Jesus' desire to involve his disciples in the mystery of his incarnation itself through participation in his bread, which is called 'flesh' (*sárx*) by John, not 'body' (*sōma*) as in the Synoptics and Paul. (The notion expressed by 'flesh' is probably closer to that expressed by the word *basar* of the Aramaic used by Jesus than the Greek notion of body.) In other words, John sees the Eucharist as expressing the ultimate expression or extension of the truth of his Christology.[33] He faithfully records how Jesus did not withdraw a syllable of the promise he made. To eat his flesh is to receive him: it is the sign of abiding by his word and of becoming one with him in eternal life. In fact, the word 'flesh' occurs six times in as many verses here. As abhorrent as this 'hard saying' must have been to the Jews' traditional religious sensitivities, Jesus remained adamant. He was being more than provocative. He was determined to break the bonds of literal-mindedness by calling for utter faith in him that frees. A subtle example of Johannine irony may be detected in this insistence on Jesus' part about his desire to give eternal life to the world which was the beginning of his historical undoing. Many no longer 'walked with him'; they walked away from the light to plan and procure his death (cf. 6:66; also 13:30). Jesus' promise of eternal life, thus, may be understood as implying a prophetic utterance of his death since, quite apart from provoking the hostility of the Jewish religious leaders against him, its fulfilment depended on Jesus giving up his life for the world as the Good Shepherd (cf. 10:11ff.).

In this whole section John implicitly teaches the sacrificial dimension of the sign or sacrament which Jesus promised – a dimension which he more clearly brings out in references to the 'lamb of God' (cf. 1:29, 36; also Rev. 5:6, 8, 12, etc.), the paschal allusions in his description of Jesus' death (cf. 19:31ff.), and the significance of the blood and water flowing from the Redeemer's pierced heart (cf. 19:34).[34] John attests that only through dying did Jesus accomplish the Father's 'work' and attain his glory (cf. 13:31). Because of his fidelity to the Father, disciples would be drawn to believe in Jesus (cf. 6:44, 65). Commenting on these verses, St Augustine penetratingly describes this movement of 'being drawn' in terms of the logic of love – that is, how the *logos* of divine love transforms the inner passions and emotions of the human psyche. This is the deepest sense of what *psychological* means:

> 'No one can come to me unless the Father ... draws him.' [Jn 6:44] You must not imagine that you are being drawn against your will, for the mind can also be drawn by love. . . . How can I believe of my own free will, if I am drawn? In reply I say this: It is not enough to be drawn of your own free will, because you can be drawn by delight as well. What does it mean, to be drawn by delight? 'Take delight in the Lord and he will give you the desires of your heart.' [Ps. 26:4] There is a certain desire of the heart to which the bread of heaven appeals. Moreover, if the poet can say: 'Everyone is drawn by his delight',[35] not by necessity but by delight, not by compulsion but by sheer pleasure, then how much more ought we to be confident in saying that a man is drawn by Christ, when he delights in truth, in blessedness, in holiness and in eternal life, all of which mean Christ?[36]

John repeatedly comes back to the image of Jesus being 'lifted up from the earth' to highlight the deepest truth of his becoming a man, that is, taking on the weakness of our 'flesh': this truth of the incarnation would draw frail and fickle human beings up to believe in him and become consolidated as his disciples in the highest level of freedom (cf. 3:14; 8:28; 12:32). Faith in this sacred sign of his sacrifice of endless love would keep believers in mind of Jesus' redemptive incarnation in all its creative richness.

This is the background, then, to Jesus' avoidance of recognition and his initial decision not to join his disciples in going up to Jerusalem for the feast of Tabernacles (cf. 7:1–10). After this the Gospel relates that he went up to Jerusalem and began teaching in the temple 'about the middle of the feast' (7:14). John describes the fresh questioning and lengthy rabbinic dispute that resulted between the Jews and Jesus, who clarifies his revelation of himself as the Messiah: the true nature of the

Christ's mission is to correct false political ideas of messianism stirred up among the crowds, such as those who came to the festival of Tabernacles. This clarification about his identity as the Christ is made in terms of Jesus' highly significant repetition of the statement 'I AM' (*egō eimi*), which occurs no less than ten times in this section – that is, more often here than in any other part of the Gospel.[37]

> This mysterious expression appears to be a deliberate reference to Yahweh's self-identification to Moses (Ex. 3:13–14); hence it is an expression of Jesus' own divinity. Of great importance is the fact that Yahweh's affirmation 'I am he' is translated as *egō eimi* in the LXX of Deutero-Isaiah (43:25; 51:12; 52:6).[38]

Various other titles are predicated of the basic 'I am' statements of Jesus: the bread of life (6:35, 51); the light of the world (8:12; 9:5); the gate or door (10:7, 9); the Good (beautiful or ideal) Shepherd (10:11, 14); the way, the truth, and the life (14:6); the true vine (15:1, 5). However, all examples of this statement in the Gospel reach their deepest significance at that climactic moment when the Jews' religious sensibilities were shocked to the core by Jesus' clearest and unequivocal appropriation of the divine Name, *Yahweh*, which means 'I AM': '"Truly, truly (*amēn, amēn*), I say to you, before Abraham was, I AM [*egō eimi*]." So they took up stones to throw at him; but Jesus hid himself, and went out of the temple' (8:58–9).

De la Potterie points out that the discourse on the Good Shepherd is aimed at the same clarification. Whereas the words 'thief', 'brigand' signify the false prophets of messianism, the 'Good Shepherd' imagery refers to fulfilment of prophecies of genuine messianic hope.[39] John borrows this imagery from Ezekiel, who applies the technical vocabulary of Exodus. The verb used regarding the Good Shepherd's activity of leading the sheep out from the sheepfold – namely, *exágei* (10:3) – is intended to recall the great work of God in leading his people from slavery to the promised land of freedom. In this context there is a yet deeper meaning, which alludes to other places in the Gospel relating to the significance of his Passover: Jesus opens the 'enclosure' – that is, frees people from ritual servitude/servility[40] – to lead them to worship in spirit and truth (cf. 4:24); he himself is 'the way, the truth, and the life' of disciples of freedom. The crux of the matter in the whole of John's Gospel is to believe in Jesus, the Word who makes the hidden God visible in his incarnation. To believe him, that is, to have trusting faith *in* him leads to true freedom, whereas not to believe in him is unfreedom, the sin of the world which leads to death: 'You shall indeed die in your sin unless you believe that I AM' (8:24). The structure of 8:31–6 clearly shows that Jesus' meaning of freedom is related to freedom from sin and revelation of true disciples as children of that freedom which Jesus, the true Son, brings about. Slavery is related especially to incredulity and blindness to God's truth revealed in and by Jesus, the incarnate Word. This liberation is realised in a growth and deepening of faith in Jesus – a growing deepening of awareness and appropriation or interiorisation of the truth revealed in the Word enfleshed in human experience.

Following John's understanding of the dynamic personal nature of truth revealed in Jesus Christ as being the basis of freedom, St Augustine understands the word 'truth' as not only propositional truth, which is accepted and believed, but truth to be believed *in*. In this respect Augustine's important three-fold distinction about belief is worth recalling as illuminating John's teaching about believing in Jesus, the living Word of God. Augustine profoundly demonstrates how the pheno-menon of language is open to theological interpretation. The great bishop points out that the word 'to believe' (*credere*) may be used as referring to: what someone tells us; or that someone or something exists; or utterly entrusting oneself to someone, which amounts to love binding one to another.[41] This is not contradictory to the somewhat different line of approach taken by St Cyril of Jerusalem, who distinguishes two senses in which the word 'faith' is used in the New Testament: 1) it is con-cerned with doctrine and denotes a person's assent to some truth; 2) a particular grace of Christ given by the Spirit to empower a person with qualities beyond human capability (cf. 1 Cor. 12:8–9).[42] While all three senses in St Augustine's analysis are involved in the act of faith, it is the last which expresses the strongest aspect of Christian commitment since it leads a person from notional assent to share in the characteristic relationship of freedom and intimacy, that relationship which is nothing less than communion of life with the mystery of the holy Trinity.[43] Trust and confidence in Christ are integral to Christian faith; and freedom, which is born of a trusting faith in him, becomes the focus of human searching and object of the Christian endeavour of love.

Furthermore, belief *in* someone is directed not only towards a person, but also involves having confidence in his or her truthfulness or 'word'. This has a particularly important relevance to our belief *in* God. Our belief in his Word means that we entrust ourselves to everything he reveals and communicates. But, our entrusting response seeks also a response from him. What is involved here is a dynamic interpersonal reciprocity which is signified by Jesus' language of 'abiding in' God, which John frequently recalls. English does not have the same sense as other languages in the use of the construction with the preposition 'in' to express this dynamic aspect of reciprocally entering into Christ and Christ into us. Christ the Word is not merely the 'object' of our belief, which is focused and terminates in this 'object'. As one writer puts it: 'He is an interiority into whom our belief penetrates and with whom it enables us to commune. The expression suggests the same interpretation of I and thou which ... underlies all human communication.'[44] The 'interiority' spoken of here is the depths of our own being. But, since these depths are created and sustained in being by the Word, who reveals that we are created in God's image and likeness, it is possible to say that Christ the Word is the radical basis of our being capable of entering into communication with God and all human beings.

The revelation of Jesus in chapters 7–10 employs and integrates different themes of the Jewish tradition, which John shows Jesus interpreting and clarifying in a new way that has important relevance for the Christian community in its celebration of eucharistic worship and especially in its living out of the consequences of this sacred sign of Christ's Passover. The profound paradox of realising this Passover is that in revealing the presence of the hidden God, John shows Jesus hiding

himself on various occasions (cf. e.g. 7:1ff., 33; 8:59; 10:40;
12:36). But, these occasions of his hiding are signs which
John presents of the total eclipse, so to speak, of Jesus' Passover
at the crucifixion as 'his hour' of supreme glory, when the
true light of his freedom dawned in the world. Especially in
his 'hour', as John brings out most poignantly, he receives
everything from the Father's hands. In this he 'becomes' Christ
– the revealer, mediator, priest or communicator *par excellence*
of the Father's eternal design of love for the world (cf. Jn
3:16). John begins his presentation of the Last Supper by
richly bringing out the new quality that Jesus gave to the
Jewish religious celebration of the Passover. This specifically
new Christian quality is that of the revelation of a kind of love
that goes beyond human expectation or capability, and, one
might be led to say, even to excess. Without this love there
is no quality of true freedom in human life, and, indeed,
without it no one can live.[45] This love reveals the whole finality
of life: 'he loved . . . unto the end [*eis telos*]' (13:1). This
refers to Jesus reaching not only the conclusion but also the
climactic moment of his life – of everything that all human
life is capable. The 'end', as indicated by the Greek word
telos, points to the purpose of living. Jesus' love alone reveals
this purpose. And, moreover, he alone – John's Word (*ho Logos*)
in and through whom all things are created and have their
being – knows life's meaning and the proper 'hour', context
and way to make it known, manifest and communicate it to
others. This 'hour' has arrived; its context has been revealed in
the new dimension given to the rite of *Passover* by the reality of
Jesus' passing from this world to the Father; its way lies open
as the exodus of a new people passing over through love to
freedom, the boundless freedom of eternal life, that is,
knowing or experiencing the quality of his love (cf. 17:3). The
'hour', context, and way – to which everything of the Last
Supper points – is the last word that John puts on the lips of
Jesus, who freely sacrifices himself to reveal God's love for the
world before breathing his spirit on the new creation: 'it is
accomplished [*tetelestai*]'.

Here one cannot help but notice the constancy of the design
and working out of the divine intentionality of love, which

nothing – neither sin nor death – can frustrate in achieving its purpose and finale (*telos/tetelestai*). What John shows is that Jesus' whole life of love – all that he sought to realise and communicate in life – is held in suspension, as it were, until the eternal 'hour' of the new Passover is revealed in the living sacrifice of love on the cross. It is to the cross that the Last Supper sacramentally pointed and to which the lives of his disciples passing over to freedom, not only their commemorative ritual, should refer. Jesus' 'hour' of his cross is the culminating point of his whole life of self-emptying, which St Paul would also emphasise (cf. Phil. 2:5–11). John depicts the supreme revelation of the meaning of God's love in Jesus giving up his breath of life and in pouring out everything of love in the blood and water from his pierced side. The cross, as Balthasar has profoundly brought out, is situated in the eternal 'primordial drama' of the divine life of the Trinity. This drama encompasses the eternal self-emptying of the three Persons.[46]

At the Last Supper Jesus prayed in his 'high priestly prayer' for his disciples to recognise the glory of his Passover sacrifice:

> 'Father, the hour has come; glorify thy Son that the Son may glorify thee, since thou hast given him power over all flesh, to give eternal life to all whom thou hast given him. And this is eternal life, that they know thee the only true God, and Jesus Christ whom thou hast sent. I glorified thee on earth, having accomplished the work which thou gavest me to do; and now, Father, glorify thou me in thy own presence with the glory which I had with thee before the world was made . . .' (17:1–5).

One is tempted to see in this prayer a spiritual, sacramental or mystical sense, which it would be, however, impossible to prove was perceived or intended by the beloved disciple, namely, that Jesus prayed as the high priest for his community of true disciples to be freed to acknowledge the hidden splendour of his work of redemption and to adore his presence as the 'Godhead here in hiding' in the eucharistic mystery. Our contemplation of this mystery enables us to perceive depths in the beloved disciple's account of Jesus' encounters with people. Pope John Paul II catches these symbolic and sacramental

depths in his poem on the Samaritan woman's encounter with
Jesus, hidden and revealed in 'the brightness of water' at Jacob's
well:

> It joined us together, the well;
> the well led me into you.
> No one between us but light
> deep in the well, the pupil of the eye
> set in an orbit of stones.
> Within your eyes, I,
> drawn by the well,
> am enclosed.[47]

4

Faith and Freedom:
Proclamation of Christ's Revelation
in the Pauline Tradition

For freedom Christ has made us free (**Gal. 5:1**)

After the essential teaching of the Gospels – particularly in Jesus' teaching in the Sermon on the Mount – no other influence has shaped the history of the world as regards the value of freedom as much as that which has been handed on as the Pauline tradition. The early Christians witness to the fundamental human right to religious freedom in their struggle against the pressures from the world outside their circle – pressures resulting not only from persecution for their faith, but also from the false values of a decadent society.[1] Thus, in many places in St Paul's letters there are indications of the apostle's encouragement to his converts to be alert, strong and steadfast in struggling for their true spiritual well-being by preserving the faith in the freedom of the spirit (cf. e.g. 1 Cor. 16:13; 1 Tim. 6:12; 2 Tim. 4:7).

A century after Paul, the urbane Justin (c. 155) endeavoured to enter into reasonable dialogue with his opponents and to demonstrate against the slanderous accusations made against Christians that not only was their way of life not anti-social, but also constructive of the true well-being of human existence as a whole.[2] Similarly, there is the often-cited passage in an anonymous author's *Epistle to Diognetus*, which shows a remarkable fidelity to the Pauline tradition regarding responsible use of freedom in fostering civic order.[3] The Epistle describes the moral enrichment brought to every place in which Christians, the 'soul of the world', abide: good citizenship in their peaceful conduct and respect for legitimate authority, the values of family life and hospitality, etc.[4] Quoting Jesus' own words, Tertullian states the Christian attitude in relation to state and legitimate authority: 'Render therefore to Caesar the things that are Caesar's, and to God the things that are God's.'[5] Nevertheless, charges against the Christian community were sporadically laid and bouts of persecution continued to break out. The favourite charges were those which were once likely to strike a note of alarm and stir up public opinion against any serious-minded group whose commitment to an alternative lifestyle presented a threat to the mediocre and, possibly also, showed up their hypocrisy. Christians were hated and denounced for various 'abominations'.[6]

In reality, though, these so-called 'abominations' refer not to the practices of the Christian community when gathering to celebrate the Eucharist, the sacramental sacrifice of the Lord's body and blood – a divine ordinance which excluded Christians from taking part in the officially prescribed practices of the state religion, especially the emperor-cult. Undoubtedly, suspicion and mistrust of the Christian community were fomented by what appeared to those outside as the secrecy and exclusiveness of this new group, particularly in their meeting to carry out the practices of its religious worship, at which its members practised a bizarre and grisly ritual of eating the flesh and drinking the blood of their leader, whom they claimed to be God; rumours spread quite rapidly regarding suspected sexual orgies at a 'love-feast' (*agapē*) later. This led on to reports and charges of infanticide and cannibalism.[7] The Eucharist made Christians into a distinctive and divinely chosen and consecrated community, freed from the false values of a corrupt secular society, since through this new kind of worship they become parts of Christ's body.

The early Christians were under severe test, however, not only in the arena of pagan persecution. In various passages of Paul's letters one detects evidence of a crucially decisive struggle taking place within their very ranks. This struggle concerned expressing the freedom which Christ taught regarding worship and the practices of religion. On the one hand, this struggle may be viewed as a defensive one on the part of converts from Judaism to preserve their religious heritage against Paul's innovatory concessions to converts from the Hellenistic world. On the other hand, it may be seen as signifying an important stage in preparing the followers of Jesus ('followers of the Way') to discern and assert their distinctive identity, not as a sect within Judaism (such as 'the Nazarenes'), but as Christians, or rather, the Church, the body of Christ.

However it may be viewed, whether as one for survival or identity, one may perhaps be justified in pointing to this struggle as the ground in which the malign roots of anti-Semitism can be traced. Later, when Christians became a publicly acceptable and socially respectable group and also after they eventually attained the upper hand with sufficient political clout, the tables were turned: the Jews found themselves marginalised in the Christian empire. This complex racial and religious prejudice in its many manifestations during the Christian era – to say nothing of the Holocaust under Hitler and the Nazi Third Reich – has resulted in some of the most atrocious crimes against human freedom. These crimes have, moreover, manifest in Christian times a direct contradiction of the central teachings of Jesus Christ – such as, to defend, uphold, and foster solidarity and the brotherhood of love between all peoples as children of the same God and Father. It must be sadly admitted that not until relatively recently was the stigma against the Jews' alleged guilt of 'deicide' officially repudiated in the wake of the Second Vatican Council.[8] But it would be quite mistaken to charge St Paul with responsibility for instigating this stigma. The accusation of 'deicide' brought against the Jews was first made not by Paul, but, most ironically, by Peter in his (Lucan edited) sermon at the Solomon's portico of the temple in Jerusalem (cf. Acts 3:12ff.).[9] Paul, indeed, seems almost to brag about having contradicted Peter to his face for taking sides with the Judaisers against pagan converts to Christianity (cf. Gal. 2:11ff.). Furthermore, it must be recalled that Paul speaks most movingly of his Jewish brethren, whose separation from the Christian community so grieved his heart that he says he would wish to be cut off from Christ for their sake (cf. Rom. 9:1–5).

Today, it seems quite wrong-headed and even futile either to level accusations at past generations for harbouring or expressing attitudes of hostility against the Jewish people. One may even question the sense of praying for 'the conversion of the Jews'. Rather, it is of primary importance that we acknowledge our part in bringing about the death of the Son of God by our sins, which in one way or another always indicate a lack of charity on our part; we must pray for our own deeper conversion to Christ. We are notorious for seeking scapegoats. But as long as we go on avoiding 'incriminating ourselves' because of fear of the truth, we have not learned to imitate Christ – to love others with the freedom in which his love freed the world. As Hubert Richards put it some years ago:

> St Paul wrote to the Romans that Israel's understanding of Jesus would have to wait until the fullness of the Gentiles was achieved (Rom. 11:25). A fullness in quantity was achieved a long time ago. Did he not mean that a fullness in quality was needed, a full sharing in the kind of love which made Jesus lay down his life for his people, before that people would be able to recognise in us his own features? St Paul also expressed his firm hope that Israel would come to that understanding of Jesus when his followers had aroused them to envy (Rom. 11:11), that is to say, when their baptism into his death and resurrection had made them die so truly to themselves that they lived, as he does, only to God. The Jews are still waiting for such a sign.[10]

At any rate, as is often the case in human affairs especially in questions concerning religious principles and traditions, struggles of this kind may be excruciatingly painful and bitter since they require that something must die, the soul itself being drained of the last drops of selfishness, in order that something may be born as a new creation. To change the metaphor somewhat, the journey to discover and enter the promised land of religious freedom involves the complete surrender of past familiar habits of mind and heart regarding religious practices and even any nostalgia for them. Both these metaphors of birth-through-death and journeying are employed everywhere in the world's great mythologies related and woven together in the legends, epic poetry, and romances, as for instance, in T.S. Eliot's *Journey of the Magi*. All this describes nothing other than a passing over towards living in hope and gratitude for that freedom of the Spirit which lies beyond sight or is perceived indistinctly and dimly.

These two metaphors seem particularly apt for describing all that followed the mysterious encounter of Saul of Tarsus with the risen Lord Jesus Christ on the road to Damascus – an encounter which may be seen as the crossroads where the meaning of being a follower of Jesus Christ took on a new and distinctive direction for faith's journey. Paul ventured such a journey that required the abandoning of his former career as a Pharisee after being blinded by the light of the risen Lord Jesus. He responded to the revelation of Christ Jesus, who called him out of the darkness of religious prejudice and attachment to the practices of Judaism to become an intrepid missionary of the gospel of religious freedom.

It should be noted that while emphasis is placed here on the importance of Paul's specific religious experience of conversion, our focusing on this experience should not be regarded as an end in itself as a matter of curiosity in or even admiration and devotion for a personality of considerable human greatness or holiness. Rather, the primary concern here is to point to Paul's conversion-experience as a crucial 'moment' of salvation history and the starting point of Christian theological reflection.[11] Moreover, our particular interest in highlighting this apostle's experience as significant for his own and, hence also, the Church's reflection is to situate the resulting reflection on his whole story of conversion within the context of the history of freedom.

Freedom: conversion to Christ's mystical body

From the time of his conversion-experience, which tradition has delighted to relate,[12] Paul became the great exponent of that distinctive quality of life in which freedom and worship are intrinsically connected. His conversion provides a pivotal point of departure for understanding the core issue of this intrinsic connection.[13] A curious providence seems to have been at work in this great apostle's conversion to Christ. On the one hand, as a Pharisee, Paul had been a member of one of the more legalistic branches of Judaism against which Jesus' most severe criticisms were levelled.[14] On the other hand, it was precisely while Paul – or rather, Saul of Tarsus as he was known as at that time – was on a hell-bent mission of persecuting Christians in his zeal for the true religion of Israel that he encountered the risen Lord Jesus. The blinding nature of this encounter – whatever it was or however it happened – enabled him to realise that God revealed to the world the fulfilment of all Israel's prophecies and its law of life and worship precisely through the 'leader' or Lord of the new group of dissident Jews, Jesus the Galilean. In that mysterious event along the road to Damascus, the risen Lord Jesus revealed to him that it was in reality *himself* who was the object of Paul's persecuting zeal: Paul, in fact, was all along pursuing him!

This revelation shaped Paul's understanding that faith in Christ's presence in the unique, but multiform, reality of his body is a gift to be cherished, preserved with responsibility, and proclaimed lovingly to others as good news. After and because of this revelation he realised that all human endeavours to do good, all our desire to worship and serve God, all our care for the welfare of others and love for one another – in fact, the entire spiritually oriented quality of human intentionality and action – is valuable only in so far as it is a response to God's saving action of revealing and bestowing his gift of love for the world in and through Jesus Christ. The realisation of this quality of faith is ultimately liberating. For the response which human persons make to the revelation of God's love is the expression of the new dimension of Christian freedom uniquely brought to living realisation by this revelation.

In other words, Paul's whole teaching must be viewed in the light of his initial grace of conversion, which enabled him to 'passover' to understand, or rather, assimilate the 'mind and heart of Christ'. This meant a total revolution of attitudes and, more importantly, a radical transformation of being, which entails, as he pointed out to others, the discovery that the depths of the freedom brought about by revealed religion are not to be found in observing the laws of ritual, but through faith in Christ Jesus. Paul's conversion-experience, thus, was transformative of the rest of his life. From being bound by religious zeal for the letter of the law he became a freeman who tirelessly proclaimed the primacy of Christ's Spirit of love. There can be no question that the new quality of freedom is the core of the apostle's teaching. This was his 'gospel' or 'good news'. He constantly related this new quality of freedom in the Christian community to his teaching regarding the implications and rich significance of sharing in the body of the risen Lord, through and in whom people discover their true worth by becoming worshippers of the true God. Only the Spirit enables them to call Jesus 'Lord', that title reserved for God alone (cf. 1 Cor. 12:3); the same Spirit emboldens them to approach God with full confidence, crying out to him 'Abba! Father!', as befits a son and heir (cf. Rom. 8:15; Gal. 4:5–7).

Faith working in love

Especially in his letters to the Romans and Galatians Paul tackles the major problem of the relationship of the law to the gospel. This problem, which was disturbing the life of the Christian community, arose because certain converts from Judaism were insistent on maintaining the Jewish ritual practices in the new community, particularly regarding the circumcision of converts from a pagan background. In his handling of this thorny problem, Paul pointed out that any kind of servile adherence to the Mosaic law was, in effect, nothing other than another form of enslavement – to sinfulness. This approach continued to place importance not on faith in God's free gift of salvation, but on the law, that is, on the Old Testament covenant which in the course of the centuries became interpreted by a multitude of prescriptions, observances and ritual customs – such as circumcision, rites of purification, observance of the Sabbath, prohibitions against defilement through contact with the Gentiles, etc. Paul recognised that all these 'works' of the law bound people to practise a way of life which only led to rigid, legalistic attitudes and which divided rather than united human beings in worshipping the one God.

Furthermore, Paul demonstrated the ineffectiveness of the law to bring about that perfect relationship with God called 'justification', for all that its observance expresses is nothing but a vain seeking of self-justification.[15] Something else was necessary, something more powerful to free all humanity – not only the Jewish people – from the power of sin. He taught what he himself had come to realise by God's grace: namely, that this something was the gift or grace (*charis*) of God manifested in Jesus Christ, who uniquely taught and lived the way of freedom. Jesus Christ's way was that of perfect obedience to the will and design of the Father in love: by freely accepting death, which was imposed on him for seeming to transgress the law, he not only really fulfilled all that the law of Moses pointed towards, but also revealed something more wonderful, namely, communion (*koinōnia*) with God. This fullness of life in the freedom of communion is the basis of the new community of Christ, that is, the Church. Paul pointed out that the pedagogical role of the law was over and done with. It had become obsolete since it is now superseded by the era of grace and faith in Christ.

Whereas Paul's teaching may be seen as being in accord with the insights of sound psychology, it goes beyond what human knowledge can offer. For he insists that an obsessive attachment to the law (even in the name of religion), which fixes people in a system of legalism and compulsive performance of ritualistic institutions, only closes them from realising something far greater and more exciting, namely, their potential to respond to the invitation of God to know the sheer generosity of his boundless love and grace in Jesus Christ. In so far as obsession of every kind is the expression of the radical condition of human sinfulness, to which it also blinds people, it prevents people from acknowledging and entering the mystery of God's love. Obsession of any kind is part of the secret working of evil – the 'mystery of iniquity' which is opposed to the lucid openness and clarity of Christ's coming to offer freedom to all humanity (cf. 2 Thess. 2:7).[16] Summing up Paul's teaching in this regard the *Catechism of the Catholic Church* states:

> Where does evil come from? ... 'the mystery of lawlessness' (2 Thess. 2:7) is clarified only in the light of the 'mystery of our religion' (1 Tim. 3:16). The revelation of divine love in Christ manifested at the same time the extent of evil and the superabundance of grace (cf. Rom. 5:20). We must therefore approach

the question of the origin of evil by fixing the eyes of our faith on him who alone is its conqueror (cf. Lk 11:21–2; Jn 16:11; 1 Jn 3:8).[17]

Transformation of the common experience

Paul, who called himself the apostle of the Gentiles (cf. Rom. 11:13), was well aware of the condition of moral degeneration and confusion in the pagan world from which many of his converts were called. He warned them against backsliding into this condition of spiritual blindness and moral enslavement. He pointed out that this condition results most radically from sin which entered the world with the first man's rebellion against God's design – the subtle rebellion of self-affirmation, which is only the expression of egotistical pride to 'go it alone'. All human beings somehow share in and contribute to a worsening of this condition, which far from liberating them only bound them in a false understanding and expression of 'self'. This 'conditioning' to enslavement affected and distorted people's ideas about the nature of God as well as their notions regarding how they might be happy and free – even if they were religiously minded, serious and sincere in their pursuit of authentic well-being (cf. Rom. 1:18ff.). Paul thus tirelessly pointed to faith in Christ as the only way out of the tyranny of ideas and an imperfect, partial understanding and carrying out of God's design for humanity in practice. He emphasised that God has shown how justification is realised apart from the law through faith in Jesus Christ (cf. Rom. 3:21f.).

In chapter 7 of his epistle to the Romans Paul gives a dramatic description of his existential experience of being confused and frustrated about his own lack of moral consistency and spiritual freedom: 'I do not understand my own actions. For I do not do what I want, but I do the very thing I hate' (Rom. 7:15).

This echoes the common experience of every person in every age – that experience of deep disappointment and, indeed, the great sorrow of being a 'divided self', in the famous expression of R.D. Laing. However, what Paul, and Augustine after him,[18] realised is a longing for the healing of a far deeper division

than that observed by psychologists especially today. This longing or yearning is focused on something even more integrating
than what the search for meaning, wholeness or coherence can
provide.[19] C.S. Lewis comments that even where Paul laments
his inability to realise the moral law he in no way denies our
perception of goodness, imperfect though our sight of it may
be.[20]

Augustine's reflection on his reading of Paul[21] enabled him
to recognise not merely the psychological but also ontological
dividedness of the human will and personality – a dividedness
which he most acutely knew by his own disconcerting early
experience of being drawn from one school of thought to
another and, above all, of vacillating between aspiring to high
ideals and being drawn back to the base attractions of the
flesh.[22] Long before Freud and the advances made by modern
psychology, Augustine, by reflecting long on his own experience and that of fellow human beings, became aware of how
the quirks of character, the manoeuvres of our subconscious
motives, tendencies and passions were all brought under the
more marvellous providence of God's grace. His insights into
the effects of habits and memory's and imagination's hold on
us – effects and habits which keep us enslaved[23] – are never
focused inward or introvertedly, but always directed on the
reality revealed by God in the expanding perspective of faith.
Like Paul, he regarded a person as a complex creature whose
constant need for the healing grace of Christ – even after the
great break with sin signified and brought about by baptism – is
oriented towards and transformed into the praise of God. The
experience of freedom through grace in the ordinary course of
the daily struggle against the tendency to selfishness becomes
an expression of worship.

More deeply, through his reflection on the apostle's teaching
Augustine discovered Christ as the providential Liberator or
Mediator of humanity. His interpretation of the epistle to the
Romans provided him, as Pelikan puts it, with his 'most
influential insight into human nature and psychology, the idea
of original sin', which was 'not only a way of speaking about the
misery of humanity, but a means of recognizing and praising
the uniqueness of Jesus. . . . Augustine found the knowledge of

the grace of Christ unintelligible without the knowledge of original sin, but he also saw that the knowledge of original sin was unbearable without a knowledge of the grace of Christ'.[24] Jesus is the unique Redeemer because of his freedom in laying down his life in obedience to the Father's will, which was not to condemn or judge, but to love and save sinful humanity (cf. Jn 3:16f.; 10:17–18).[25]

Following the Pauline tradition expressed in Augustine's insight, the Church sings its praise of Christ's freedom-giving triumph of grace in the *Exultet*. The Welsh artist-poet David Jones discerned the universal symbolism of those two words *felix culpa* at the centre of this great Easter hymn – a symbolism which he hears echoed in Coleridge's 'The Rime of the Ancient Mariner':

> This expression, owing to its own happy conciseness, has for many centuries been used as a kind of code-phrase for the whole dogma of the Fall and the Redemption. It is used with its fullest poetic effect during the Blessing of the Paschal Candle on Holy Saturday: '. . . O truly necessary sin of Adam . . . O happy fault, that merited such and so great a redemption.'

In the light of the mystery of Christ sin becomes recognised as a *felix culpa*, a 'happy fault', because sin and all the misery and pain that flows from it have been enveloped and transformed in the fullness of divine love's embrace.[26]

Augustine understood well the apostle's whole balanced teaching on the intrinsic necessity for that dialogue of co-operation between human freedom and God's grace, which the Holy Spirit nurtures and enriches in prayer and Christian worship. His position can be summed up in the following sentence: 'He who brought you into being without your assistance, does not justify you without your co-operation.'[27] The dialogue of divine–human co-operation found expression in his well-known prayer in the *Confessions*: 'Give what you command; command what you will' (*Da quod iubes; jube quod vis*),[28] six words which triggered off the famous Pelagian controversy, which in substance resembled Paul's controversy with the Judaisers. As Henry Chadwick notes, when the British monk Pelagius heard the passage in which this prayer appears, it seemed to him: 'to be condoning the number of Christians whose sexual life appeared unregenerate'.[29] The sentiment expressed in the six words of this prayer smacked of everything that Pelagius considered was opposed to the rigorous moral demands in the gospel about striving for perfection. Augustine's emphatic insistence on the primacy of grace suggested to the ascetically minded monk the promotion of passivity and laxity in moral endeavour – a slackening that simply pandered to the easy-going lives and disordered passions of people in the sun-kissed Mediterranean lands. But, so important is this prayer as regards the acknowledgement of the necessity for divine grace that frequently its influence is seen in the Collects of the liturgy.[30] The significance of these prayers cannot be missed for they gather the community in celebrating the greatest gift of God's liberality, the Eucharist, which enables or empowers us to live and to fulfil freely the new command of love as members of Christ's mystical body.

In his writings on the Donatist schism in the African church and especially in his sermons, Augustine constantly drew on Paul's teaching on the necessary unity of those who share the one bread, the one body of Christ the Redeemer, whose grace empowers Christians both to revere (admire) and imitate (follow) him.[31] The grandeur of Augustine's development of Paul's teaching on offering 'a living sacrifice, holy and acceptable to God, which is your spiritual worship' (Rom. 12:1) can be seen in his sacramental theology of turning towards or being converted to Christ's body. Conversion, the constant need of Christians, is thus a moral process which is only possible because it is intrinsically linked to the mystical, sacramental reality of Christ's paschal mystery celebrated in the Eucharist. A fine example illustrating this teaching can be seen in his commentary on the great psalm in praise of the law. Peter Brown points out that in this commentary Augustine proposes a teaching on how the process of conversion leads to true integrity, that is, a healing and integration of knowledge, thought, feeling, imagination, memory, will, etc. which are brought into harmony under the influence of the grace of Christ's Holy Spirit of truth.[32]

Worship in the body of Christ

The quality of being enabled to co-operate freely with God's grace revealed by Christ is related to many expressions in Paul's letters which express or imply the unity of the Christian community in worship – for instance, 'the body of Christ' (cf. Rom. 12:4; 1 Cor. 10:17; 12:12f., 20; Eph. 2:16; 4:4; Col. 3:15); 'the temple of God' (cf. 1 Cor. 3:16ff.; 6:19; 2 Cor. 6:16; Eph. 2:19ff.); 'the dwelling-place of God in the Spirit' (Eph. 2:20–2). The special context in which worship comes into its own as characteristically Christian is that of 'giving thanks', offering *eucharist* in the body of Christ. This theme of thanksgiving dominates the apostle's thought, especially in the epistles to the Ephesians and Colossians. The hymns and spiritual canticles, which he mentions (cf. Eph. 5:19; Col. 3:16), may be regarded as the ways the early Christian communities gave liturgical expression to the divine gift of their newness of life in Christ. There is no dearth of evidence scattered throughout the Pauline letters of hymns directed to Christ the Saviour as the One who brought the freedom of redemption to humanity (cf. e.g. 1 Tim. 3:16; Eph. 5:14, and especially Phil. 2:6–11).[33] It is not unlikely that he has in mind the Christian celebration of the Eucharist when he exhorts Christians to become strengthened to endure everything patiently 'while joyfully giving thanks to the Father (*eucharistoûntes tōi patrì*)' (Col. 1:12). Thanksgiving is the pre-dominant theme and tonality of Paul's magnificent exordium, which is like a *hymn of freedom* at the beginning of the letter to the Ephesians:

Blessed be God the Father of our Lord Jesus Christ,
who has blessed us with all the spiritual blessings of heaven in Christ.
Before the world was made, he chose us, chose us in Christ,
to be holy and spotless, and to live through love in his presence,
determining that we should become his adopted sons, through Jesus Christ
for his own kind purposes,
to make us praise the glory of his grace,
his free gift to us in the Beloved,
in whom, through his blood, we gain our freedom, the forgiveness of our sins (Eph. 1:3–7, JB).[34]

These words recall the hymn to Christ cited in the epistle to the Colossians 1:15–20, which was sung possibly at the rites of Christian initiation.[35] It is interesting to notice the immediate context of this hymn, which is situated between two statements in which the author of the letter speaks of redemption:

> He has rescued us from the power of darkness and transferred us into the kingdom of his beloved Son, in whom we have redemption, the forgiveness of sins [*through his blood*] (vv. 13–14).[36]

> And you who were once estranged and hostile in mind, doing evil deeds, he has now reconciled in *the body of his flesh* through death, so as to present you holy and blameless and irreproachable before him . . . (vv. 21–2: cf. Greek for italicised words).

According to many scholars these statements are most probably an allusion to baptism through which Christians are illumined and given access to the grace of redemption. The hymn itself exultantly affirms the absolute supremacy of Christ, in whom the whole of creation is held together because he is its efficient and final cause in the unfolding of history. In this passage all the verbs refer to the work of the incarnate Son, who is the image of the invisible God.[37] Paul presents in this way a fine synthesis of two themes regarding human knowledge of God. Although the term 'invisible' (*aopátos*) applied to God appears most rarely in the scriptures,[38] the idea of God's transcendence (his 'hiddenness') finds expression in the prophetic tradition (cf. especially Is. 45:15), whereas the Wisdom tradition speaks of God being known through the traces of his reflection in creation (cf. Wis. 7:26; cf. Ps. 18; cf. Rom. 1:19f.). It is particularly in and through the mystery of the incarnation, however, that God's image is fully manifest for Christ has uniquely revealed the Invisible God, as was seen above in John (cf. Jn 1:18; 14:9).

Certainly Paul was referring here to the biblical teaching regarding God creating human beings in his 'image and likeness' (cf. Gen. 1:26–7; 2:7; Wis. 1:13–15; 2:23–4; 15:7–8, 10–11). However, by mentioning only the word 'image' it would seem that the apostle of the Gentiles was accommodating this teaching to his converts from the Greek world (cf. Rom. 8:28–30; 1 Cor. 15:44–9; 2 Cor. 3:18–4:6). For whereas the word *eikón* (image) was familiar to the intellectual world of Hellenism,[39] that of 'likeness' is absent in the Greek philosophers regarding human life. The composite expression ('image and likeness') was peculiar to the Semitic tradition of the divine revelation, which nonetheless borrowed and integrated into its teaching whatever it found compatible and valuable in surrounding cultures. Paul Ricoeur has pointed out that the underlying notion contained in this expression is an utterly dynamic, developmental one in the understanding of many of the Fathers who built on Paul's reworking of the archaic simplicity of the original potter-imagery in Genesis to bring out the progressive *élan* of redemption.[40] By having slipped into an overly individualistic idea of and approach to the remission of sins and salvation, we have somehow tended to lose sight of the Greek Fathers' 'grandiose vision of the growth of mankind which God orients, in the very midst of evil and by means of grace toward divinization'.[41] In Paul, to whose world-view and tradition these Fathers were faithful, redemption from sin is no trivial matter of individualistic security, but a question of collective discernment and discovery of that awareness of hope for freedom. 'Redemption' is, in Ricoeur's memorable description, that word which 'is inscribed in letters of fire and joy' on human awareness.[42] But, the depths of this awareness consist in the religious awe and adoration, praise and gratitude, which follow human beings' conversion and transformation of their sinful way of life into one of worship after encountering the living God who freely reveals himself in Jesus Christ. Professor Dodd finely describes this life of worship in referring to Paul's doxology at the end of Romans 11:33–5, which leads to the apostle's exhortation to Christians to offer their very bodies as a 'living sacrifice . . . spiritual worship' (cf. Rom. 12:1–2):

> The religious consciousness, after its highest flights of speculation returns to the simple 'numinous' feeling of awe before the Mystery. 'Verily Thou art a God that hidest Thyself, O God of Israel, the Saviour!' (Is. 45:15). This *Deus absconditus* remains the Object of our worship. But when we can start from the religious experience of redemption by the love of God, which Paul has eloquently expressed in 8:18–30, the feeling of awe has a joyous and not a

gloomy colour. We are assured that the 'fathomless wealth' of the 'wisdom and knowledge of God' is at the service of everlasting mercy, and we are content that 'all comes from Him, all lives by Him, all ends in Him' (cf. Rom. 8:33, 35).[43]

Freedom of expression in Christian worship

Paul encouraged Christians to celebrate their joy for the gift of redemption in no trivial way. Their celebrations in hymns and spiritual canticles manifest a deep sense of participation in the life of the Spirit, which was not merely a social 'together-ness'. Following the Pauline teaching about care to observe the sacredness of intimacy with God in worship, Clement of Alexandria warns that the singing at Christian gatherings should not be allowed to degenerate into an excuse for mere rowdy sociability. He links the eucharistic feast with fulfilment of the two sides of Jesus' new law of love.[44] Clement's view about the use of wine and song (to say nothing of women!) sounds very severe. He was certainly concerned about respect for the sacred. For he understood the scriptural sense of wine in a mystical way, 'as a symbol of the holy Blood'.[45] But, there were also more immediate pastoral reasons for his admonitions. These were not dissimilar from those of Paul, who had to repri-mand the community of Christians at Corinth, not because they had a tendency to forget themselves and get carried away by the fervour of religious intoxication, but because there were divisions at these gatherings between the rich and poor, the latter being the object of discrimination since they were unable to provide fare for the social side of the gatherings.

Paul's exhortations of Christians to live in unity were not merely moral admonitions or directives regarding external conduct, but a teaching calling them to discern the activity of the risen Lord Jesus' Holy Spirit present in their midst. Through this Holy Spirit Christians are enabled to live in the hope of enjoying 'the glorious freedom of the children of God' (Rom. 8:21). This hope is particularly expressed in their communal celebrations of prayer. One of the oldest prayer-formulas recorded by Paul was: *marana tha* – 'Our Lord, come!' (1 Cor. 16:22). This acclamation seems to have originated from the liturgy of the Aramaean-Palestinian community, which had an important centre at Antioch – the place to which Paul was brought by Barnabas and spent a whole year, meeting with the Church and teaching many. It was possibly in this place – where the disciples were first called 'Christians' (cf. Acts 11:26) – that Paul learnt this prayer.[46] *Marana tha* combines both a lively yearning and hope for the 'second coming' of Christ (the parousía) among the first Christians and also their deep intimate devotion to him as Lord. Whereas worship was given to Christ, who was recognised as present among those who gathered to pray in his name, Paul's teaching emphasised that it was especially directed through him and in his Spirit to the Father.[47]

Paul deepens the sense of Christian prayer by teaching that all acts of prayer, praise, and adoration are addressed to God in the name of or through Christ. Because of Christ Jesus believers are enabled to worship God in a new way: through him worshippers have access to the presence of the Almighty in the intimacy of confident familiarity and the serene joy of freedom. Paul's word for this new attitude of boldness or directness of approach in utter confidence is *parrēsía* (cf. 2 Cor. 3:12; Eph. 3:12; also 1 Jn 2:28; 3:21). This word has been etymologically linked with those three words relating the open showing or appearing of the Lord: *parousía, epiphany* and *doxa*.[48] Here we may suggest a connection with John's theology concerning the uniqueness of Jesus' showing of the Father in his flesh: God as *Father* is *outspoken* in his Word! Paraphrasing Paul's imagery and the language of the letter to the Hebrews, Professor Moule says: 'In this sense, Christ's own "flesh" is a new way into the presence of God – a way which is "alive", for the way *is* the living Christ: incorporate in His humanity our humanity now enters the presence of God (Heb. 10:20).'[49] He goes on boldly to state that 'a new epoch is marked in the history of prayer to God' with the invocation 'Abba, Father'.[50] This 'new epoch' is one of freedom – a freedom of belonging to and being in communion with Christ's body, through which and in which Christians are united by the Spirit in their corporate worship of thanksgiving and prayer to the Father for his 'glorious grace which he freely bestowed on us in the Beloved' (Eph. 1:6).

Especially in the epistle to the Romans Paul relates those three great themes of law, grace and redemption (freedom) by his teaching on the way Christ's Spirit is given to lead towards 'the glorious freedom of the children of God' (8:21), for which we cry out 'Abba! Father!' (8:15; cf. also Gal. 4:5–7). Paul significantly uses the verb 'cry' (*krázomen*), not only because it suggests the inarticulate poignant sound of a little child claiming its parent's attention, but also because it particularly calls to mind the inner dispositions of Jesus in his anguished hour of discerning the Father's will, which is graphically described in Mark's Gospel (cf. 14:36).[51] Cardinal Ratzinger highlights the importance of Paul's teaching for appreciating the intrinsic connection between the Church's prayer and Christ's:

> A fundamental word in the mouth of 'the Son' is 'Abba'. It is no accident that we find this word characterizing the figure of Jesus in the New Testament. It expresses his whole being, and all that he says to God in prayer is ultimately only an explication of his being (and hence an explication of this one word); the Our Father is this same 'Abba' transposed into the plural for the benefit of those who are his.[52]

Paul repeatedly implores the members of the Christian communities to share 'the mind of Christ Jesus' (cf. Phil. 2:5; 2 Cor. 8:9). It is this 'mind', or rather, this inner attitude that constitutes Christians as worshippers, united or *at-one* in the deepest freedom of their vocation to share Christ's redeeming sufferings in order to know the power of his resurrection in building up his body, the Church (cf. Phil. 3:10; Col. 1:24).

It has been suggested that the Hebrew and Greek words (*Abba, Páter*) placed side by side in St Paul's great epistles on Christian freedom and grace (cf. Rom. 8:15; Gal. 4:5–7) might well signify the unity in prayer and life which Jesus Christ's sacrifice brought about between Jews and Gentiles. Moreover, his unity or communion is realised in the new life and worship of the earliest Christian communities which were made up of people drawn from the culturally different and religiously distinct and divided Jewish and pagan worlds.[53] This suggestion would seem to be well-founded on Paul's insistence, particularly in the epistle to the Galations, that Christ has freed humanity by manifesting the universal outreach of God's love to all people from the divisive force of those narrow religious laws and customs which arise from ethnic, national or political interests (cf. also Eph. 2:14ff.). Many Fathers of the Church developed Paul's fascination with the profound significance of the cross of Jesus' sacrifice as the powerful symbol of the universal extent and the limitless dimensions of the Father's Spirit of love that frees.[54] Jesus' cross cancels out every form of limiting selfishness and self-assertiveness – religious intolerance being the worst form of unfreedom. The cross of the Redeemer of humanity points horizontally to human brotherhood because it simultaneously reveals the vertical direction of the vocation of all persons to acknowledge God as 'our Father'. This cross of Christ's sacrifice of love is thus like an indispensable compass in our pilgrimage to the kingdom of freedom.[55]

The Pauline proclamation of the revelation of the new covenant of the freedom of God's children is closely related to the apostle's teaching on that restoration of the whole creational reality of the cosmos. The Church constantly celebrates this new creation of the covenant of grace in its greatest moment of praise and thanksgiving in the Eucharistic Prayer.[56] The Eucharist is the measure of all Christian experience. St Irenaeus developed Paul's great insight regarding all things being restored in and through Christ, who 'recapitulates' all things, that is, who becomes the 'head' or Lord of creation and history (cf. Rom. 13:9; Eph. 1:10).[57] The *Catechism of the Catholic Church* cites Irenaeus' terse statement: 'the Eucharist is the sum and summary of our faith: "Our way of thinking is attuned to the Eucharist, and the Eucharist in turn confirms our way of thinking."'[58]

Discerning and ministering to Christ's body

In various places in his letters we see Paul working out a theological approach to specific concerns and problematic pastoral issues in terms of linking his dominant interest and intuition about the newness of Christian freedom with worship in the eucharistic celebration, which constituted the identity

of the Christian community as the body of Christ. A salient
example illustrating this is evident in the first letter to the
Corinthians. Concern for communion in the vibrant reality of
the body of Christ is the deep truth proclaimed throughout this
letter. Pastoral questions and problems regarding befitting
Christian conduct – such as those pertaining to marriage and
sexuality, consideration of the poor, hope concerning the dead,
etc. – are all an elaboration of the implications of the truth of
being united to Christ through the sacrament of his risen and
glorified body.[59] This appears clearly in what is considered the
earliest witness to the institution of the Eucharist in Paul's
first letter to the Corinthians (cf. 1 Cor. 11:23–6). Let scholars
continue to debate whether this was a piece of catechesis or
evidence of primitive liturgical usage.[60] In 1 Corinthians 11:29
Paul insists on the crucial importance of discerning the
body and blood of Christ when celebrating the Eucharist.
The traditional Catholic interpretation, which regards this
verse as referring to the doctrine of the real presence,[61] has
been contested by Protestants, who read it as indicating the
community of Christ, 'the body of Christ'.[62] Francis Moloney
considers that:

> both interpretations are involved. . . . Thus, a further meaning to
> 'the body' must be discerned. If the Corinthians ignore the context
> of the whole community in their Eucharistic meals, they are failing
> to discern 'the body' that is the community itself. They would be
> proclaiming the presence of the Lord in a way that ran counter to
> that very 'rhythm' of the offering of Christ that they claimed to be
> 'remembering' in their celebration.[63]

Paul's account of the institution of the Eucharist cannot be
taken in isolation from another passage at the end of the same
great letter (cf. 1 Cor. 15:3–8).[64] For the introductory phrase of
each passage is strikingly similar in vocabulary, structure and
content: In chapter 11 of Corinthians we read: 'For I received
[*parélabon*] from the Lord what I also delivered [*parédoka*] to
you . . .'; while in chapter 15: 'For I delivered [*parédoka*] to
you as of first importance what I also received [*parélabon*] . . .'.[65]
Paul's credentials for being a faithful communicator and
minister or servant of the sacred mysteries of God (cf. 1 Cor.

4:1) are that he is himself a deeply grateful recipient – of communion of life through Christ's sacrifice, which is at the same time the sacrament of hope in the resurrection. One cannot give what one has not oneself received (cf. 1 Cor. 4:7)! The essential truth of being a Christian pertains to belonging to and being part of the body of Christ.

Faith in the mystery of Christ Jesus, who communicates authentic freedom, opens the way to hope by uniting Christians in his and the Holy Spirit's communion of love with the Father. This communion of life is what constitutes the Christian 'tradition', handed on in doctrine and worship. 'Tradition' refers to and links the Christian community of every age with the evangelising activity of the Church from apostolic times.[66] It signifies handling with care what has been received. Its content is in essence not merely a set of propositions or truths, but the mystery of Christ who is Truth itself, the Way to the life of communion with God (cf. Jn 14:6). As Bishop Christopher Butler says:

> the real content of Tradition is Christ himself, transcending all human attempts to 'put him into words' or express him in rites, ceremonies, poetry and art. Tradition thus understood lives not so much in the so-called 'monuments of tradition' as in the heart and mind of the Church, and its life is connected with the gift of the Holy Spirit to the Church as its, so to speak, animating principle.[67]

Tradition points always towards the 'mystery of Christ', a phrase dear to St Paul and contemporary theology, as the essential focus of catechesis.[68]

The relevance of the apostle's message today has been highlighted in the Basic Text of the Forty-sixth International Eucharistic Congress in Wroclaw (1997). This Congress focused on the theme of the Eucharist and Freedom by highlighting Paul's arresting sentence: 'For freedom Christ has set us free' (Gal. 5:1). Particularly in our present situation in which various false interpretations of freedom have provoked a disturbing religious and cultural crisis in the lives of individuals, families and society, it is important to reflect on and take to heart Paul's proclamation. For today, perhaps even more than in the past, there is 'the need for human freedom to be freed from sin, redeemed by grace. . . . Freedom itself needs to be set free. It is Christ who sets it free.'[69]

Paul's realisation of the transformative grace of Jesus Christ who rose from death in the power of God's love might be rightly regarded as the key to understanding the Christian approach to that vitally important issue which, especially in our own century, has come to occupy the central stage of serious consideration – the intricately complex issue that has been treated under different headings: 'religious freedom/liberty', 'freedom of conscience', 'religious toleration', etc. The Second Vatican Council strenuously debated this issue and on 7 December 1965 promulgated, together with its last documents, the *Declaration of Religious Liberty*, which stands as one of the more successful achievements of that Council.[70] The very opening words of this Declaration are highly significant of its whole tone, content and message: *Dignitatis humanae* – which loosely translated means, '*The dignity of the human person* exercises the consciousness of people of our times more and more . . .'. The Council's whole statement offers a monumental witness to Christians' growth in respect not only for the human endeavour for freedom, but also for persons in their individual and collective right and responsibility to exercise freedom of religion and, indeed, freedom in their search for religious truth.[71] Needless to say, such an exercise should be understood as seeking truth and its intrinsic relationship to God's revelation that the dignity or worth of being fully human consists in people collaborating together to discover common recognition and expression of the significance of worshipping him, who is the source, focus, end and fullness of the life of communion.[72] The Second Vatican Council's openness to cultural dialogue was prepared by persons of vision such as Barbara Ward, who already in the mid-1950s wrote that

> there is infinitely more understanding and respect for other traditions and cultures than was the case even a hundred years ago . . . There is now, with greater learning and greater humility, a new readiness to follow the wisdom of those Jesuit missionaries who held that the essence of Christianity could be given to Indians and Chinese only if Christianity were stated in terms of their own religious tradition and philosophy. We in the West, who

are convinced that time has meaning and that God works in history, cannot believe that the thousands of years of Confucian social discipline, of Hindu mysticism, of Buddhist charity and compassion, have had no significance and were not intended to give their own special light to the general illumination of mankind. For the philosophers and scholars of Christianity today the task is, then, still the task of Paul interpreting Greek philosophy to the Hebrews and Hebrew tradition to the Greeks.[73]

Such an approach in no way indicates a concession to relativism or a weakening of the Church's sense of responsibility in its mission to proclaim the gospel to all peoples. But it does signify a major shift in emphasis from an identification of the Christian faith with European culture.[74] It shows a widening of perspective in seeking to understand the important need to incarnate the essential message of God's revelation in Christ in a diversity of indigenous cultural situations, in which all wholesome religious traditions and practices that are compatible with the values of the gospel become recognised as preparatory to the coming of Christianity and incorporated into its new cultural expressions.

In recent years this process has claimed no little attention. It is called *inculturation*, 'which the spreading of the faith "must involve if the Gospel is to take flesh in each people's culture", as the recent *Catechism of the Catholic Church* puts it.[75] Inculturation means the implanting of the Christian faith, of the Good News of Jesus and of his church, in a given culture in ways that are effectively built into that particular culture.'[76] However, because it has been forgotten that the original use of the word 'Christianness' (*Christianismos* in Greek) referred primarily 'not to an institution but to the manner of living of a true disciple . . . including the disciple's reception of the gospel',[77] there are still many steps that have to be taken in the process of relating evangelisation and inculturation – as emphasised at the Synod of the African churches in Rome in 1994 – before people can come to a maturity of faith and freedom. Mature freedom implies trust and hope and love in which we realise Jesus' vision of worship in spirit and truth (cf. Jn 4:24).

The process of inculturation is more than pluralism; but rather, it is an expression in our times of the Christian Church's essential characteristics or 'marks' of pastoral charity: namely,

its *catholicity* or universal outreach and embrace, which began
in *apostolic* times, when the Lord's disciples and particularly
Paul, 'the apostle of the Gentiles', were impelled and strengthened by the Spirit of truth to go to the ends of the earth to
proclaim the good news and celebrate the sacramental mystery
of faith, the mystery of our religion or *holiness* (cf. 1 Tim. 3:9,
16), that is, Christ's Passover sacrifice, through which human
beings are called to be at-one in Christian *unity* in the truth and
freedom of the risen Lord Jesus' body.

PART III

RESPONSE TO THE
GIFT OF GOD

Our beloved Mother, Jesus, feeds us with himself, and, with the most tender courtesy, does it by means of the Blessed Sacrament, the precious food of all true life. And he keeps us going through his mercy and grace by all the sacraments. This is what he meant when he said, 'It is I whom Holy Church preaches and teaches.' ... Strengthened in this fashion by his working in us we freely choose to serve him and to love him, by his grace, world without end.

Julian of Norwich, *Revelations of Divine Love*[1]

Freedom is an expression of that spark of truth and life with which humanity was created in the image and likeness of God. ... Freedom is God's gift made to humanity in creation, and even more in redemption. It is, indeed, to the mystery of redemption that Paul is referring when he says: 'For freedom [*eleutheriai*] Christ has set us free [*eleuthépôsen*]' (Gal. 5:1) ... so that we may remain free, Christ himself willed that the mystery of redemption and our liberation – his and our Passover – should be sacramentally presented to us in the Eucharist at all times and in all places until his glorious and definitive return, when *freed from the corruption of sin and death, we shall sing the glory of the Father with every creature.*

Basic Text of the 46th International Eucharistic Congress[2]

I can only celebrate freedom if I *am* free; otherwise it is tragic self-delusion. I can only celebrate joy if the world and human existence really give me reason to rejoice. *Am* I free? *Is* there cause for joy? Where these questions are excluded, the 'party' – the post-religious world's attempt to rediscover the feast – is soon revealed as a tragic masquerade. ... But in the background there is the number one question concerning the power of suffering and death which no freedom can resist. ... We have said that liturgy is festal, and the feast is about freedom, the *freedom of being* which is there beneath the role-playing. But where we speak of being, we also raise the question of death. ... The freedom with which we are concerned in the Christian feast – the feast of the Eucharist – is not the freedom to devise new texts but the liberation of the world and ourselves from death. Only this can make us free, enabling us to accept truth and to love one another in truth.

Joseph Cardinal Ratzinger, *The Feast of Faith*[3]

Liturgy: The Dynamic Rhythm of Freedom in Christ's Paschal Mystery

Since God has declared himself freely and openly in Jesus Christ, his living and abiding Word (cf. Heb. 1:1–4; 1 Jn 1:1–4), human language and life and history can never again be the same. Humanity is called to listen, to believe, and to respond to the truth of the presence of God's redemptive or life-liberating action. The quality of human life depends on the reciprocal interaction of God's and our freedom. The liturgy is the expression *par excellence* of this interaction. The logic of the divine power of love in the liturgy far exceeds what can be humanly said or thought. It cuts through the barriers of communication, such as indicated in the philosopher Wittgenstein's famous statement which sums up the *impasse* of modernity: 'The limits of my language mean the limits of my world.'[4]

Josef Pieper reminds us that God's freedom-giving power in the sacred sphere of the liturgy enables human language to achieve its proper dynamic function, namely, to refer to and communicate reality:

> The spoken word and the proclamation do indeed constitute a beginning, but such a beginning has to be accomplished ever anew. And yet, the spoken word in itself is not central here. All speech by its very nature refers to something that is not speech. What is it? It is reality! . . . I attend Church, not because of all the talking and preaching but because something happens there. . . . And the Church, too, declares the center of her liturgy to be indeed an action, something that 'happens' . . . an event that utterly transcends all human imagination: God himself becomes man, and – in the New Testament language of nomadic shepherds – 'pitches his tent among us'.[5]

In other words, the ensemble of symbols, gestures and words of the liturgy point beyond themselves and lead us beyond the prosaic into the sacred sphere of encountering the divine mystery of God's life of pure communication. The dynamic rhythm of the liturgy opens us to perceive and enter the sacred sphere of *being-in-relationship*, that is, God's domain of *being-in-Love* or communion. This communion is where freedom is fully realised.

In this chapter we must consider the implications of Christ's 'work of our redemption' which is realised in the sacred liturgy. For God's Word is utterly different from all other words in so far as it demands a response of faith leading to commitment, or rather, participation in the deepest sense of the word. Here we focus on how freedom is realised through participating in the proclamation of Jesus Christ's gift of God's redemptive action in the Church's sacred liturgy – that action which achieves incomparably more than all human words or endeavours can bring about. Since the signs and symbols of the liturgy bear the divine guarantee of communicating what they signify, they both refer to and realise the ultimate dimension of the reality of communion in a more perfect way than even the most sincere human hopes or promises can achieve.

The signs and words of liturgy express and realise the worship of God and humanity's sanctification in the celebration of a 'sacred action surpassing all others'.[6] For this reason the Second Vatican Council, following the rich tradition of the Fathers of the Church, described the sacred liturgy as the 'summit and source' (*culmen et fons*) of the Church's entire life.[7] In its Decree on the Ministry and Life of Priests the Council implicitly distinguishes two senses in which the word 'Eucharist' is used: as referring to the Church's principal action (*actio*) of celebrating Christ's paschal mystery and as the fullest expression of the Church's spiritual good, namely, Christ himself who is its paschal sacrifice as the living and life-giving bread (cf. 1 Cor. 5:7).[8] The first sense is linked to one of the earliest names of the action which the Christian community gathers to carry out in obedience to Jesus' command: 'Do this in memory of me' – that is, to offer 'eucharist'.[9] As this verb itself means in the original Greek, 'eucharist' signifies *giving praise and thanks* for God's wonderful works and especially for the greatest act of his redeeming love in Christ. By the middle of the second century the word 'eucharist' came to be used also as a noun referring to the Lord Jesus Christ's special mode of presence in the Church's *Blessed* or *Most Holy Sacrament*, which refers to the second sense of 'Eucharist'. The Council states that all the other sacraments, all ministries and apostolates, and, indeed, the whole spiritual life of the Church are ordained to, hold together and reach the fullness of their purpose in the celebration of the holy Eucharist.[10] Thus, the Constitution on the Sacred Liturgy, the great first document of the Council, states the whole meaning and twofold purpose of divine worship:

> From the Liturgy therefore, [and] especially from the Eucharist, grace flows towards us, as from [its] fountainhead (*ut e fonte*), and in the most effective way there results in Christ that sanctification of humanity and the glorification of God, towards which, as to [their] goal (*uti ad finem*), all the Church's other activities (*opera*) are directed or converge (*contendunt*).[11]

Discovering the depths of Christ's paschal mystery

The words just quoted clearly indicate the need for consistency between Christian worship and life. They are preceded in the same paragraph by references to the prayers of the Easter season in which the Church teaches that the liturgy impels the faithful, 'filled with "Paschal sacraments"' to live united in 'the concord of piety',[12] and also that the lives of the faithful 'may express what they have received through faith'.[13] Elsewhere, namely, in the section of the Dogmatic Constitution on the Church dealing with the bishop's ministry of sanctifying the faithful especially through offering and overseeing the worthy offering of the Eucharist, the following quotation from a sermon of Pope St Leo the Great is included: 'Participation in the body and blood of Christ achieves nothing other than that we may be transformed [literally, *pass over*] into what we receive.'[14] The verb *transeamus* employed here is most significant. It recalls another splendid passage in the same Father's second sermon on the ascension, in which he states that 'the

visible presence of the Redeemer has passed into the sacraments [*transivit in sacraments*]'.[15] In other words, the very basis
of our transformation into the mystical body of Christ is his
passing over into the sacred signs of the liturgy.

The English word *Passover* expresses exactly what the Hebrew
word *Pasch* signifies. This word literally means 'to leap/pass
over'; it is related to the idea of passage. In early catechetical
Easter homilies we find great care exercised in explaining the
original meaning of the Hebrew word, as for instance in the
following text by a second-century anonymous author:

> The very name of the feast points to the way in which it [the Jewish
> Passover] is surpassed, if it is carefully explained. The word 'Pasch'
> means 'passage', because when the angel of death was striking
> down the first-born, he passed over the houses of the Hebrews. But
> with us the passage of the angel of death is a reality, for it passes
> over us once for all when Christ raises us up to eternal life . . . the
> sacrifice of the true Pasch is the beginning of eternal life for us . . .
> Now Christ is sacrificed for him [the Christian] when he recognises
> the grace and understands the life this sacrifice has won for
> him.[16]

The Fathers delighted to explore the double sense expressed
here of 'passover': the figure (or type) and the reality of the
angel's/Christ's deliverance. In virtue of this Passover other
deeper levels of the quality of human life are made possible:
the exodus or passage from the condition of every kind of
bondage to freedom – from slavery and sin to new life in the
promised land and/or the new creation in Christ.

Throughout the long homily of the second-century Melito of
Sardis on the Passover, the idea of the permanence of Christ's
eternal sacrifice is poetically contrasted with the transitory
quality of its Old Testament antecedents and all imperfect or
incomplete attempts to worship God fittingly. Three centuries
later St Augustine energetically explained to his congregation
that, despite the corruption of the sense of *Pascha*, it really
meant 'to pass over' (*transitus*) since it is derived from the
Hebrew, and not – as was commonly thought in his day – from
the Greek verb '*paschein*' ('to suffer').[17] Augustine was not being
merely pedantic about the correct use of language, but he was
making an important point regarding the way that the faithful

understand and live the liturgy must be in accord with the
reality of Christ's paschal mystery. In our own day we, perhaps
more than the Greek- or Latin-speaking Christians of Melito's
or Augustine's time, have greater need to realise our religious
roots and to recover a lost sense of the traditional symbols of
the sacred.

St Augustine may be taken as representing the mature
patristic tradition which indicates the celebration of Christ's
paschal mystery as determining the focus and the essential
rhythm of the Church's entire life. In his two letters (c. AD 400)
to a certain layman called Januarius, who was perplexed at
coming across differences in liturgical practice in various places,
Augustine points out what must be held regarding the essential
ordinances of the Lord and the sacred tradition of the Church:

> I want you in the first place to hold onto this as fundamental: that
> our Lord Jesus Christ gave us a 'light yoke' and an 'burden easy to
> bear', as he declares in the Gospel (Mt 11:30). In accordance with
> this statement he bound his people under the new dispensation
> together in a fellowship by sacraments, which are very few in
> number, most easy to observe, and most excellent in significance –
> such as baptism solemnized in the name of the Trinity, communion
> of his body and blood, and similar things enjoined in the canonical
> Scriptures. . . . There are other practices which we hold because of
> the authority, not of Scripture, but of tradition: these are observed
> throughout the whole world; they are rightly held as approved and
> instituted either by the apostles themselves or by plenary Councils,
> which have a most useful authority in the Church. These practices
> are, for instance, the annual solemn commemoration of the Lord's
> passion, resurrection, and ascension, and of the descent of the Holy
> Spirit from heaven, as well as whatever is similarly observed by the
> whole Church wherever it has been established.[18]

Briefly, the whole Christian life is shaped by the rhythm of
Christ's Passover or paschal mystery, which in its sacramental
fullness is celebrated in the Easter Vigil, called by Augustine
'the mother of all vigils'.[19] On another occasion, the same great
pastor explains to his congregation in a sermon:

> We keep vigil on that night because the Lord rose from the dead;
> that life . . . where there is no longer the sleep of death, began for
> us in his flesh; being thus risen, death will be no more nor have

dominion . . . If we have kept vigil for the risen one, he will see that
we shall reign with him for ever.[20]

However else we may regard the celebration of the sacred
liturgy today,[21] we cannot ignore or neglect to see it as characterised by the essentially God-ward rhythm of Christ's Passover.
This truth still needs to be better and more deeply appreciated
as shaping the inner structure of the Eucharistic Prayer before
attempting to substitute the approved prayers with innovations
or other free improvisations.[22] Cardinal Ratzinger points out
that such attempts are tangential to the central serious purpose
of the paschal mystery celebrated in the Eucharist: 'The
freedom with which we are concerned in the Christian feast –
the feast of the Eucharist – is not the freedom to devise new
texts but the liberation of the world and ourselves from death.
Only this can make us free, enabling us to accept truth and to
love one another in truth.'[23]

Participation in Christ's sacrifice

Already more than thirty years have slipped by since the 'new'
Order of the Mass (*Ordo Missae*) became mandatory for use
in the Western Church.[24] The purpose for revising the Roman
Missal was clearly to enrich the sense of active participation of
all in the central act of Christian worship and, hence, to bring
about that renewal and deepening of the whole Church's life of
holiness in Christ's Spirit which was called for at the Second
Vatican Council.[25] Active participation (*participatio actuosa*) is at
the nub of the theology of celebrating the sacred liturgy since it
refers to the close relationship between the significance of
liturgical celebration and the nature of belonging to the
Christian community or fellowship (*koinōnia*). This relationship
comprises both internal and external dimensions and depths,
which pertain both to the Christian community and also to
the celebration of the source and fullness of its life in the
liturgy. The recognition and appropriate expression of this
relationship is crucial for understanding the precise way that
the Christian community and its liturgy gather up and
transform the fragments of human life – those fragments which
are constituted by all that is genuine in human experience: the

grief and anguish about alienation as well as the joy and hope for freedom in the hearts of every man and woman of every group and nation.[26] Cardinal Ratzinger has described this relationship between the Church's liturgy and life in the following magnificent paragraph:

> In order to do justice to our humanness, 'participation' and 'activity' must be seen in the perspective of the individual and the community, of inwardness and external expression. For community to exist, there must be some common *expression*; but, lest this expression be merely external, there must be also a common movement of *internalization*, a shared path inward (and upward). Where man operates *only* at the level of expression, at the level of 'roles', he is only 'playing' at community. This 'acted' community only lasts as long as the playing of the roles. We can see this in the writings of Sartre, Simone de Beauvoir and Camus. As representatives of a whole generation they have described the feeling of isolation, the sense of man's essential loneliness and the impossibility of communication between separate selves ... the total impossibility of real relationship. Christian liturgy could and should take up this very point. But it cannot do so by exhausting itself in external activity. The only way is to open up these separate selves through the process of interiorization, by an entering into the liturgical word and the liturgical reality – which is the presence of the Lord – and by enabling them inwardly to communicate with him who first communicated himself to us all, in his self-surrender on the Cross.[27]

After thirty years of the Council's challenging reforms, however, we still need to be reminded that the dignity and depth of the sacred liturgy become compromised when the 'celebration' is turned into a kind of jamboree and the Church becomes like a noisy piazza or bustling city thoroughfare. While Christ can be and *is* certainly present in these places too, the primary purpose of our coming together in the liturgy is not to create the same atmosphere of hubbub as in places of daily commerce or amusement, shopping arcades or nightclubs, etc. We gather, or rather, we are assembled not to be 'loud' or 'showy', nor to find or celebrate ourselves, nor even 'to be ourselves', but above all to discover and celebrate Christ, the *font and fullness* of our lives and of our reason to rejoice in the confident freedom of the children of God. The deepest meaning of 'participation' in the liturgy, which the Council intended, consists not in everyone 'doing something', but in partaking in Holy Communion, when we receive, welcome and listen to him, the Word of Life. This sense was made clear in the following statement in the post-conciliar Instruction on the worship of the eucharistic mystery: 'the faithful achieve a more perfect participation in the Mass when, with proper dispositions, they sacramentally receive the Body of the Lord in the Mass itself, in obedience to his words "take and eat"'.[28] One must avoid decrying the tendency of Christian spirituality since the Middle Ages to concentrate more on the humanity of Christ and his passion and death, than on his glory as the risen Lord. For, it cannot be denied that this tendency certainly manifests the living development of doctrine and devotion within the overall scope of the Church's history. The lives of many generations of saints bear eloquent witness to devotion to the sacred humanity of Christ.[29]

However, difficulties may be detected as foreshadowed in the failure of some of the greatest of the scholastic theologians to integrate this valid tendency to respond to the humanity of Christ into a sound theology of the Eucharist as the celebration of the whole paschal mystery. Even the genius of St Thomas Aquinas for theological synthesis did not sufficiently relate the resurrection and ascension to the eucharistic mystery, but tended to focus on the passion of the Lord's sacrificial death.[30]

A notable exception is found in the approach of Baldwin of Ford, who, quoting the hymn of Venantius Fortunatus, *Pange lingua gloriosi proelium certaminis*,[31] points out that the events of Christ's whole life – his birth, miracles, discourses, passion, resurrection, ascension – are integrally represented in the eucharistic mystery. Baldwin's rich theology of the Eucharist offers one of the finest examples of mediaeval monastic theology which is nourished on the *lectio divina*. For Baldwin, the crowning glory of Christ's whole life was not only the passion and cross, but the resurrection. Thus, he sees the Eucharist as enabling us to participate in Christ's entire freedom-giving mystery, which the gospel announces. In giving us access to this integral mystery, the Eucharist is itself a proclamation and extension of God's communication of 'good news': 'The word of God – or the body of Christ – is our nourishment according to the limited manner of our capacity to participate in it until we can better appreciate it after our sojourn in this desert and arrival in the habitable land of the living.'[32]

Nevertheless, it is regrettable that this approach played little part in influencing the general teaching handed on – a teaching which came from the scholastics, rather than the monks. Emphasis on Christ's sacrificial death has been closely linked (as both effect and cause, from different points of view) to a diminution in the sound sense of liturgical piety and to a separation between popular devotions and liturgical worship. Thus, despite the clarity of its apologetic approach in the polemic context of dealing with the Reformers, the Council of Trent did not adequately integrate the questions of the sacramentality of the Eucharist, sacrifice of the Mass, and Real Presence. It was precisely to foster a rediscovery and deepened awareness of the riches of Christian tradition that the Second Vatican Council's reforms were directed.[33]

Freedom in 'the work of our redemption'

It is helpful at this point to examine more closely how the rhythm of the paschal mystery in the sacred liturgy is related to and affects our realisation of the freedom for which Christ has set us free (cf. Gal. 5:1). The deepest and fullest meaning of freedom consists in living in harmony with the truth of his Passover. The expression 'the paschal mystery' is almost synonymous with another theme recurring in the documents of the Second Vatican Council, namely, 'the work of our redemption' (*opus nostrae/humanae redemptionis/salutis*). The meaning of the phrase 'the paschal mystery', dear to the Fathers of the Second Vatican Council,[34] is seen in its connection with the Council's teaching on 'the work of our redemption'.[35] Thus, the two expressions are linked in the Constitution on the liturgy, which quotes the words of the Memorial (*anamnesis*) of the Roman Canon and the Easter Preface in its terse description of the sacred liturgy as presenting the paschal mystery:

Christ the Lord fulfilled this work of human Redemption and God's perfect glorification – to which the marvels God did for the people of the Old Testament were a prelude. He accomplished this principally through the paschal mystery of his blessed Passion, Resurrection from the dead and glorious Ascension. In this paschal mystery he [Christ] 'destroyed our death by dying and by rising restored our life'.[36]

First of all we need to be clear about the meaning of the sentence, 'the work of our redemption is carried out', or its equivalent expressions. The sentence derives from part of a quotation of a liturgical text, namely, the Secret Prayer for the ninth Sunday after Pentecost of the old Roman Missal – now the Prayer Over the Gifts of the second Sunday of the Year. The idea expressed in this prayer can be traced back to St Leo the Great.[37] It must be admitted that it is almost impossible to translate into English the rich conciseness of the patristic Latin idiom in the phrase: *opus nostrae redemptionis exercetur.* It is rather misleading to render the phrase as: 'the work of our redemption is accomplished'. For while this translation does justice to the unique, 'once-for-all' character of Christ's saving action, it is ambiguous in that it fails to convey clearly the important theological point that this action is accessible and, moreover, continued in the sacramentality of the Church's liturgy. For a correct translation of the meaning expressed by the verb *exercetur* it is necessary to appreciate that what is precisely at issue is that the eternal mystery of God's salvific will, which was historically disclosed perfectly and uniquely in Christ's Passover, is made actual or rendered present in the sacramental signs of the liturgy.[38] Hence, a rough translation of the idea expressed in this phrase might be: the work of our redemption is set in motion or is being actualised and made manifest (sacramentally).

It cannot be sufficiently emphasised that the key to a sound appreciation of the continuity of Christ's Passover rhythm in the liturgy is the notion of sacramentality.[39] The vocabulary of sacramentality at the time of the Fathers included such words as 'figure', 'image', 'likeness' (*figura, imago, similitudo*).[40] But in the course of time these terms lost their strong sense as indicating the reality signified and came to mean 'merely a copy'. Hence there arose misunderstanding and disagreement regarding the

Church's faith in eucharistic presence and actuality of Christ's sacrifice even long before the Reformation. The original use of these terms, however, took into account the rich biblical context and especially Pauline theology of imitation (*mimesis*) and memorial (*anamnesis*) of the essence of what the Lord Jesus said and did at the Last Supper. To *imitate* did not signify merely reproducing a 'copy' or ritual observance; but rather, it also implied realising the very presence of Christ's Passover mystery which was liturgically celebrated. The Church's obedience to the will of Christ ('Do this as my memorial')[41] is charged with the same dynamic power which became released in virtue of the rhythm of his own lifelong loving obedience to the Father's will unto the climatic moment of his sacrifice on Calvary.

Rather than being a *mere* symbol or subjective kind of 'remembering', to keep or do the memorial of Christ's entire paschal mystery – similar to the Jewish celebration of God's wonderful saving deeds – *reali*ses (makes real) Christ's 'work of our redemption' as present to the Church, the community of the *mystery of faith*.[42] Authentic Christian faith is never subjective. The criterion that faith is authentic is that it always flows from, expresses and remains in communion with the faith of the Church,[43] which acknowledges the presence of God who saves us from individualism, subjective or private interpretation, and sinful refusal to recognise that God calls us to praise him for his saving love. The 'alignment' of individual persons with the Church's faith is expressed in the prayer that follows the Our Father just before the sign of peace in the Communion of Rite of the Mass: 'Look not on our sins, but on the faith of your Church.'[44] The Church's faith leads us to the realism of the present moment in the strong sense of the word – that is, into the freedom of God's redeeming presence in the sacrament of his and the Church's sacrifice. This is what the *anamnesis* or memorial signifies in the Eucharistic Prayer, the text of which is understood in the context of the Church's intention to be faithful both to the Lord's command and his Holy Spirit's unfolding of revelation.[45]

The complementary sense of the two themes, 'the paschal mystery' and 'the work of our redemption', may be further illustrated by examining them in the light of a verse of St Paul's epistle to the Romans where it is thought that the apostle is quoting from an early hymn in praise of Christ: 'The death he died, he died to sin, once for all; but the life he lives, he lives to God' (Rom. 6:10, NRSV). This sentence dramatically brings out the absolute break between death and life, which is more strikingly evident in the Greek of St Paul's text than our English version can convey. The tenses of the Greek verbs highlight the radical change in Christ's state: the aorist past tense in the repetition of 'he died', emphasised by the adverbial expression 'once for all [*ephápax*]', stands in stark contrast against the reiteration of the continuous present tense in 'he lives'. Furthermore, the repetition of the crisp monosyllabic *zē* ('he lives') suggests, as it were, a staccato-like note of hopeful vitality that overcomes and takes over from the languid tone of the repeated polysyllabic *apéthanen* ('he died'). It would hardly seem an exaggeration to see, or rather, hear in this sentence a hint of the quickening rhythm of Christ's Passover to life, which is freed from the lengthened syllables of the sentence expressing the letter of the law of death.

St Paul describes Christ's attainment of the fullness of 'actuality' by being raised up to and in God. His attainment gives him lordship over death. As he puts it, 'death no longer has dominion' or rather, 'lords it [*kurieúei*] over him' (v. 9). The break between death and living is absolute. This applies much more in the moral and spiritual senses, than in the natural, physical sense. But, the moral and spiritual senses are founded on the reality of Christ's resurrection from death. The law of *being-in-Christ* is the 'source and summit' of freedom to obey God's covenant of life joyously. We may be permitted to regard the 'grace and truth' of the Redeemer's presence as the *metaphysical* foundation of human moral and spiritual reality.[46] Christ's paschal mystery is the ultimate basis for the raising up of all those baptised or plunged into the mystery of his Passover. The Church's celebration of this *mystery of faith* is the basis of Christian hope for authentic freedom.

Turning our attention to the context of Romans 6:10, we note that this verse occurs in the section of the apostle's teaching on becoming conformed to the sacramental *pattern/form* of Christ's paschal mystery. Paul's instruction draws out the practical consequences of faith in God's free gift received through sacramental initiation into Christ's life. The consequences of this cannot be ignored as superfluous because Christ has done everything. Rather, the very proclamation of Christ's generous achievement on our behalf does not merely impel us to follow his good example or to be attracted to obey his teaching as an admirable 'ideal';[47] but, more radically, it effectively empowers us to imitate what we receive and handle in the sacraments, as we have already indicated the Fathers of the Church constantly emphasised.[48]

Christ's death is the great passage or Passover through and from our human condition of every kind of limitation and enslavement into the eternal presence of God's life of unlimited love.[49] His Passover is the eternal event of love which generates a new pulse or rhythm in the human heart. This pulse quickens the heart's deepest desires and hopes for deliverance from every sinful form of selfishness and pride, whether of an individual or corporate kind – such as racist or religious discrimination, prejudice and enmity. The celebration of the paschal mystery both signifies and creates a bonding in brotherhood and friendship, because it contains the source and summit of communion with the Father in the Lord Jesus' Spirit. Jesus Christ 'brothers', so to speak, the whole of humanity which he alone is capable of representing before and leading to his Father's life of love, since he restores human beings to his image and likeness, in which they are originally created and which they are called to resemble. He would not and could not be detained in the thickets of time by death, the effect of humanity's common condition of pride and lovelessness; he was, rather, single-mindedly intent upon realising his Father's business – namely, the 'work of our redemption', which reveals, reconciles and re-creates the world into the kingdom of love. He brought this loving business to its fulfilment in the intense atmosphere of his passion, death, resurrection, ascension and sending of his Spirit. The atmosphere of this Passover is that of our rite of passage to life, which the Church celebrates in the sacred liturgy and proclaims with tireless joy in the Eucharistic Prayer.

Eucharist: thanksgiving hymn
in praise of Christ who frees us

The freedom, which is offered and made available through
the liturgical celebration of Christ's paschal mystery, is a gift
requiring our reception with thanksgiving and the greatest
reverence of worship to God the Giver. The need for a rediscovery of the sense of the sacred has been repeatedly
emphasised in recent times. The following words from Pope
John Paul II's pastoral exhortation are worth citing at some
length since they highlight the positive value of the liturgical
renewal since the Council:

> It is therefore very opportune and necessary to continue to actuate
> a new and intense education, in order to discover all the richness
> contained in the new liturgy. Indeed, the liturgical renewal that has
> taken place since the Second Vatican Council has given, so to speak,
> greater visibility to *the Eucharistic sacrifice.* One factor contributing
> to this is that the words of the Eucharistic prayer are said aloud by
> the celebrant, particularly the words of consecration, with the
> acclamation by the assembly immediately after the elevation. All
> this should fill us with joy, but we should also remember that *these*
> *changes demand new spiritual awareness and maturity,* both on the part
> of the celebrant – especially now that he celebrates 'facing the
> people' – and by the faithful. Eucharistic worship matures and
> grows when the words of the Eucharistic prayer, especially the words
> of consecration, are spoken with great humility and simplicity, in a
> worthy and fitting way, which is understandable and in keeping with
> their holiness; when this essential act of the Eucharistic liturgy is
> performed unhurriedly; and when it brings about in us such
> recollection and devotion that the participants become aware of
> the greatness of the mystery being accomplished and show it by
> their attitude.[50]

The spirit of reverent thanksgiving and praise in the celebration
of *eucharist* requires us to turn to the Lord above all, rather than
towards ourselves or our own resources. This turning to the
Lord, that is, being converted and reconciled is the primary
focus of Christian worship. The whole rhythm of the eucharistic
celebration always implies the dynamic movement of conversion and reconciliation, that is, being made *at one* through,
with and in Christ. This rhythm is evident in the very structure

and flow of the celebration: from the assembling of the faithful
to listen to God's design for human freedom, which, in a word,
calls them to 'repent and believe in the gospel' (cf. Mk 1:15), to
the offering and entering into communion with Christ's
sacrifice.[51] To offer the eucharistic sacrifice is nothing other
than to enter ever more deeply into the most radical level of
the Passover process, that process which draws us towards
realising Jesus' prayer at the first Eucharist for Christian unity
(cf. Jn 17:11, 22–3). This process is primarily a sacred response
to God's offer of redemption or freedom to all people. It is
sacred because it turns us to acknowledge and worship God,
whose *at-oneing* love of Christ's Spirit draws us together not
only towards one another in mutual respect and the reciprocity
of service in charity, but also, more deeply, towards seeking
the truth of God's *holy communion* in worship. This was the
whole point of many of the Fathers' teaching on the symbolism
of turning in prayer to face the East, since the East was once
considered as the region signifying the coming of spiritual
light into the world, Christ the 'Splendour of Truth', 'Sun of
Justice' (*Sol Iustitiae*) and 'Light of the Nations' (*Lumen
Gentium*).[52]

The liturgical expression of thanksgiving or *eucharist* for the
whole sweep of God's wonderful deeds of salvation which
culminated in Christ, however, is not enough. It also involves
our co-operation in the Passover process of conversion. This
process signifies that all things become reconciled and integrated into the harmonious perspective of God's design in 'the
work of our redemption'. Conversion involves the transformation of all our fragmented experiences, all our disjointed
and painful memories, all our divisive and frustrating moments
of unachieved hopes, yearnings and dreams, as well as our
failures and loss of self-esteem or sense of worth resulting from
the destructive power of evil. In every eucharistic celebration
the Church's proclamation of Christ's new and eternal
covenant calls us to receive the grace of conversion, which most
radically means *being turned* together towards living Christ's
Passover, that eternal instant of his power of love's dynamism
manifest and communicated in human history.[53] Thus, every
eucharistic celebration manifests the sacramental quality and

dynamic nature of the Church's identity. Christ's paschal mystery celebrated in the eucharistic liturgy reveals the centre of the Church's identity and purpose as enabling us to become more credibly a community of reconciliation, while it is also the source of the inspiration and energy in the Church's mission of pastoral charity to announce and celebrate the abundant life of communion with God, which Christ, the Good Shepherd, came both to reveal and give through freely laying down his own life in the perfect sacrifice (cf. Jn 17:3f.; 10:10). Every celebration bears witness to the deepening grasp of the truth of becoming the mystical body of Christ. The Christian celebration of the Passover is possible and realised because of the power of the Holy Spirit who draws us to Christ, the Light of the Nations, in the *mystery of faith.*

The Spirit of the Word

The Western perspective of the priest's special sacramental relationship to the Word of consecration, which Karl Rahner admirably expresses,[54] needs to be balanced by that of the Eastern Church's recognition of the Holy Spirit's role in the Church. In the profound – but regrettably little known – first statement of the Joint Commission for Theological Dialogue Between the Roman Catholic Church and the Orthodox Church, there is a particularly beautiful and important section describing the mission and action of the Holy Spirit in the Church. This section includes a passage which highlights the eucharistic co-operation, so to say, between the Word and the Spirit – the joint interaction of the silent inexpressible mystery of God's love and his disclosure in the mystery of the Church receiving his body. The following sentences richly present the rhythm of the Church's liturgical celebration, which resembles and utterly depends on the action of the blessed Trinity in leading unto the fullness of freedom in the divine communion of life:

> Taken as a whole, the eucharistic celebration makes present the Trinitarian mystery of the Church. In it, one passes from hearing the Word, culminating in the proclamation of the Gospel, the

apostolic announcing of the Word made flesh, to the thanksgiving offered to the Father, to the memorial of the sacrifice of Christ and to communion in him thanks to the prayer of *epiclesis* uttered in faith. For the *epiclesis* is not merely an invocation for the sacramental transforming of the bread and of the cup. It is also a prayer for the full effect of the communion of all in the mystery revealed by the Son. . . .

[T]his Spirit . . . is communicated to us particularly in the eucharist by this Son upon whom he reposes in time and in eternity (Jn 1:32).

That is why the eucharistic mystery is accomplished in the prayer which joins together the words by which the Word made flesh instituted the sacrament and the *epiclesis* in which the Church, moved by faith, entreats the Father, through the Son, to send the Spirit so that, in the unique offering of the incarnate Son, everything may be consummated in unity.[55]

These words point to the vitality of the Word of God and the silent energy of the Spirit of the Father's and the Son's reciprocal love which become recognised in the dynamic rhythm celebrated in the sacred liturgy. Moreover, in virtue of the Word and prayer in the Spirit the liturgy impels and strengthens Christians to move towards and to experience the depths of 'the work of our redemption' being carried out or taking place in the spiritual harmony of Christian worship – that harmony which fully manifests the freedom of participating in the holiest communion of God's life of unity, for which Jesus prayed to the Father (cf. Jn 17:11, 21f.).

The meaning of the Christian *memorial* – 'sacrifice of praise'

While an understanding of the liturgical memorial celebrated in the Eucharist has opened the way to significant ecumenical agreement about the nature of the Church's sacrifice, the depths of this memorial are far from being exhausted. Just as the search for roots and the depth analysis of human memory offer much insight into human behaviour, so too the riches of the notion of religious memorial are the focus of ongoing modern investigation from various points of view: biblical, liturgical, theological and anthropological. David Power has usefully described the six features of Jewish religious practice of keeping memory or memorial (Hebrew: *zikkaron*; Greek: *anamnesis*):[56]

1) worship is based on ordinances received from God;
2) worship is a reciprocal covenantal relationship between Yahweh and his people – Yahweh being the initiator;
3) continuance of worship is a sign of *God's* remembrance of his people and saving deeds of past;[57]
4) Israel's remembrance in worship proclaims God's marvellous deeds in praise;
5) certain recurrent elements: narrative of deeds remembered, recital of divine command to keep memorial, prayers of blessing, ritual actions which have a covenantal significance;
6) expression of eschatological hope in anticipation of God's reign (kingdom) to come is integral in the significance of memorial.

All these features are implied in the event of Jesus' revelation of the new covenant which passes into historical truth through the Church's proclamation of the Institution Narrative. In Power's words, the ancients' use of memory in the art of storytelling

allows the accounts to place the events surrounding Jesus of Nazareth into the history of the covenant and to show the link of the church's memorial action with this history and with the anticipation of God's reign. Much of the accounts' power lies in their use of the historical master images of covenant, pasch, suffering servant, and sacrifice. These images give the words and actions of Jesus at the supper their density and their eschatological value.[58]

C.S. Lewis throws light on this manner of employing imagination through faith in God, whose light of revelation is filtered even through great literature. Thus, Lewis evaluates most highly Tolkien's genius because of this author's gift for situating our ordinary experiences within the vast perspective of reality opened by myth and storytelling:

The value of the myth is that it takes all the things we know and restores to them the rich significance which has been hidden by 'the veil of familiarity'. The child enjoys his cold meat (otherwise dull to him) by pretending it is buffalo, just killed with his own bow and arrow. And the child is wise. The real meat comes back to him more savoury for having been dipped in a story; you might say that only then is it the real meat. If you are tired of the real landscape, look at it in a mirror. By putting bread, gold, horse, apple, or the very roads into a myth, we do not retreat from reality: we rediscover it. As long as the story lingers in our mind, the real things are more themselves. . . . By dipping them in myth we see them more clearly.[59]

These words can be applied, without difficulty, to the eucharistic mystery, which relates, or rather, proclaims the greatest story ever told – the revealing love story of God's eternal love for the world (cf. Jn 3:16). The story of the Eucharist – the gift of Christ Jesus' sacrifice of love – is, as it were, the finest motif woven into the story of human beings' longing for freedom. The Institution Narrative at the centre of the eucharistic celebration establishes the design of the whole rich tapestry of religious memory and hope. It points to the reality underlying and revealed in all the myths of human memory and hope. Its proclamation by the Church creates that utterly new environment of the splendour of grace and truth which the divine liturgy celebrates as 'heaven on earth'. This environment of the liturgy may thus be regarded as the true ecumenical crossroads of history, where Jesus Christ meets all the memories and hopes of humanity for authentic justice and peace, freedom and unity.

The essential form of the eucharistic celebration consists in the sacrifice of praise of God's people. The basic structure of the Mass is that of *eucharist*, that is, the prayer of *anamnesis* or 'memorial' whose shape is that of thanksgiving for Jesus' unique gift of self to the Father out of loving obedience for the life of the world. Love is what is unique in Christ's sacrifice and must be the distinctive character of the Christian sacrament of his sacrifice as well. Jesus' sacrifice brought about the world's redemption or freedom from the selfishness and pride of sin because he alone was free and capable of loving totally. Thus, the various theories about sacrifice – immolation, oblation, etc. which exercised the ingenuity of Scholastic theologians in recent centuries – seem to have missed the point and caused confusion in a tangle of distinctions and verbal precisions about the moment of the consecration, the sacramental manner of representing the separation of the body and blood of Christ in the mystical and 'unbloody' division of the species of bread and

wine by the words of consecration, etc.[60] What is represented in
the Eucharistic Prayer is neither Calvary as such nor even the
Last Supper. The Church cannot repeat what is unique to the
life of Christ. As Ratzinger puts it:

> As such, the Christian Eucharist is not a repetition of the Last
> Supper (which was in fact unique). . . . We might put it like this:
> the eucharistic actions are taken out of the context of the Passover
> and are placed within the new context of the 'Lord's Day', i.e. the
> day which marked the first meeting with the Risen Lord.[61]

It is a mistake, therefore, to strain to explain the eucharistic
sacrifice of praise in terms of the destruction or immolation of
the 'elements' of bread and wine. Likewise, it is quite wrong-
headed to attempt to turn the Mass into a meal that mimes the
Last Supper.[62] For Christ's Passover was unique. But the Church
can and must give thanks and praise in response to his unique
love. As utterly different from all human endeavours to offer
sacrifice, the Christian sacrifice is unique in so far as it
sacramentally represents the free, eternal and unique offering
of Christ in the thanksgiving act of memorial. While Christ's
self-offering is eternal, since love can have no end, the Church's
offering extends in time its sacrifice of praise and thanksgiving.
In offering this new act of divine worship, the Church realises
the freedom by which and for which Christ freed us in love.
The loving act of the sacrifice of praise and thanksgiving
expands the hearts of Christ's faithful to be free in a way that
only worship can open human beings to rejoice in being
united with the Lord and with one another. This joy of the
(comm)union of heaven and earth is the fruit of the sacrifice of
praise, that is, the hymn of freedom of the mystical body of
Christ.

In one of the most beautiful passages of his writings Pope
John Paul II states:

> In the liturgical experience, Christ the Lord is the light which
> illumines the way and reveals the transparency of the cosmos,
> precisely as in Scripture. The events of the past find in Christ their
> meaning and fullness, and creation is revealed for what it is: a
> complex whole which finds its perfection, its purpose *in the liturgy*
> alone. This is why the liturgy is heaven on earth, and in it the Word

who became flesh imbues matter with a saving potential which is fully manifest in the sacraments ... Cosmic reality also is summoned to give thanks because the whole universe is called to recapitulation in Christ the Lord. . . . To those who seek a truly meaningful relationship with themselves and with the cosmos, so often disfigured by selfishness and greed, the liturgy reveals the way to the harmony of the new man, and invites him to respect the Eucharistic potential of the created world. That world is destined to be assumed in the Eucharist of the Lord, in his Passover, present in the sacrifice of the altar.[63]

The expression 'heaven on earth' recalls the striking teaching of St John Chrysostom who sums up the purpose of the sacred liturgy: 'so that earth may become heaven'.[64] These words of this great Eastern Father indicate not only his deep sense of awe for the splendour of the sacred mysteries – a sense which was creative of the liturgy that to this day bears his name in the Greek Church – but also his emphasis on the power of the liturgy's beauty both to challenge and transform the social conditions of our lives through the works of mercy and justice, especially in caring for the poor.[65] Chrysostom's emphasis on the intrinsic relationship between liturgy and life, which earned him exile from the corrupt and decadent imperial court of Constantinople at the beginning of the fifth century, presents no less a challenge to the complacency of modern consumerism which is directly related to the false values, materialistic orientation in the systems and structures of Western capitalism as its sterile and destructive by-product. Unless this challenge is taken to heart and brings about the Passover movement of conversion to God the Giver of life – a movement which also means a turning towards serving Christ in the poor – then our recitation of the words of the Lord's Prayer before Holy Communion – 'Thy will be done on earth as it is in heaven' – will surely have the hollow ring of hypocrisy about it; and, far worse, our celebration of the Eucharist will become in effect a perpetuation not of Christ's sacrifice, but of humanity's sinful divisions as old as time and as multiple as legion.

Heaven is not only 'up there', out of sight, out of the mind's reach. It is the 'new creation' glimpsed in the gift of Christ's sacraments – especially the Eucharist. From ancient times, at the solemn moment of entering the Eucharistic Prayer the celebrant calls the congregation to behold this reality: *Sursum corda* – *Lift up your hearts!* This summons implies an image signifying not an escape, but the sense of dynamism and urgency about entering the movement or dynamic rhythm of Christ's Passover. Christ's Spirit uplifts and inspires our hearts to respond to his stirring in this invitation at the threshold of entering into the eucharistic mystery.

Much depends on the response we make both during this great Prayer and also to its implications in the rest of our lives. Our response is somehow mysteriously a continuation of the Blessed Virgin Mary's 'yes' from Nazareth to Calvary.[66] Much more, however, is offered by the Spirit-filled Word, Jesus Christ, who expressed God's affirmation of humanity (cf. 2 Cor. 1:19f.; Rev. 1:7; 22:20), since all he desires is to raise all creation to the Father in a hymn of freedom. Only the Passover-imagination of faith, hope and love can liberate our hearts from the negative, heavy downbeat of this world's materialism and hedonism. In the joy of praising God for his gift of Christ's mystery of Passover in the Eucharistic Prayer we rediscover with the freshness and innocence of childlike simplicity the world's true value – its worth and reality as the sign of God's nearness in creative love.

The eucharistic tradition, the source of renewal

Genuine renewal involves that transformation of minds and hearts through worship which St Paul repeatedly calls for (cf. Rom. 12:1f.; Eph. 4:23; 5:10). This renewal is achieved through a discovery of Christian memory, that is, fidelity to the tradition received from the Lord in celebrating the Eucharist (cf. 1 Cor. 11:23). In his eulogy of Eastern monasticism Pope John Paul II reminds us, who are too often bound as 'prisoners of the present moment',[67] that we need to discover a healthy attitude to tradition. Herein lies the well-spring of genuine renewal since it focuses our yearning and hope on the eschatological perspective of the gospel. The agenda of hope is succinctly expressed in the well-known phrase from the antiphon of Evening Prayer in the Office of Corpus Christi, where the Eucharist is called 'the pledge of future glory' (*pignus futurae gloriae*).[68] It hardly seems necessary to point out the importance of this perspective of hope for the realisation of human freedom.

The Church's vitality becomes regenerated and open to future development precisely by recourse to the unique source of divine revelation, which is communicated through the living voice of the Word of God, namely, tradition. Thus, as the Church develops an understanding of its mystery, it learns to appreciate that tradition, in its profoundest sense, is 'never pure nostalgia for things or forms past, nor regret for lost privileges, but the living memory of the Bride [of Christ], kept eternally youthful by the Love that dwells within her'.[69] All Christ's faithful have the responsibility of being mindful of the Lord Jesus' great gift of the Eucharist. The practical exercise of this sense of responsibility is part of the sense of the Church's celebration of the Lord's memorial until he comes again in glory (cf. 1 Cor. 11:26). Responsibility for the gift of the Eucharist means fidelity to Christ the generous Giver of the source and summit of our life as God's children; and fidelity implies trust and gratitude for this sacrament leading to the fullness of our glorious freedom:

> We cannot, even for a moment, forget that the Eucharist is a special possession belonging to the whole Church. It is the *greatest gift* in the order of grace and of sacrament that the divine Spouse has offered and unceasingly offers to his bride. . . . We should remain faithful in every detail to what it expresses in itself and to what it asks of us, namely, thanksgiving.[70]

The Lord's Day: celebrated in festive freedom

The celebration of the Eucharist introduces the Christian community to the liturgy of the heavenly banquet.[71] All the holy scriptures, which are called 'the table of the Word', point to this great banquet in the heavenly Jerusalem.[72] This is especially true of the Gospels, which originated in the context of the eucharistic assembly and which were primarily written for this same gathering. Frequently the Gospels refer to the ancient Jewish symbolism of the meal as the sign of the messianic banquet.[73] The reality of Christian hope to share in the ultimate

goal of this heavenly communion springs from the Eucharist.
For the Eucharist *realises* the true and deepest significance of
the Church, namely, the reality of humanity being *called* by God,
as the Greek root (*ek-kaléo*) of the word 'church' signifies. The
Church points to 'the goal of all things'; it is also 'the sign
and instrument ... of the full realisation of the unity yet to
come'.[74] The Church is never a 'finished' reality, but a
reminder always of the pilgrim nature of human existence.
Our attention is constantly directed, therefore, in the
Church's eucharistic celebration to realise our vocation or
calling before the world as a people imbued with a deep,
realistic sense of hope. The Eucharist commits us, in other
words, to be responsible witnesses to the hope of eternal life,
which contradicts the pessimism of the world's myopic time-
bound preoccupations with materialism, productivity, success,
etc. By celebrating the Eucharist we are schooled gradually to
realise the truth for which Christ taught us to yearn: 'thy will
be done on earth *as it is in heaven*'. The Eucharist, thus, sets
the agenda of hope for those called and assembled in the
presence of Christ's Spirit to acknowledge the Father 'in the
glorious freedom of the children of God' (Rom. 8:21). The
Second Vatican Council described the sacred liturgy as
expressing the Church's freedom of access to and participation
in the divine liturgy of heaven:

> In the earthly liturgy, *by way of foretaste*, we share in that heavenly
> liturgy which is celebrated in the holy city of Jerusalem *toward which
> we journey* as pilgrims, and in which Christ is sitting at the right
> hand of God, a minister of the sanctuary and of the holy tabernacle
> (cf. Apoc. 21:2; Col. 3:1; Heb. 8:2); we sing a hymn to the Lord's
> glory with all the warriors of the heavenly army; venerating the
> memory of the saints, *we hope* for some part and fellowship with
> them; we *eagerly await* the Savior, our Lord Jesus Christ, *until* He,
> our life, *shall appear and we too will appear* with Him in glory (cf.
> Phil. 3:20; Col. 3:4).[75]

This perspective of hope is deepened particularly through the
Christian community's weekly celebration of the Eucharist on
Sundays, 'the Lord's Day' (*kykiaké*). There is some obscurity re-
garding the exact origins of the relation of the Eucharist to
Sunday, especially in the New Testament period. Acts 20:7–11 is

a key text. It opens up the discussion as to exactly when the Christians (of Troas in this instance) gathered through the night and ended their assembly with 'the breaking of bread', an expression which is generally accepted as referring to the eucharistic celebration. Was it on Sunday evening leading into Monday morning or, as is usually thought, on Saturday evening into Sunday morning? The relationship with the Jewish custom of keeping holy the Sabbath seems clear; it expressed a profound sense of cultic time and the re-creational aspect of commemorating God's integral relationship to the world, in which he involves humanity. Building on this, the Christian practice developed its own tradition in relation to the day of the Lord's resurrection.[76] By the beginning of the second century, however, the Eucharist was the principal and primary way of marking Sunday as a day apart – the 'Lord's Day'. An early witness to this practice was St Ignatius of Antioch.[77]

McPartlan introduces us in the West to the rich approach of the Orthodox Church, which carries on the tradition of the Fathers regarding the link between the celebration of the Lord's Day and the eschatological expectation at the heart of Christian worship and life:

> Assembled on Sunday at the Lord's table, we anticipate our membership of that great final assembly on Mount Zion; we experience, in other words, what it is to be the Church. As John Zizioulas memorably says, the Church 'is what she is by becoming again and again what she will be'.

He goes on to bring out the cosmic dimensions of the Christian community's sanctification of time:

> [W]hen Jesus instituted the Eucharist, he did so not just . . . in the light of his coming sacrifice, so that we might be participants in its mystery, but also and crucially in the light of his Resurrection, such that henceforth the principal day for its celebration will not be Thursday or Friday but Sunday, the paschal day (cf. SC 106). We celebrate our salvific incorporation into the Son of Man and the Suffering Servant on the day of his triumph, which is not the seventh day, the sabbath day of God's rest, but the *eighth* day, the first day of God's new cycle of creation, in which '[t]he first creation finds its meaning and its summit' (CCC 349, cf. 1166, 2174–5).[78]

Since today the importance of Sunday is reduced and under severe threat by the materialistic interests of our consumer society the Basic Text for the International Eucharistic Congress in Wroclaw makes a strong appeal for the rediscovery of the value of celebrating the Lord's Day:

> Sunday, as the memorial of the Lord's Resurrection, should also be a joyful expression of the Paschal freedom of the people of God. All through the week we should learn to prepare for Sunday – in the *scholae cantorum*, in choirs, schools, catechetical and other groups of Christian formation, as well as in the family. In this way the Eucharist will be experienced as a living memorial of Christ's Resurrection, the source and summit of our spiritual and cultural life. In short, it will be experienced as the most intense moment of our ecclesial, parochial, family and social reality.[79]

Moreover, everyday recalls the eternal 'Today' (*hodie*) of freedom revealed by Christ's sacrifice. St Augustine uses the word 'day' in a double sense: historical and sacramental. Thus, for instance, in his Commentary on St John's Gospel, he brings together the significance of the opening words of Jesus' 'sacerdotal' prayer: 'Father, the hour is coming, glorify your Son' (Jn 17:1) with three verses regarding God's favourable time: Isaiah 49:8, 2 Corinthians 6:2 and Galatians 4:4.[80] Frequently in his sermons St Leo the Great makes capital of the sense of this word as expressing the Church's daily reliving of the mysteries of Christ – particularly his central paschal mystery.[81] Time is charged or 'weighted', as it were, with a dynamic density. It is pregnant with the presence of Christ who was born, lived, died and rose from the dead at a particular moment of time to reveal and communicate eternal life. Time is the condition of human existence through which it is essential to pass in order to become free. Time marking the rhythm of the fragmenting changes in living, which we so fear, challenges us to seek transformation. Time is that terrible condition of struggle between the unknown and intelligibility, conflict between determinism and will, darkness mingled with light. Against this background the entire span of human endeavour and willing is staged. But, by his assurance to be at hand Christ frees us from fear of all that passes: he has thrown in his lot with us and tabernacled in the midst of our provisional condition of existence. He is really present always! The *Catechism of the Catholic Church* sums up the Christian life drawn into the daylight of the *mystery of faith*:

> When the Church celebrates the mystery of Christ, there is a word that marks her prayer: 'Today!' – a word echoing the prayer her Lord taught her and the call of the Holy Spirit (cf. Mt 6:11; Heb. 3:7–4:11; Ps. 95:7). This 'today' of the living God which man is called to enter is 'the hour' of Jesus' Passover, which reaches across and underlines all history:
>
>> Life extends over all beings and fills them with unlimited light; the Orient of orients pervades the universe, and he who was 'before the daystar' and before the heavenly bodies, immortal and vast, the great Christ, shines over all beings more brightly than the sun. Therefore a day of long, eternal light is ushered in for us who believe in him, a day which is never blotted out: the mystical Passover.[82]

Passover to the vision of God

Death approaches stealthily – whether we are prepared or not. The whole art of living, however, consists in much more than stoic resignation to the inevitability of the surest fact of existence – as for the sages of Eastern religions or philosophers, like Boethius, who wrote his treatise *On the Consolation of Philosophy* while awaiting execution in the dungeon of Ticinum.[83] We are not free about choosing for ourselves whether we wish sacrifice to be part of worship or not, no more than we are free about discovering our deepest worth by avoiding to give of our best or by seeking to escape that 'condition of complete simplicity', which T.S. Eliot reminds us means total surrender of everything else.[84]

Paradoxically by accepting sacrifice as integral to worship we discover the deepest dimensions of our worth and freedom. To will the one thing necessary signifies discovering and actualising all the deepest energies of our being in the rhythm of sacrifice. Sacrifice, as the root meaning of the word means, is nothing other than the art of *making life sacred* in the spiritual dynamism of the supreme value of love. Nothing could be more central to Jesus' teaching on the completeness of love – that teaching he lived out – than that of the way of the cross: 'For whoever would save his life will lose it; and whoever loses his life for my sake and the gospel's will save it.' (Mk 8:34–5; cf. Mt 10:38–9; Lk 14:27; Jn 12:25, etc.) The paradox expressed in these essential words of the gospel is no mere stoicism in the face of the inevitability of dying. Nor is it a perverse denigration of the worth of human living or denial of the goodness and beauty of creation. Rather, it presents the existential paradox which transfigures cloying desire into the greatness of the human spirit; that is, it invites human beings to become enlivened by the Lord's Spirit who leads them to the fullness of freedom in the truth of his risen life.[85]

The life–death tension, which Freud called the 'Oedipus complex', defies resolution by psychoanalysis or any human means whatsoever. Despite a certain logic of yearning to live at every stage of human experience – from the springtime of childhood and adolescence to the serene maturity of old age – death presents the most terrible irreconcilable contradiction. It is the one 'illogical element' in everything we find meaningful in existence. Death is that single factor of which we cannot make any sense. Coming up against this opaque face of existence, especially in the climate of atrocities experienced in this century of two World Wars, some modern writers have called the whole of life 'absurd'. Death is meaningless not only because it is inexplicable and even unintelligible to the whole pattern of experience of living in which, for the most part, we expect and discover or impose meaning, but also, and especially, because it wrests from us our jealously and tenaciously held capacity to make choices. Over death we ultimately have no freehold! But paradoxically a word of hope for human life sprang from the very soil of our desperation about the commonly experienced tragedy of death. This Word is God's revelation of the resurrection from death of his beloved Son Jesus Christ, the Word incarnate, who broke through the vicious circle of the tragedy of existence by expressing that quality which human beings lacked so badly – namely, the quality of godliness which is the mystery of love, the dynamic energy of all life. This is purely and simply God's meaning, as

Julian of Norwich realised at the end of her contemplation of the crucified.

At the Last Supper Jesus prophetically expressed his serene freedom in the proximity of death. He stated the paradox of the sacrifice of one's life which he would live out in freely giving up his life for the world: 'Greater love has no man than this, that a man lay down his life for his friends. You are my friends if you do what I command you' (Jn 15:13–14; cf. Rom. 5:7f.). Looking to Jesus Christ's transformation of the archetypal experience of the Hebrew exodus, celebrated in the Jewish Spring rites of the Passover, Balthasar says: 'Time seen as a descent toward a final catastrophe implies an element of futility and nothingness, but this element is inserted in a superior logic of grace, since God has abased Himself to this abyss made by the creature, not the Creator.'[86] The Christian response throughout life – a response sacramentally given in the liturgy – enables our free Passover or entry to a higher state of awareness, namely faith, hope and love. Echoing St Paul's teaching in the first letter to the Corinthians, Balthasar warns against daring to exceed this threefold parameter, or better, this logic of God's wisdom and his salvific design of grace:

> Faith, hope, and love together make up the form of time-bound man. This is the starting point he must use in each effort to understand his existence; we have nothing to work with beyond hope that seems so tiny, faith that is self-abandonment, love that gives itself and loses itself. Any attempt to go beyond the glory and misery of these three, *tria haec* – and every non-Christian religion would like to go beyond them – leads us astray into gnosis.[87]

This sobering warning is obviously a check against the over-emphasis sometimes given to what is called 'human fulfilment', 'self-awareness' or 'progress', etc. – or any of the other varieties of experience (religious and otherwise!), which are promoted by an ever growing number of movements, methodologies and techniques of pseudo-spirituality of the 'new age' – an age which is scarred perhaps more deeply by anxiety, escapism and self-indulgence than any other. Perhaps never before than in our experience-craving and self-satiated times has there been a more urgent need for the Spirit of truth to guide us to discern responsibly between the genuine yearning for what the freedom of children of God entails and a presumptuous and hasty seizing of liberties with the sacred revealed gift of religious 'conscience' and human dignity. The euphoria of individual and subjective 'religious experience' is quite alien to and ultimately destructive of Christian discipleship. For it lacks the discipline of the Spirit who guides the community of Christ's disciples to the truth of the eucharistic mystery. The rhythm of the truth of the eucharistic mystery is discerned in the obedience of faith to God's revealed Word Jesus Christ, who empowers his disciples to pattern their lives on his obedience to the Father, which he expressed in the paschal mystery by his double-edged commandment of love: 'Do this as my memorial . . . Love one another *as* I have loved you . . .'. This commandment, which reveals Jesus' love for the Father and the world, constantly challenges our naive claim to sincerity. For sincerity can never replace the divine vocation we have as human beings to go on seeking his truth in the community of faith, hope and love. Otherwise, by deceiving us in assuming one or other of its various guises and masks, sincerity itself can degenerate into myriad forms of self-love. Only the Eucharist guarantees freedom by rendering all pride and self-sufficiency impossible. For, it is the Sacrament *par excellence* of charity, and where there is charity pride must bow out: *Ubi caritas . . . ibi Deus est.*

In the first of three meditations on 'What Corpus Christi means to me', Cardinal Ratzinger sums up the essence of the eucharistic mystery in commenting on the Council of Trent's teaching on Christ's triumph, that unqualified victory over death represented in the celebration of the Eucharist:

> The purpose of Christ's campaign was to eliminate death, that death which devours time and makes us cultivate the lie in order to forget or 'kill' time. Nothing can make man laugh unless there is an answer to the question of death. And conversely, if there *is* an answer to death, it will make genuine joy possible – and joy is the basis of every feast. At its very heart the Eucharist is the answer to the question of death, for it is the encounter with that love which is stronger than death.[88]

Only those who are truly free know how to celebrate the meaning and experience of authentic joy.[89] But, to know this joy of freedom paradoxically entails experiencing something of 'the sorrow of God' in encountering Jesus Christ in his paschal mystery.[90] There is just no way of bypassing the cross of Christ. For this is the signpost of the 'life in abundance' which he came to give (cf. Jn 10:10). The desolation of the Redeemer cannot be ignored if human beings are to experience the glory of his risen life. Faith in his resurrection – and our incorporation in it – does not, however, flee from or cancel the realism of the essential Christian experience of the *via crucis*. The Church's mystery of faith offers something far greater than a false path of delusory optimism: it transforms the whole existential drama of negativity and frees us to transcend realistically sin and death itself in the perspective of Christ's Passover to eternal life. For what is crucially realised here is the transforming encounter of our limited human freedom with the infinite and transcendent freedom of God's love stretched out towards and reaching us.[91] The whole rhythm of the paschal mystery entails and enables our Passover with Christ from the obscurity and horror of dying to self to know that by remaining faithful to his word we become freed by his truth in the glorious freedom of God's children (cf. Jn 8:32; Rom. 8:21). The sacrifice of the cross, which the Church celebrates faithfully, does not cast a shadow of gloom over human existence, but transforms it with the mystical light of God's love. To recognise the existential paradox of life through death requires the grace of this spiritual enlightenment (*photismos*), which was how the great Eastern Fathers described the experience of the paschal mystery in baptism and the Eucharist. Only this quality of enlightenment purifies the human heart, that is, both makes it utterly single-minded to seek above all Christ's splendour of truth and endows it with the blessedness of freedom to see God (cf. Mt 5:8).

6

Eucharistic Adoration:
Extending the Grace of the Sacrifice

The post-conciliar Instruction on the Eucharistic Mystery,
Eucharisticum Mysterium, pointed out that all aspects of this sacrament must be properly understood. This document highlights
the importance of manifesting the closest relationship that
exists between the sacramental sacrifice of the Mass and the
reception of Holy Communion and adoration of the sacrament.[1] After listing the principal doctrinal points taught by the
Church's Magisterium regarding the Eucharist, the Instruction
states: 'The Eucharistic Mystery should, therefore, be considered in all its fullness, both in its celebration of Mass, and
also in the external worship [*in cultu*] of the sacred species,
which are reserved after Mass to extend the grace of the
sacrifice.'[2] The phrase 'in all its fullness' recalls the Council's
teaching on the Eucharist as the 'source and summit' or 'font
and fullness' of the Church's worship and life. The Eucharist is
the font and fullness of the liturgy and the whole life and
mission of the Church since it contains our Lord himself in the
manner of a 'substantial presence', as Pope Paul VI insisted in
his beautiful Encyclical Letter *Mysterium Fidei*. From Christ's
fullness, that is, from God's revelation and communication of
his 'grace and truth' we receive and know eternal life. This
communication takes place at both the communal and personal
level of human experience. The Church's Magisterium has
repeatedly emphasised with pastoral patience that in the sacred
mysteries of the liturgy as well as through his sacramental
presence in the Blessed Sacrament Jesus Christ reveals and
communicates to us the unimagined depths of the freedom-

giving joy of union with him and the Holy Spirit in their communion of life with the Father. The Church thus also encourages a deepening of devotion towards Christ's eucharistic presence as an indispensable means for discovering our true sense of freedom against the scenario of multiple pressures and idols thrust upon our awareness today.[3] A deepened personal sense of devotion not only extends the Church's song of thanksgiving and praise, but it also enables us to realise that we are not alone, for Christ is with us as our *Emmanuel*, God-with-us.[4]

Christ's purpose in instituting the Eucharist

Much has been said and written in the last few decades about the purpose for which Christ instituted the Eucharist and no little discussion has taken place for and against the 'traditional' practices of adoration, Benediction, Corpus Christi processions of the Blessed Sacrament, and 'Forty Hours Devotion', etc. This is not the place to discuss the extremely complex factors of the social and religious crisis which has disturbed the devotional life of Christian communities during the last thirty or forty years of rapid and abrupt changes. However, during this same period, it must also be acknowledged, there has been much positive good realised through the maturing of an intelligent faith, the deepening of a sense of dialogue at different levels, the growth in sensitivity and generous response of many (especially among youth) to the call to become committed in serving the urgent needs of society. While one observes a diminution in the 'traditional' Catholic devotional practices in many places, one cannot be blind to many heartening signs of the emergence of new forms of prayer and also of a renewal of interest in eucharistic contemplation. Perhaps it is no bad thing that the trimmings and external style of a bygone baroque age are no longer in evidence. The significance of the manner of exposition of the Blessed Sacrament, as has been reordered by the Church, is not just a matter of taste, aesthetic sensibility or style – a move from the baroque to a simpler, plain style. Nor is it merely a question of theological emphasis or preference of piety. There is much need for catechesis of the sacred signs and also for mystagogical penetration through contemplatively 'gazing', or rather, looking deeply into (not merely at!) Christ's sacramental body. This body is the sacrament of his mystical body present in the world. This mystagogical catechesis enables us to read the signs of the Eucharist. It does not stop at explaining the natural significance of bread and wine in their human usage, but is essentially a matter of fostering the art of discernment, by which we perceive the reality of symbolism as integral to human understanding and endeavour. The sacred signs Christ entrusted to his Church contain and communicate reality. Today we need to rediscover a sense of the spiritual such as the Fathers of the Church possessed so richly.

In these times of worldwide spiritual hunger it is fitting that Christ, who chose to become flesh in the womb of Mary of Nazareth and to be born in a stable at Bethlehem, the 'house of bread', is adored and received in simple and humble devotion by people who at the same time bear in their hearts compassion for their sisters and brothers in dire poverty. There is nothing in this that can be said to smack of anything of the spirit of Catholic 'triumphalism' once severely criticised. But, it is nonetheless a true triumph: both the triumph of the Lord Jesus in winning hearts to acknowledge the power of his love, and also the genuine triumph of the faithful who claim their right to religious freedom in rejoicing in their Redeemer's presence. Only people who know the spirit of freedom delight to contemplate and adore the sacramental presence of Lord Jesus Christ.

The new form or style of presenting the Blessed Sacrament for adoration on the same altar-table on which the eucharistic sacrifice is celebrated, as the liturgical reforms advocate, offers an impressive teaching regarding the Church's desire to be, like the Virgin Mother of God, a servant of its Lord, who himself came not to be served but to serve. In this spirit of service the faithful discover the true significance of Christ's manifold presence in the Church and purpose for which he instituted this sacrament for the life of the world.

The above-mentioned Instruction of Eucharistic Worship points out that the external marks of devotion during exposition of the Blessed Sacrament should be consistent both with the Mass and also Christ's intention in instituting the Eucharist:

> Care must be taken that during exposition the external worship [*cultus*] of the most Blessed Sacrament should highlight, by signs, its relationship to the Mass. . . . In the decoration accompanying exposition, one must carefully avoid everything which in any way could obscure the desire of Christ, who instituted the most holy Eucharist above all in order to be present to us as food, healing and strength [*ut nobis praesto sit in cibum, remedium et levamen*].[5]

This description of the purpose for which Christ instituted the Eucharist focuses exclusively on the sign of bread as pointing to his spiritual nourishment in holy communion. While such a description of our Lord's purpose is undeniably true, it is incomplete. It expresses the mentality of the members of the committee appointed by the Congregation of Rites which drew up the Instruction – a mentality reflecting the spirit, concerns and eucharistic controversies of the 1960s. At that time it is quite understandable that a concerted effort was necessary in introducing the liturgical reforms to bring out the centrality and primacy of the eucharistic celebration of the Mass in the Christian life.

The *Catechism of the Catholic Church*, some twenty-five years later, at different places presents a broader teaching regarding the purpose for which Christ the Lord instituted the mystery of the holy Eucharist. (It is interesting to note that the *Catechism* does not quote or refer to the said Instruction – except once in which the paragraph of the Instruction is made up of various quotations from Conciliar documents regarding the power of the Eucharist to bring about communion with God and the unity of his people, a communion which realises divine worship and at the same time the sanctification of human beings.)[6] In at least three places the *Catechism* states the reason or purpose for which Christ instituted the holy Eucharist:

> in order to perpetuate the sacrifice of the cross throughout the ages . . . and so to entrust to his beloved Spouse, the Church, a memorial of his death and resurrection: a sacrament of love, a sign of unity, a bond of charity, a Paschal banquet . . .[7]

> In order never to depart from his own and to make them sharers in his Passover, he instituted the Eucharist as the memorial of his

death and Resurrection, and commanded his apostles to celebrate it until his return . . .[8]

It is highly fitting that Christ should have wanted to remain present to his Church in this unique way. Since Christ was about to take his departure from his own in his visible form, he wanted to give us his sacramental presence; since he was about to offer himself on the cross to save us, he wanted us to have the memorial of the love with which he loved us 'to the end', even to the giving of his life. In his Eucharistic presence he remains mysteriously in our midst as the one who loved us and gave himself up for us, and he remains under signs that express and communicate this love . . .[9]

Particularly in this last description one is struck by the emphasis placed on Christ's desire to remain present to his Church. This sense is strengthened even further by the personalist language of Pope John Paul II, whose words immediately follow the paragraph just quoted:

The Church and the world have a great need for Eucharistic worship. Jesus awaits us in this sacrament of love. Let us not refuse the time to go to meet him in adoration, in contemplation full of faith, and open to making amends for the serious offences and crimes of the world. Let our adoration never cease.[10]

This quotation leaves no doubt whatsoever regarding the interpretation to be given to the words of the *Catechism* regarding Christ's desire to *remain* with the Church: it is not merely to perpetuate the memorial of his sacrifice or give himself in sacramental communion, but also to be present to be adored by his faithful.

A distinction must be made between gradual development of the Church's practice of adoration of the Eucharist and the fullness of Christ's intention in instituting this sacrament. This distinction is implicit in the following words of the *Catechism*:

The tabernacle was first intended for the reservation of the Eucharist in a worthy place so that it could be brought to the sick and those absent, outside of Mass. As faith in the real presence of Christ in his Eucharist deepened, the Church became conscious of the meaning of silent adoration of the Lord present under the

Eucharistic species. It is for this reason that the tabernacle should be located in an especially worthy place in the church, and should be constructed in such a way that it emphasizes and manifests the truth of the real presence of Christ in the Blessed Sacrament.[11]

While it is true that the cult of adoration and public veneration of the eucharistic sacrament developed in the thirteenth century, it is quite erroneous and would show a lack of historical knowledge to say that Christ's sacramental presence was not discerned in faith and adored with love from the earliest Christian times.[12] We do well to reflect deeply on Pope Paul VI's words:

> No-one is unaware that the divine Eucharist bestows an incalculable honour on the Christian people. It is not only while the sacrifice is being offered, the sacrament constituted, that Christ is truly Emmanuel, 'God with us'. He is so after the offering of the sacrifice, the making of the sacrament, as long as the Eucharist is kept in churches and oratories. For day and night he is in our midst, he is dwelling among us full of grace and truth (cf. Jn 1:14). He is giving formation to morals, sustenance to virtue, comforting the sad, strengthening the weak. He stimulates all who approach him to imitate him so that they may learn from his example to be gentle and lowly of heart, to seek not their own ends but God's.[13]

Emmanuel

The 'Emmanuel' notion, contained in Jesus' last recorded words in Matthew's Gospel, certainly expresses his assurance to be really present to his people in a diversity of ways, such as described in the teaching of the Second Vatican Council.[14] The theologian Jean Galot goes further in linking Jesus' various 'I am' (*egō emi*) statements with the gift of his permanent presence in the Eucharist. As seen above in the chapter on John, these statements have a direct resonance of God's covenantal revelation of being near his own people. Galot's argument can be summed up in the following paragraph:

> In applying to himself at various times the name of God as it was revealed at Sinai (see Jn 8:24, 28, 58; 13:19), Jesus has identified himself not only as the absolute Being but as the absolute Presence. He is the presence definitively established in the midst of humanity.

By declaring his name as that of 'I am', the God of Exodus had already wished to affirm not only his absolute existence and his complete independence and sovereignty but also his active and faithful presence together with the aid he will give to Moses. The 'I am' guarantees the promise 'I am with you.' In the same way Christ affirms the indefectible presence of his 'I am' in order to guarantee to his Apostles his perpetual assistance: 'I will be with you.' He is the presence that will never abandon men. . . . It must be emphasized that 'divine presence' says much more than 'divine being'. It signifies that the divine being is turned toward men, comes forward to meet them, and desires to enter into communion with them.[15]

Later in the same article, the author reflects on the relationship between the permanent eucharistic presence in Christian times and its various foreshadowings in the experience of Israel.[16] Thus, while Christian experience is in continuity with the religious history of salvation, it also introduces all humanity to a new stage of awareness of the reality of 'God-with-us' in the perceptible signs of the Church's life of worship 'in spirit and truth'.

Galot's particularly rich contribution to modern eucharistic theology merits careful consideration and warrants emphasis. It is refreshing to find this modern theologian highlighting the fact at the heart of the Lord's intention to *be* with us always – a fact which, though deeply rooted in biblical covenantal theology, has not received the attention it rightly deserves. Galot persuasively argues that Christ's *being with us* is not only realised in the multiple modes of his presence, but also particularly in the unique sacrament of God's permanent covenant, the divinely mysterious reality of the Blessed Sacrament. It is true that the very 'words of consecration' are indicative of and pronounced in view of the communion of the faithful with God, which is the whole purpose of the Church's new covenantal form of sacrificial worship.[17] However, this does not contradict the point Galot makes: that these words establish first of all the sign and real means of this union, namely, the reality of God's initiative in coming to meet us in Christ's sacramental presence. In his words:

Moreover, in the way in which Christ expresses himself there can be perceived a sign that the presence of his body and his blood, while implicated in a sacrifice and destined for a repast, is not merely functional but has an absolute value. According to the version of St Matthew, Jesus says: 'Take and eat: this is my body.' He does not say: 'Take and eat my body' – words that would have been suitable for the institution of the Eucharistic repast. From the words 'Take and eat' He detaches the affirmation: 'This is my body,' thereby giving to it a more independent value. The reality of the presence of his body is affirmed in itself.[18]

Remembrance of Christ is the heart of our prayer and the source and summit of that particular kind of awareness in which we experience freedom through worship. In a meditative work, Galot outlines the significance of Jesus' words 'Do this in memory of me' for the Christian who prays:

> They should express the sentiments of those who turn towards the 'Me' of the Lord as the centre of their lives. They will bear witness to the fascination which this 'Me' exercises over people of all times. They should also proclaim repeatedly and forever the love with which the Saviour wishes to gather the whole human race around his person. It must be added, however, that these words do not envisage simply a subjective remembering by those who are celebrating the Eucharist. Their aim is to bring about objectively the memory of Jesus by the Eucharistic act itself. Sometimes they have been translated as, 'Do this as my memorial'. A memorial has more objective consistency than a simple memory. In the Book of Exodus God, when speaking of the day of the Passover when the people knew that they would be delivered, said, 'This day shall be for you a memorial day, and you shall keep it as a feast to the Lord' (Ex. 12:14).[19]

Further on in this meditation the implications are drawn out of Christ's desire to abide with the members of his mystical body and they in him:

> And so it was that he [Jesus] wanted to foster the development of contemplation in Christian piety. This contemplation is an essential way of being attached to his person. In his revelation Jesus first of all unveiled what he was: the Christian religion is the religion of a person, the Son of God made man, who is the primary object of faith. The repeated statements, 'I am', or 'It is I', draw attention to his personal identity. The 'I am with you all days', makes us understand that the 'I am' is a call to a meeting, to a reunion. Jesus

offers himself continually to our gaze and for dialogue. . . . In this way, the permanent Eucharistic presence is the sign of Christ's commitment in the development of the life of the Christian community, of its expansion and in all the events of each disciple's life. . . . The Eucharistic heart of Jesus seeks contemplatives in order to make missionaries of them.[20]

This is how the saints understood Jesus' words about being always with his own – as, for instance, St Francis of Assisi. His words are worth recalling here:

'. . . daily [the Son of God] humbles himself as when he came from the royal throne into the womb of the Virgin; daily he comes to us in a humble form; daily he comes down from the bosom of the Father upon the altar in the hands of the priest. And as he appeared to all the apostles in true flesh, so now he reveals himself to us in the sacred bread. . . . And in this way the Lord is always with his faithful, as he himself says: Behold I am with you even to the end of the world.'[21]

After quoting from these sentences, David Power goes on to comment:

Francis wanted his followers to constantly reverence Christ in the Sacrament, even as they travelled along the roads and turned at opportune moments to the churches where the sacrament was kept. He found a reason for the institution of the sacrament in the promise given by Christ in Matthew 28:20 to remain always with his followers . . . the visual role that the Eucharist had begun to assume as a public symbol in the life of the church fitted the devotion of the followers of Francis and allowed them to keep the sacrament at the center of their practices, despite the disparity between what was prescribed by the liturgy of the official books and the more popular practices that Francis followed. These diverse examples of Eucharistic piety are good illustrations of how the Eucharist could in the manner of the time become part of emerging forms of spirituality, even as frequent communion was on the wane. Indeed it may well be its accommodation to the diversity that shows best how the Eucharist was such a powerful and vibrant common symbol. In the new forms of practice, it was a focal point of reverence for all, a symbol of ecclesiastical and even civic unity, and at the same time a support for new forms of the spiritual life.[22]

The 'disparity', which Power speaks off, had to be solved. And it was, in due course. Within fifty years after St Francis died the Feast of Corpus Christi was instituted by Pope Urban IV's Decree *Transiturus*.[23] In this important document the words at the end of Matthew's Gospel are interpreted in this eucharistic sense. Also here for the first time in an official teaching is the phrase 'real presence' applied to the Blessed Eucharist.

Contemplative listening: spiritual childhood

Pope John Paul II, who doubtlessly has in mind the powerful grace of the sacramental sacrifice of the holy Eucharist, insists on the Church's essential focus of attention being directed daily to contemplation of Jesus crucified. In this way it comes to understand and live the full meaning of its freedom. By means of this contemplative gaze we are enabled to discover the meaning of freedom, which the Pope calls: 'the gift of self in the *service of God and one's brethren*'; he adds: 'Communion with the Crucified and Risen Lord is the never-ending source from which the Church draws unceasingly in order to live in freedom, to give of herself and to serve.'[24] He also indicates that the 'secret' of the Church's teachings is based on contemplation of the presence of the Lord Jesus. The contemplation of Jesus holds a greater educative value than what even the documents or pastoral appeals of the Church's Magisterium can offer.[25] One should note that there is no contradiction between the meaning of contemplation – in the sense of looking to Christ in the liturgy, as the Pope emphasises – and the privileged place given in the holy scriptures (especially in the Gospel of John) to listening to the Word of God. For it is not a matter of contemplation in the Neoplatonist, Greek sense, but a question of experiencing the intimacy of being near God. This is what the faithful are encouraged to experience through the liturgy.[26]

The grace of the paschal sacrifice of Christ is what is received when one encounters the Lord by listening to his word in the liturgy, during the intimate silence of his presence in Holy Communion, and also in contemplating him with love during eucharistic adoration. This grace is the truth of his presence which opens us to all facets of reality – facets to which we remain blind, like the man born blind, or rather, like the Pharisees, because being bound in the slavery of pride. In encountering the reality of the presence of the Lord in the mystery of faith we become freed from the power of the evil one in order to live in the full freedom which Jesus promised and gave by the gift of his Spirit of childhood. In the opening of the section on prayer in the Christian life, the *Catechism* quotes the words of St Thérèse de l'Enfant Jésus: 'For me, prayer is a surge of the heart; it is a simple look turned toward heaven, it is a cry of recognition and of love, embracing both trial and joy.'[27] Later in the same section the *Catechism* recalls the simplest teaching of all on prayer learnt in the presence of the Blessed Sacrament:

> Contemplation is a *gaze* of faith, fixed on Jesus. 'I look at him and he looks at me': this is what a certain peasant of Ars used to say to his holy curé about his prayer before the tabernacle. This focus on Jesus is a renunciation of self. His gaze purifies our heart; the light of the countenance of Jesus illumines the eyes of our heart and teaches us to see everything in the light of his truth and his compassion for all men.[28]

'The mystery of piety' (1 Tim. 3:16)

The paragraph from the mediaeval English mystic Julian of Norwich, which was cited at the beginning of this section, refers to the moment of encounter with the sacramental presence of Christ in terms of courtesy.[29] Throughout her *Revelations* Julian continually emphasises the exquisite 'courtesy' of our Lord. She is at pains to make known to others what our Lord revealed to her: namely, that God's love for us, especially manifest in Jesus' 'motherly' love in the Blessed Sacrament,[30] frees us from preoccupation with our own sinfulness and from the fear of what we imagine this condition deserves.[31] Nothing can be more depressing – in the psychological and spiritual sense of the word – than being imprisoned in a sense of morbid guilt, the worst kind of melancholia. Julian's *Revelations* insist repeatedly that nothing is more utterly opposed to the radiant hope which our Lord shows us in his gospel than this guilt-syndrome; nothing is less appreciative of God's gracious 'courtesy' towards humanity. From discovering that we are freed by God's love we are raised up to love and serve him in joy and freedom. In passing we might observe that a similar notion, borrowed from the imagery of mediaeval chivalry, is expressed by the converted John Donne, the Dean of St Paul's, in the couplet which concludes the poem *Hymne to God my God, in my Sicknesse* and in his *Holy Sonnet 14*, where he states that he cannot be free from his weakness to succumb to the attractions of pleasure and the flesh except that God ravish him. The same theme is, of course, evident throughout St Teresa of Avila's great work on the spiritual life, *The Interior Castle*.

Intrinsically linked with the notion of remembering this limitless love of God's 'courtesy' towards us in his Christian gift of forgiveness is gratitude. In Julian's little treatise on prayer – which comprises the central chapters of her *Revelations of Divine Love* (41–3) – she says that thanksgiving is a special, intimate kind of knowledge uniting us to God who is the source of everything experienced in our lives, the very *ground of our beseeching*:

> With prayer goes gratitude. Thanksgiving is a real, interior, knowledge. With great reverence and loving fear, it turns us with all our powers to do whatever our good Lord indicates. It brings joy and gratitude within. Sometimes its very abundance gives voice, 'Good Lord, thank you and bless you!' And sometimes when the heart is dry and unfeeling – or it may be because of the enemy's tempting – then reason and grace drive us to cry aloud to our Lord, recalling his blessed passion and great goodness. And the strength of our Lord's word comes to the soul, and fires the heart, and leads it by grace into its real business, enabling it to pray happily and to enjoy our Lord in truth. Thanksgiving is a blessed thing in his sight.[32]

The whole of human living, whose 'real business' is worship in gratitude and praise, thus, becomes 'Eucharist-hearted'.[33] The depths of thinking plunge us into an attitude of thankfulness, praise and wonderment or adoring love. This attitude bespeaks an openness to Being-beyond-ourselves. It implies *being* with enormous possibilities, bringing us into contact not merely with some abstract 'First Principle', but with the personal God and Father, whom Jesus revealed. The attitude of adoring love turns us to the divine 'Thou', who is the personal source or 'love-causality' of freedom in the world.[34] In Julian's language, more precisely, it empowers us to turn towards recognising and acknowledging the infinite 'courtesy' or grace of God the Father shown towards us in Christ by his Holy Spirit. By enabling our hearts – the inner depths of our whole selves – to respond to God's graciousness, thanksgiving elevates and transforms our dull prosaic processes of thinking and the dreariness of our whole lives into participating in the divine 'courtesy'.[35]

Julian's repeated references to the divine 'courtesy', which comes from the mediaeval world of romantic love,[36] should not be off-putting to our appreciation of her teaching today. Despite all the insistence today on democracy and recognition of personal freedom, this century has paradoxically been accompanied by a diminution of a sense of respect. The theologian Zoltàn Alszeghy points out that quite contrary to what Catholic devotion to the sacrament is accused of being – namely, a making of the Eucharist an *object or thing, reification* – it is focused on Christ as the *Kyrios*, the Lord, to whom the Church continually and in different ways submits itself. In fact, he says, the unique manner of the act of prostrating oneself in worship (*proskynōsis*)[37] that is conserved in this world, which is so marked by an absence of respect, is in eucharistic adoration and frequent visits to honour Christ in the Blessed Sacrament not only on special occasions and feastdays, but at the centre of the daily life of Christian piety.[38]

Cardinal Ratzinger likewise speaks eloquently of the deep significance that gestures and marks of reverence towards the Blessed Sacrament – especially that of genuflection – have in expressing the fullness of human freedom:

> Nor is it contrary to the dignity, freedom and greatness of contemporary man to bend the knee, to pledge obedience to him, to adore and glorify him. For if we deny him lest we should have to worship, all we are left with is the eternal necessity of matter. Then we are really *not* free, then we are only a tiny particle of dust, continually thrown around in the vast mill of the universe, trying in vain to persuade itself that it is free. Freedom is the foundation of everything, and we too can be free *only* if he is the Creator. When our freedom bows before him, it is not taken away: only then is it really accepted and made definitive. But there is something else on

this day [*Corpus Christi*] that we are celebrating: the One we worship is not some remote power. He himself has knelt before *us* to wash our feet. That gives our adoration a relaxed quality, an atmosphere of hope and joy, because we are bowing before him who has bowed before us; because in bowing we are entering into a love which does not enslave but transforms.[39]

In another meditative passage he says that bending the knee to Jesus expresses entering into the cosmic gesture, imitating him who humbled himself to our earthly condition, descended to death and the nether regions for the sake of his obedience to the Father's will to save creation and restore its dignity and freedom.[40]

In seeking the presence of Christ in the Church, which is his body, we discover our true identity. This identity was described by the theologians of the Middle Ages as becoming

an *anima ecclesiastica* – a personal embodiment of the Church. This is both identity and purification, it is a surrendering of oneself and a being drawn into the innermost nature of what we mean by 'Church'. . . . We are given an anticipatory share in the Church's perennial dialogue of love with him who desired to be one flesh with her, and this gift is transformed into the gift of speech. And it is in the gift of speech, and not until then, that I am really restored to my true self; only thus am I given back to God, handed over by him to all my fellow men; only thus am I free. . . . Isolation and the loss of a basic sense of fellowship in prayer constitute a major reason for the lack of prayer. . . . And it is precisely why it is impossible to start a conversation with Christ alone, cutting out the Church: a christological form of prayer which excludes the Church also excludes the Spirit and the human being himself.[41]

Extending the grace of the sacrifice

The Russian Metropolitan Anthony Bloom sums up the attitude which is fundamental to the gospel teaching regarding the radical change brought about in a person through the experience of being loved – that change which amounts to that total transformation of a person's outlook and energies which should result from the freedom received in being forgiven:

One should not expect to be forgiven because one has changed for the better; neither should one make such a change a condition for forgiving other people; it is only because one is forgiven, one is loved, that one begins to change, not the other way round. And this we should never forget, though we always do.[42]

And yet, we do forget! To counter the mystery of the hold sin has on us – the mystery of forgetting God's goodness in creation and his utter prodigal and extravagant generosity towards us in redemption, as the very words for-*giveness* and par-*don* imply[43] – we constantly must return to ourselves in extending our religious sense of memorial when we celebrate and contemplate the Eucharist, the Sacrament of remembering in love our Saviour's body 'given up for you' and blood 'shed for you and for all so that sins may be forgiven'. The Eucharist, as the sacred sign of God's disclosure of mercy and forgiveness in Christ, keeps us ever mindful in praise and gratitude of the wonder of his eternal covenant of immense love. This remembrance is quite different from the Platonist doctrine of reminiscence.[44] The Judaeo-Christian memorial is not mere recollection of the past, but introduces us to the real and deepest significance of the quality of renewal; it plunges us into the mystery of God's reality of eternal presence in the communion of love – his presence which has no memory of our sinfulness, but only, as the psalmist says, of his 'faithful love'. It would be not only a pity to forget to remember the truth of this mystery of immense love; it would be to live, or rather, to pretend to live, while forgetful of what is most important for hope, namely, that God has pledged himself to free humanity and, indeed, to *be* our 'pledge of future glory' (*pignus futurae gloriae*) in the sacrament of Christ's sacrifice 'for the remission of sins'.

We thus 'extend the grace of the sacrifice' by remembering to adore the presence of Christ the Redeemer of humanity. Eucharistic memorial is all about remembering that the Father's tender mercies towards us are ever present, available, inviting us to turn to him simply and freely in the praise and gratitude of Christ's Spirit for his generosity in creating and forgiving us. Such a response of gratitude enables us to participate most deeply in Christ's gift of 'Eucharist', that is, praise and thanksgiving for the most intense, deepest and fullest sense of God's giving.

St Peter Julian Eymard, the founder of two congregations focused on the Eucharist and the inspirer of international eucharistic congresses, saw visits and adoration of the Blessed Sacrament as spiritual communion.[45] In a conference on adoration he reads Revelation 5:12–13 regarding adoration of the Lamb in relation to eucharistic adoration, which here on earth joins in the divine liturgy of heaven. This adoration expresses thanksgiving and praise for Jesus' love to the end (cf. Jn 13:1).[46] In an article published in the periodical he began editing he expressed the conviction that the nineteenth century is the age of the Eucharist and that the eucharistic cult is the 'grace of our times' to counteract the rationalist denial of religion and faith and, above all, in the attack on the basis of Christian religion, namely, the divinity of Jesus Christ. He regarded the Eucharist as the extraordinary means required to heal the distortion of human reason and freedom. Only devotion to Christ can integrate the whole human person – heart, seat of emotions, affections, interior energies of persons.[47] Eymard teaches that the secret of prayer in the presence of the Blessed Sacrament (*oraison*) consists in reflecting lovingly on and contemplating all the mysteries of Christ in order that one relives them and also appropriates the truths of faith and virtues in the light of this sacrament, which is as it were a 'divine prism'. He calls the Blessed Eucharist 'the royal mystery of Faith into which flow all the truths like rivers into the ocean'.[48] In this way the Eucharist becomes the dominant passion of the Christian life.

The Spirit of prayer in service

Adoration is the only adequate response to the annunciation of the mystery of presence. But, this annunciation being received also impels one to become witnesses whose whole lives of worship announce to others the good news of praising God in deeds of charity. After receiving the world-creating *Logos* into her womb with adoring love – 'Immensity cloyster'd in thy deare wombe', as John Donne puts it,[49] – the Virgin of Nazareth was impelled to go forth to be with, to be also present to her aged cousin in her difficult hour of childbirth – an hour of communicating life! She dared this potentially hazardous journey into the brigand-ridden hills of Judaea, because she was spirit-filled with the 'immense charity' of the Word-incarnate, empowered by the Word of Life. Both Mary and Elizabeth shared the joyous news of life coming into the world; both, freed from the stigma of disgrace in the opinion of neighbours, shared in worshipping God for the marvels he had done for them. The Magnificat is the Virgin Mary's – as the Eucharist is the Church's – 'hymn of freedom'. Thus, the cloister of contemplation, the inner Cenacle of spiritual communion and intimacy of adoring love, becomes transformed by the Holy Spirit's invasion of our disproportionate and jealous sense of privacy and individuality. The Spirit of God's love opens closed hearts to become instruments of communication of the good news of God-with-us – Emmanuel.

In a particular way special ministers of the Eucharist should draw close to Jesus in the sacrament of his 'immense charity' through adoration. The Blessed Virgin Mary may be regarded as their prototype and *icon*. For they, like her, bring the presence of Love to the aged, the housebound, the sick – the presence of him who uniquely comforts, that is, strengthens those in their hour of urgent need.[50] Like the Virgin Mary, special ministers bring the Saviour who uplifts the sick in the Spirit of the risen Jesus' desire to share his truth of freedom (cf. Jn 8:32) – the full and enriching truth of his presence in the sacrifice of the Eucharist, into which the same Spirit alone can lead us (cf. Jn 16:13).

'Behold the Lamb of God'

I saw what appeared to be a sea of glass mingled with fire,
and those who had conquered the beast and its image . . .
standing beside the sea of glass with harps of God in their
hands. And they sing the song of Moses, the servant of God,
and the song of the Lamb, saying,
'Great and wonderful are thy deeds,
O Lord God the Almighty!

Just and true are thy ways,
O King of the ages!
Who shall not fear and glorify thy name, O Lord?
For thou alone art holy.
All nations shall come and worship thee,
for thy judgments have been revealed' (Rev. 15:2–4).

Whatever may be the liturgical source of this early Christian hymn or the inspiration of John's various visions recorded in the book of Revelation, one thing is clear: worship fittingly belongs both to God the Father and also to Jesus Christ. For Jesus Christ, the Lamb of God's eternal Passover covenant of love for the world, shows us the Father to whom he is equal and with whom he is one (cf. Rev 22:1–5). Thus too, in the eucharistic mystery of the new Passover he remains the sacrament of the Father's revelation of saving freedom to the world: he continues to reveal in a marvellous way that God dwells among his people because of his authority to renew, sustain and refresh all creatures as the Alpha and the Omega, the beginning and end of all things, for he *is* without beginning and without end (cf. Rev 21:3, 5–6). By worship we are indeed drawn into the heart of this revelation and realise our human freedom.

In a splendid article on 'The Eucharist and the fulfilment of the World in God',[51] the great Dominican theologian Yves Congar poetically reflected on the mystical vision of the New Jerusalem described in the book of Revelation. The eucharistic mystery contains a glimmer of this vision; it invites us to delight in penetrating the heart of its reality in the gaze of contemplative faith; it attracts us to hasten ever onwards, towards the communion of the life of divine love, which is the essence of eternity – to know the Father and the one whom he sent, Jesus Christ (cf. Jn 17:3). Near the end of his sketch of the eschatological design of God for the outcome of history, Congar quotes – with 'particular pleasure', he notes – a passage written in 1893 by Maurice Blondel, whose mark on Catholic thought and culture has not until recent times begun to be rightly recognised.[52] In this passage Blondel speaks of Christ becoming the bond of creation through transubstantiation in the Eucharist, which is the prelude of the spiritual configuration and incorporation of the order of creation with the incarnate Word – an incorporation which in no way threatens or suffocates the identity of each person or thing but is, as it were, like the embrace and kiss (*osculum*) of Christ's Spirit consummating the unity of the Trinity. Congar concludes by recalling the last scene in R.H. Benson's poetic novel, *Lord of the World* – a scene describing in apocalyptic manner the consummation of all things as the world ends during the singing of the *Tantum ergo* before the Blessed Sacrament at Benediction.[53] Père Congar comments that through the divine action of transubstantiation our bread – the fruit of the earth and work of human hands – 'is absorbed into the supreme reality of Christ who is about to make all things new'.

In reflecting on Benson's imagery we may see how the mystery of the Word-become-sacrament surpasses and transforms the meaning of all things which human thought, art and endeavour attempt to discover and describe. Benson's faith regarded the finality of all human thought, words and action as drawn into the praise-song of the Word made flesh who is manifest in the mystery of the holy Eucharist. The *Mysterium Fidei* points to and beckons us towards entering the luminous reality of the risen Lord's presence in the mystical body which reveals 'God all in all' (cf. 1 Cor. 12:6; 15:28; Eph. 1:23; Col. 3:11). In and through this *mysterium*, the Lord's Spirit invites all people to unite in the canticle of the new creation – the eucharistic *hymn of freedom*. To cite Benson's own words:

> the priest understood; for thought was no longer the process of a mind, rather it was the glance of a spirit. He knew all now; and, by an inevitable impulse, his throat began to sing aloud . . . They were all singing now; even the Mohammedan catechumen who had burst in a moment ago sang with the rest, his lean head thrust out and his arms tight across his breast; the tiny chapel rang with the forty voices, and the vast world thrilled to hear it.[54]

CONCLUSION

FREEDOM
A NEW REALITY?

Beloved, we are God's children now; it does not yet appear what we shall be, but we know that when he appears we shall be like him, for we shall see him as he is.

1 John 3:2[1]

Indeed, contrary to what a humanism incapable of understanding its own metaphysical implications supposes, there is every reason to think that the relationship between God the Father and God the Son is not in any way the product of a sublimation of strictly human relationships. It seems much rather that these relationships themselves, in the course of history have been deepened and renewed under the action of a transcendental idea, without which what we call our nature would never have been able to evolve fully.

Gabriel Marcel[2]

It is only through Christ that we come to the Father. When speaking of God the Father, we ought to add that we mean Him whom Christ means when He says 'My Father'. Thus we would signify that we were not thinking of a vague concept of deity whose power one may suspect behind the government of the world, but that holy countenance which revealed itself for the first time in the words of Christ. When we 'go to the Father', we must go together with Christ, along His path and in His spirit. There can be no other way to the Father than the one on which the Son came to us.

Romano Guardini, 'Prayer to the Father'[3]

7

The Spirit of Freedom

The opening chapter of this book sketched the crisis of culture resulting from various attempts to rationalise the authority of the tradition of Christian faith regarding the meaning of freedom. The crisis of culture has been brought upon us precisely because the very methodology of rationalism has emphasised to such an exaggerated degree the licensing of private interpretation and subjectivism in the interests of promoting the freedom of the individual. Even the sound principle of democracy becomes virtually jeopardised as the good order in society today is threatened by every kind of disorder as well as by the widespread disruptive near-chaos witnessed in the rise not only of violence in cities, but also of the unprecedented phenomenon of international terrorism, whose protagonists are often persons driven by their subjective self-justifying notions and ideologies regarding individual 'rights', rather than justice.

The following chapters presented a picture of human dignity as revealed by God's loving design not only to restore human beings to the authentic worth for which they were created by him, but also to communicate to them something more wonderful, namely, that freedom of faith, hope and love, by which they become empowered to respond, enter into and enjoy his own intimate life of communion in the mystery of the Trinity. The revelation of the truth of freedom in the gospel and new covenant of Jesus Christ, requires a response. It invites and challenges human beings to accept or reject the freedom by which Christ frees us. In affirming the truth of his freedom Christians proclaim Christ's Passover to freedom in the Church's sacred

165

liturgy, especially in the paschal sacrament of the Eucharist; they also enter more deeply into this mystery of faith by adoring the presence of Christ the Redeemer, who transforms and empowers them to become more fully what they receive in the Eucharist, that is, 'adorers of the Father in spirit and truth' who enjoy 'the glorious freedom of the children of God'.

As was seen in the first part of this book, the importance of individuality was not recognised until the humanist movement of the Italian Renaissance. This recognition helped to correct various negative influences which Christianity inherited and borrowed from the world-fleeing and body- (matter-) disparaging views of the Neoplatonists, Stoics, Manichees, etc. However, it would be a mistake to forget or neglect to take into account one vitally important consideration about the Christian Middle Ages: namely, that the value and grandeur of the self was seen as being a part of the whole – a microcosm of the macrocosm. The *summas* produced in those centuries were not intended as attempts to say everything or as arithmetic feats in summing up all conceivable points of view; they were primarily oriented towards relating human intelligence to its highest goal, God, the unique summit. The Latin title of these treatises, *summa*, was fitting since it richly signifies 'highest', 'principal', 'most perfect'. Their perspective was concentrated on the vision of God, the *Summum Bonum*, who reveals the unity of human existence with the cosmic order of God's design and integrates all beings in worship. Medieval artists thus delighted to depict Christ presiding over all orders of creation, such as seen in the triptych of *The Adoration of the Lamb* in Ghent. This same perspective may be seen depicted at the height of the Renaissance in Raphael's fresco of the Eucharist in the *Stanze* of the Vatican. For this painting may be interpreted as showing Christ's reality in the sacrament of the altar as freeing human intelligence from self-centred pursuits to contemplate and be united with God made visible in the bread of life. This seems evident from the artist's own title of this famous painting, namely, *The Triumph of the Eucharist* – not, as Vasari called it, *The Dispute*.

In an enquiry into the social history of the Middle Ages Miri Rubin has attempted show that the Eucharist was the central unifying symbol of European culture prior to the beginning of the Renaissance. The implication of this thesis would seem to be that after the Renaissance, Reformation, and especially because of the emergence of the emphasis on reason in an age of scientific investigation and the Enlightenment, Europe or the world at large has never again known or been capable of recovering any unifying focal point, religious, political, or of whatever kind.[4] However, Rubin's presupposition that the Eucharist was employed by ecclesiastical and secular power-brokers in the late mediaeval period to weld society together has been seriously challenged by the historian Eamon Duffy. He finds this perspective questionable as somewhat anachronistic since it indicates signs of being coloured by contemporary ideological preoccupations. In his major revisionist study of the pre-Reformation Church in England he definitively demolishes the once commonly held notion that the faith and devotional life of people lacked vigour or showed signs of decadence. He thus questions the recent tendency to regard the communal aspect of eucharistic worship as missing in mediaeval devotion, and contends that it was not a Vatican II (re)discovery of the heritage of the great Fathers of the Church, but handed down through the Middle Ages.[5]

Although we may be aware of the mediaeval perspective of society hierarchically ordered towards a wholeness of a unified faith-vision, it is immensely difficult for us today to grasp the complex ethos of that age in which political and religious issues were intricately entwined. However, while it is indeed quite embarrassing to recall the climate of religious intolerance of those times, in which in the name of Christian truth many individuals were denied their human rights and freedom of expression, it is even more difficult to explain the religious persecution carried out in the 'enlightened' times of our own century. Thus, for instance, while Communism was born out of the 1917 October Revolution in order to liberate the serfs oppressed under an outdated Russian feudal system, it soon turned into a totalitarian régime more terrible than that of the Tsars. For while it sought to satisfy the needs of the masses with material benefits, as the Caesars of Rome had once tried with bread and the circus, Communist dictators such as Stalin denied people freedom to aspire to those irreplaceable spiritual qualities such as religious belief and any shred of hope for a better world than that which was programmed by the State. This has been well expressed by the poet Yevgeny Yevtushenko, who became one of the fearless spokesmen of his generation in the Soviet Union after discovering that his ardent beliefs in the aims of the early Revolution had been betrayed by the political dogmatism that followed. He pointed out that whereas bread can never be a substitute for ideals, an ideal can sustain people even when lacking basic material commodities and see them through the darkest hours of deprivation and suffering. An ideal may free and empower the human spirit to endure persecution even to the point of death.[6]

The well-spring of the powerful human yearning to realise the ideal of freedom must ultimately be a source of energy greater than that of human reason. The history of religious experience repeatedly shows that the 'worldly wisdom' of every strain of Gnosticism lacks the needed impetus and sustaining power to confront the problems of ordinary existence; it wanes and shies away from the vigorous challenges and testing of life's sacrifices.[7] Gnosticism – of which there are many modern movements such as the rise of religious sects and naturalistic cults – vainly attempts a false 'self-transcendence'. Its failure or 'sin' stems from what is even worse than the pride of every form of moralistic voluntarism, classically represented in Pelagianism. For, at its core, Gnosticism rejects truth. It is a 'know-all-ism' that refuses to listen to the Word, that is, to obey and submit to the authority of God. As a consequence it festers in its indulgence of the delusion that human reason and intelligence alone are supreme: it rejects any encounter with the gift of the wisdom of the crucified and risen Word incarnate, who uniquely can make us free in the rhythm of his Passover mystery.[8]

The divine call to dialogue in personal intimacy and communion

The story of the transformation of our yearning for freedom begins in God, whose love for humanity gradually unfolded through the history of salvation until it becomes fully revealed through Jesus Christ's communication of his Spirit of intimate and transforming dialogue with the Father. The Bible describes this love-initiated dialogue which leads to freedom and the transformation of human experience. This dramatic redemptive dialogue has been described in terms of the dynamic art of asking questions – that art which is manifested in the narratives of the holy scriptures. By taking the initiative, as he always does and must as Creator, God entices human being into a liberating dialogue with him.[9]

The quest for freedom is implicitly a yearning for the God who saves, yet who remains silent. This double-edged quest, however, is itself the existential response to that question which God has etched into human awareness from the original attempt of human beings to flee and hide from him: 'Adam [Man], where are you?' (Gen. 3:9). This question cannot be ultimately evaded. It has not ceased to echo in the tortuous corridors of the heart and mind of humankind – 'down the arches of the years . . . , down the labyrinthine ways', as Francis Thompson put it. As long as there is an attempt to flee from this terrible question there is fear. This question bespeaks above all the divine questioner – 'the Stranger', as T.S. Eliot calls him[10] – who is adept at raising questions of ultimate concern. He is the One who all along is seeking out his human creature. Pope John Paul II describes the existential drama of God's eternal fatherly search to address and enter into the dialogue of freedom-bestowing communion with humanity:

> *In Jesus Christ* God not only speaks to man but also *seeks him out.* The Incarnation of the Son of God attests that God goes in search of man. Jesus speaks of this search as the finding of a lost sheep (cf. Lk 15:1–7). It is a search which *begins in the heart of God* and culminates in the Incarnation of the Word. If God goes in search of man, created in his own image and likeness, he does so because he loves him eternally in the Word, and wishes to raise him in Christ to the dignity of an adopted son. God therefore goes in search of man who *is his special possession* in a way unlike any other creature. Man is God's possession by virtue of a choice made in love: God seeks man out, moved by his fatherly heart.[11]

This teaching recalls the same Pope's words in summing up the long tradition of reflection on the quality of the quest for freedom as intrinsically connected with the paradox of responding to God's call to faith: 'It is the search of the Magi under the guidance of a star (cf. Mt 2:1ff.), the search of which Pascal, taking up a phrase of Saint Augustine, wrote so profoundly: "You would not be searching for me, if you had not found me".'[12] The silent presence of God mysteriously lurks, as it were, in the deepest crevasses of human beings' longing to be loved until they awake to the discovery that the answer to the disturbing question, 'Where are you', consists in accepting the amazing grace that their 'life is hid with Christ in God' (Col. 3:3). As soon as they encounter and surrender themselves completely to the presence of the divine questioner, an incredible dialogue begins and issues in that song of freedom whose theme is *Eucharist*, the sacrifice of praise of God's greater and more wonderful love.

The dynamic interaction of God the questioner and human beings implies some invisible and spiritual, but real bond of relationship. Through sinning human beings severed this bond; they, so to speak, 'lost the thread' of this spiritual current of the life of truth and love in which freedom is realised. It was necessary, therefore, that God regenerated the life-line of communication by his Word, which found fullest expression in Jesus, 'the Word of Life'. From the beginning of their new experience as 'worshippers whom the Father seeks', the disciples of Jesus realised that their capacity to relate to God as Father and to him as Lord was due to the work of the Spirit of truth, who had been promised to them at the Last Supper in order to lead them into all truth (cf. Jn 16:13; Rom. 8:16; 1 Cor. 12:3; Gal. 4:6;). In the words of the Fourth Eucharistic Prayer, the disciples of the Word experience the Holy Spirit as 'the first Gift to those who believe'. This Spirit of the risen Lord restores the freedom of human persons' access to God and among themselves and the whole of creation by communicating the grace of communion.

The Spirit of Truth

This book on the Eucharist as the *Hymn of Freedom* would be seriously deficient if it failed to speak of the Holy Spirit's mission and action in bringing about that spirit of freedom without which we cannot become related either to God in the worship of the eucharistic mystery or among ourselves in the world. As seen above in the chapter dealing with the liturgy, the Holy Spirit – 'the forgotten Person of the Holy Trinity'[13] – enables the Church to recall, deepen, and also develop its experience of the full truth of the Lord Jesus' sacrifice for freedom or redemption. For it is especially here that the Spirit of the risen Lord comes to the aid of our weakness and the cries from out of the depths of a condition of aliena-tion (cf. Ps. 130[129]; Rom. 8:26): here above all in the swiftness of divine love he realises the eucharistic memorial when the Church invokes his action to transform both the gifts of bread and wine and also our lives. Indeed, the whole of Christian life can be rightly described 'as one long epiclesis'.[14] In virtue of the presence of the Spirit of Truth, the Church, the Bride of Christ, becomes constantly rejuvenated and enabled to discover the true riches of its tradition as 'the living memory of the Risen One' so that it does not cling nostalgically to forms of the past,[15] but presses forward to interpret the gospel and adapt the liturgy in new situations where Christianity must become inculturated. The Spirit of the risen Lord thus empowers the Church not merely to be an instrument of change, but to be the sacrament of salvation in exercising and experiencing a freedom of conversion analogous to the wondrous transformation of material creation in the eucharistic mystery.

The Anglican Bishop John V. Taylor has therefore called the Holy Spirit, who brings about the transforming freedom of the life of communion, 'the Go-Between God'.[16] The expres-sion 'Go-Between God' is certainly quite an original and appropriate one for approaching the Holy Spirit, the principle of all transformation or renewal both of the lives of the community of all Christ's faithful, and also, through their collaboration in prayer and service, of the world at large. It is worth recalling here Bishop Taylor's explanation for taking this approach, because it has an important bearing on our understanding of freedom as realised through the eucharistic mystery:

I have already started to talk about this force of influence in very personal terms. I am bound to do so because the effect of this power is always to bring a mere object into a personal relationship with me, to turn an *It* into a *Thou*.

So Christians find it quite natural to give a personal name to this current of communication, this invisible go-between. They call him the Holy Spirit, the Spirit of God.[17]

The Go-Between God just will not permit the world to fall asunder! He will not allow human beings to disintegrate into a situation of faithlessness, which is the ultimate irreverence since such a situation denotes a denial of the radical relationship between things and between persons themselves and God. The Go-Between God inspires, invites, enables us to discover the joy of believing in God's creation of 'all things visible and invisible'; he disturbs and deepens the shallowness of our materialistic way of approaching reality; he awakens and confirms – that is, strengthens – the weakness of our vision; he discreetly draws us together, as it were, in the interdisciplinary art of a new ecumenism which dares to break through the barriers of age-old racial, national and religious prejudices; he enables us to discover the exciting new common ground of convergence between science and religion, reason and faith; he reveals mysteries which are hidden from the naked eye and buried in our accustomed preference for empiricism or mere appearances and which lie beyond the scope of human imagining – mysteries which God prepares for those who receive his power to love (cf. 1 Cor. 2:9–10). He does all this – and much more than can be drawn up in any listing of the innumerable ways of hope permeating human history[18] – by anointing and illumining the faith of believers without impairing their freedom in the slightest. Rather, he extends and enhances the scope of human freedom from being a matter of making choices, to a way of delighting in the law of love. He can do this precisely because he is the Go-Between Father and Son, God who is love (cf. 1 Jn 4:8). Being Spirit, who is as invisible as a breath of fresh air, he is the Father's and Son's secret agent, as it were, who initiates and facilitates the dialogue which leads to and expresses personal dignity. He raises the tone of human considerations and conversations above the pettiness of self-interest, sectarianism and party-politics, in order that we become focused in seeking that quality of communication which is, in reality, the gospel or good news of communion. Communion – this is the abundant, eternal life of freedom which the Holy Spirit – fosters in God's children when they participate in and live the Eucharist, the *hymn of freedom.*

The mission of the Go-Between the Father and Son in the world consists in revealing the presence of God's dynamic power of love reconciling and freeing people to become united in the mystical body of Christ. It is the function of the Go-Between God to gather and transform all creation into the cosmos of relationship, where the chaos of oppression, injustice, and alienation is definitively overcome by the freedom of divine love. Thus, under the inspiration of the Holy Spirit the Fathers of the Church delighted to interpret the action of the Spirit in the history of salvation as that of the divine Person who delicately begins, fosters and brings the relationship between God and humanity to completion; the Fathers discern his presence-in-action everywhere: hovering over the primaeval depths (cf. Gen. 1:2), overshadowing the Virgin Mary (cf. Lk 1:35), reposing over Jesus 'the anointed one' at his baptism and initiation of proclaiming good news to the poor (cf. Lk 3:21–2; 4:1, 18), presiding over the disciples gathered in the Cenacle with Mary the Mother of the Church at Pentecost, the day of fullness of the grace of communication (cf. Acts 2:3–4). From the beginning to the end the Holy Spirit's revelation of God's self-giving in the history of salvation concerns human beings and their freedom to realise themselves fully as created in God's image and likeness.[19] In a particular way the eucharistic mystery celebrates our being drawn into the new beginning of Christ's Passover by the Holy Spirit. The Go-Between reveals that the truth underlying God's self-communication to humanity is not merely rationality, but *relationship*, that is, communion in the holy (*communio in sacris/communio sanctorum*).

Relational-being is the new definition of the truth about being human that the Go-Between God bestows on rationality. Being-in-relationship is the unique newness of Christian spirituality. The dimension of 'relational-being' is the divine basis of the gift of freedom.[20] For it is intimately linked with that personal quality and manner of relating to God which is the spirit of the Christian prayer of praise, thanksgiving and adoration. The fine distinction between non-Christian paths of meditation and the way that Jesus lived and taught is expressed well in the following paragraph from a Roman document:

> Christian prayer is always determined by the structure of the Christian faith, in which the very truth of God and creature shines forth. For this reason, it is defined, properly speaking, as a personal, intimate and profound dialogue between man and God. It expresses therefore the communion of redeemed creatures with the intimate life of the Persons of the Trinity. This communion, based on an attitude of conversion, a flight from 'self' to the 'You' (*Thou*) of God. Thus Christian prayer is at the same time always authentically personal and communitarian. It flees from impersonal techniques or from concentrating on oneself, which can create a kind of rut, imprisoning the person in a spiritual privatism which is incapable of a free openness to the transcendental God. Within the Church, in the legitimate search for new methods of meditation it must always be borne in mind that the essential element of authentic Christian prayer is the meeting of two freedoms, the infinite freedom of God with the finite freedom of man. . . . in the Holy Eucharist, as in the rest of the Sacraments – and analogically in his works and in his words – Christ gives himself to us and makes us participate in his divine nature, without nevertheless suppressing our created nature, in which he himself shares through his Incarnation.[21]

The Christian Eucharistic Prayer especially enables believers to be explicit in their confession of Christ and the mystery of being-related to the Father in the Holy Spirit. There can be no more hiding or groping in the shadows of worshipping an 'unknown god' – no more anonymity.[22] This is far from saying that God cannot be known and loved at least implicitly in everything. For through the incarnation of his Word, 'the true light . . . coming into the world' (Jn 1:9), God is revealed as present in the world.[23] We can truly say that in the light of the Eucharist, which extends the mystery of the incarnation in time, all human experience – like the fruits of the earth and the work of human hands – becomes gathered into the eternal presence of God.[24]

The Spirit of dialogue leading to unity in Christ

The eucharistic mystery both expresses and leads to unity in
Christ.[25] The steps to unity, however, imply a journey to
freedom, along which fidelity to the commandments and
especially to Christ's all-bracing command of love is essential.[26]
The journey of freedom towards unity, furthermore, involves,
as Pope John Paul II points out, '*a dialogue of conversion*, and
thus, in the words of Pope Paul VI, an authentic "dialogue of
salvation'". He goes on to state that:

> Dialogue cannot take place merely on a horizontal level . . . It has
> also a primarily vertical thrust, directed towards the One who, as
> the Redeemer of the world and the Lord of history, is himself our
> Reconciliation. This vertical aspect of dialogue lies in our acknow-
> ledgment, jointly and to each other, that we are men and women
> who have sinned. It is precisely this acknowledgment which creates
> in brothers and sisters living in Communities not in full com-
> munion with one another that interior space where Christ, the
> source of the Church's unity, can effectively act, with all the power
> of his Spirit, the Paraclete.[27]

Only by the power of the Spirit can we gain access to the
kingdom of the Father of life – that kingdom or *divine milieu* in
which our lives and whole sense of relationship to God, others
and our environment become transformed so that in freedom
and with the trustfulness of little children we can say: 'Abba,
Father'. The experience of acknowledging God as one's own
father – that is, of being 'fathered' by God – is not merely a
negative renunciation of all that is human or natural, but it
evokes the profoundest sense of Christian freedom which is
founded on and grows through worship in spirit and in truth
(cf. Jn 4:24). Christian worship schools us in the deepest attitude
of fear or awe, tender love, gratitude and praise of God, while at
the same time it impels us with the energy of divine love to the
ecumenical task of service as brothers and sisters of the same
God and Father of all. The discovery of this sense of freedom
through spiritual worship together with service (cf. Rom. 12:1–
2) presents the great challenge and exciting prospect to which
the Spirit of the risen Lord is leading the Christian Church and
all people. To quote Pope John Paul II words:

The greatest homage which all the Churches can give to Christ on
the threshold of the third millennium will be to manifest the
Redeemer's all-powerful presence through the fruits of faith, hope
and charity present in men and women of many different tongues
and races who have followed Christ in the various forms of the
Christian vocation.[28]

This attitude of freedom in Christian worship and service is
made possible and constantly renewed and deepened in the
Church through the Holy Spirit. For, in the perfect worship of
the Son's Spirit of loving obedience to the Father's design in
creation and redemption, we discover the basis for true
harmony and freedom.

The love-causality of the Father's Spirit breaks a rigid,
mechanical and deterministic view of reality; it breaks down and
breaks through our hard and fast notions about what can or
should happen. It breaks into our hardened hearts, immobile
and perhaps embittered by individualistic motives or self-
centred hurts, and calls us to be converted and to become
transformed into a community characterised by the freedom
that flows from the forgiveness and reconciliation of his Son's
freely given new covenant-sacrifice. The action of the Go-
Between God in bringing about spiritual freedom is expressed
in the noble simplicity of the Gregorian chant of Stephen
Langton's Sequence for Whitsunday:

> Flecte quod est rigidum,
> Fove quod est frigidum,
> Rege quod est devium.
> (Stubborn wills to thine subdue,
> Hearts grown cold to fire renew,
> Warped and selfish lives make true.)[29]

Towards realising the Spirit of brotherly love

Every person is part of the overall human struggle to become
and be free. In virtue of the risen Lord's Spirit-given power to
love, he or she is, for better or worse, implicated in the drama
of existence and must realise being called to take that
qualitative leap of faith towards freedom as that gift by which
and for which Christ has set us free (cf. Gal. 5:1). Over the

Christian centuries many strides have been taken towards engaging in the exciting adventure and daring exploration into how the meaning of freedom and human dignity are interwoven in the mystery of that love which God has revealed through Jesus Christ. The Christian story of this exploration includes many pages which cannot be read without a sense of embarrassment and shame for betraying Christ's gospel of freedom – pages of intolerance and religious prejudice and bloody persecution.[30] Pope John Paul II urges a spirit of repentance for all expressions of '*intolerance and even the use of violence in the service of truth*'.[31] What is at issue here is the dark chapter of history, which concerns the persecution Christians inflicted on one another. It may be almost impossible for us to comprehend the meaning of this in these fairly comfortable ecumenical days. The pages of this chapter cannot and must not be torn out of the human memory because they record important lessons to be learned by us today and by people in the time ahead. These are hard-bought lessons, which we may be disinclined to heed or consider unnecessary or superfluous in our complacency about our achievements in ecumenical 'Joint Statements' and collaboration. Yet these lessons cannot be evaded. They concern the two faces of zeal, which someone of the calibre of St Paul knew well regarding so great a good as Christ Jesus' gift of freedom. On the one side, zeal can generate a fanatical energy to deny others the right to interpret and live the meaning of freedom's truth according to conscience; and, on the other, it can fire an ardent pursuit of this precious gift, for which it enriches and deepens an appreciation the more that we discover the joy of sharing it and learning about it through the experience and collaboration of others.

The story of both these faces of zealous yearning for freedom may perhaps be recognised symbolically in the famous Liberty Bell on display at Philadelphia, the city of 'Brotherly Love'. For the bell is severely cracked so that it remains a mute witness to the cause of freedom, over which so many voices have been clamorously raised, so many lives violently lost, and so many books written! In fact, the original bell cracked the very first time it was rung – on the occasion for which it was cast, namely,

the fiftieth anniversary of the William Penn's Charter of
Freedom for the State which is named after this great pioneer
of religious tolerance. After being melted down and recast –
this time in Philadelphia instead of at Whitechapel in London
– it tolled for a good many years, joyfully welcoming the
signing of three important documents in the state buildings
of Penn's city, which was founded on the principle of religious and civic freedom for all people: the Declaration of
Independence (1776), the new nation's Constitution (1787)
and the Bill of Rights (1791). But in 1835 the Liberty Bell
cracked again, and again had to be recast. In a similar way,
should we not learn that endeavours for freedom must
constantly be remade?

Furthermore, just as the real significance of the bell's name
is not known by many, we may well ask whether the significance
of freedom is also only understood by a few – those few who
have given their lives for it. The liberty the bell commemorates
is not, as is often thought, the Declaration of the American
Colonies' Independence from Britain; but it was baptised, so to
speak, with its popular name when its voice was needed to be
heard as a symbolic rallying point, calling for the freeing of
slaves. Thus, we may ask whether tourists who pass by and look
at the Liberty Bell reflect on the deeper significance of the
many forms of enslavement in which their lives are ensnared
and held captive: materialism or consumerism, ideologies and
preconceptions and subtle prejudices, fears and false securities,
etc. Do we, who may never have seen this bell, realise that the
root of every form of slavery is selfish pride, from which there is
deliverance and freedom, or rather, a Redeemer – the risen
Lord Jesus Christ – who liberates captives of every kind, and,
moreover, calls all men and women today to share the joy and
freedom of being the children of God?

In the same city of Brotherly Love during the celebrations of
the bi-centennial year 'of the day when the hunger for freedom
ripened in the American society and revealed itself in liberation
and the Declaration of Independence of the United States', the
Polish Cardinal Karol Wojtyla, delivered an address at the Forty-
first International Eucharistic Congress on the congress theme,
which remains dear to the heart of one coming from a nation

whose history is marked by the struggle for freedom: 'The
Eucharist and Hungers of the Human Family.' On that occasion, he spoke most movingly of freedom as that insatiable
hunger which is basic to every human being and which is both
inspired and satisfied solely and uniquely by Jesus Christ. From
the beginning of his public ministry and throughout his whole
life and, now, until the end of history, Jesus Christ abides in our
midst in the Eucharist as the Lord sustaining and transforming
the vision and energies, the hearts and very lives of all people –
especially the poor, oppressed and marginalised. These truly
seek to become freed from every form of degradation caused,
at root, by sin and the sinful structures of tyranny and enslavement, which disfigure the complex network of dimensions and
dynamics making up human existence – that delicate living
network of intrinsically related factors such as the political and
social, moral and psychological, material and spiritual, personal
and communal.

The same man, Karol Wojtyla, who spoke at Philadelphia,
namely, Pope John Paul II, deemed it most opportune to focus
more deeply on 'The Eucharist and Freedom' as the appropriate theme for the Forty-sixth International Eucharistic
Congress at Wroclaw in Poland in 1997 on the threshold of the
Third Christian Millennium.

Though human freedom may be flawed, though the cry for
it muffled or strident, though the endeavours to realise it
shoddy or made of poor stuff, the Lord's command to his
chosen people – as etched on the rim of the famous bell in
Philadelphia – rings forever true: 'Proclaim Liberty throughout
all the Land unto all the Inhabitants thereof' (Lev. 25:10).
More than merely giving us a command, however, the Father of
all mankind graciously gave us his beloved Son, whose Spirit
transforms our meagre yearnings and tawdry efforts and very
hearts so that we become empowered to live his new covenant
of brotherly love, which we celebrate in the Passover mystery of
the Eucharist, our *hymn of freedom*.

On Easter Sunday 1990, that is, at the beginning of the
decade of evangelisation leading to the Third Christian
Millennium, Pope John Paul II made this eloquent appeal,
which itself is a confession of faith in Christ who has set us free:

Man of our day!
You, man, who live immersed in the world and think you are its
    master
while perhaps you are its prey,
Christ frees you from every form of slavery
in order to propel you towards self-conquest,
towards love . . .
Christ sets you free because He loves you,
because He has given Himself up for you,
because He has conquered for you and for all.
Christ has restored the world and you to God.
He has restored God to you and to the world.
Forever!
'Be of good cheer, I have overcome the world!'[32]

Notes

PRELIMINARY PAGES and A PRETEXT FOR WRITING?

1 From Karol Wojtyla's poem 'I reach the heart of drama' in *The Place Within* (tr. Jerzy Peterkiewicz), Hutchinson, London, 1995, p. 145.

2 Pope John Paul II, Post-Synodal Apostolic Exhortation *Familiaris Consortio*, n. 11; (ET) CTS S 357, p. 21.

3 See Dr Chandra Muzaffar's critical examination of the stance of the United Nations in this war-torn country; cf. 'Human rights and hypocrisy in the international order' in *Dominance of the West Over the Rest*, Just World Trust (JUST), Penang, Malaysia, 1995, pp. 97f.

4 Cf. Pope Paul VI, Allocution on 31 December 1975. In this context of remaking civilisation, Pope Paul VI stressed Christians' responsibility to become healers: 'We are called to be physicians of that civilisation.'

5 Cf. Robert Sokolowski, *Eucharistic Presence: A Study in the Theology of Disclosure*, CUP, Washington, DC, 1994, pp. 183, 193. Since completing this book my attention has been drawn to Donald Keefe's massive critique of the rationalistic method inherited from Greek thought, whose influence somewhat distorted Catholic theology until relatively recent times so that an undue emphasis was placed on a speculative rather than a practical approach, as demanded by divine revelation. Cf. *Covenantal Theology: The Eucharistic Order of History*, Presidio Press, Novato CA (USA), 1996 (rev. ed. two volumes in one). While pursuing a different methodology and line of argument, I am in general agreement with Keefe's conclusion.

6 Cf. OL 8; (ET) Libreria Editrice Vaticana, p. 15.

7 Address at the Sixth Symposium of the European Bishops, 11 October 1985; cf. *Briefing 85*, Catholic Media Office, London, Vol. 15, No. 20 (25 October 1985), p. 316.

8 Cf. *Eucharistic Prayers,* I and IV.

9 Cf. LG 9.

10 *Four Quartets: Burnt Norton,* I; cf. also *Murder in the Cathedral,* Part II. Cf. also *Chorus from 'The Rock',* X.

11 *Four Quartets: Burnt Norton,* III.

12 Ibid., II.

13 Sutherland's words quoted on a card beside his painting.

14 *Orthodoxy,* Unicorn Books, London, 1939, p. 36.

15 As Raymond Gawronski summarises the great Swiss theologian's stance before the crucified: *Word and Silence: Hans Urs von Balthasar and the Spiritual Encounter Between East and West,* T&T Clark, Edinburgh, 1995, pp. 216f. Cf. also Balthasar's Preface to *Heart of the World,* (ET) Ignatius Press, San Francisco, 1979, pp. 13f.

16 *Pensées:* 'The mystery of Jesus', (ET) Penguin ed. n. 919 – éd. Brunschvicg 553. Likewise, see George Bernard Shaw, *St Joan,* Epilogue: 'Must then a Christ perish in torment in every age to save those that have no imagination?' In *Choruses from 'The Rock',* VI, T.S. Eliot also sees Christ's sacrifice continued in Christian martyrs and saints.

17 Address to delegates for the 46th IEC, paragraph 3 – OR, 19 May 1995, p. 5.

18 Cf. RMi 3; in paragraphs 7 and 39, he speaks of the freedom revealed by Christ; in paragraph 86, in Cardinal Newman's image, he heralds the 'new springtime' brought about through the new evangelisation.

19 SRS (30 December 1987) 46 (end); (ET) *Briefing* 88 (4 March 1988) Vol. 18, No. 5, p. 112 quoting Congregation for the Doctrine of the Faith, Instruction on Christian Freedom and Liberation, *Libertatis Conscientia* (22 March 1986), 24: AAS 79 (1987), p. 564.

20 Letter to the Bishops of Europe on relations between Catholics and Orthodox in the new situation of Central and Eastern Europe, 31 May 1991; (ET) Paul McPartlan (ed.), *One in 2000? – Towards Catholic–Orthodox Unity,* St Pauls, 1993, p. 181. Cf. also UUS, which is devoted entirely to the vitally important task of realising the gift of Christian unity through dialogue.

21 Paragraph 4, OR, l.c.

22 *Finita iam sunt proelia,* Hymn *Simphonia Sirenum* (1695); (ET) R.A. Knox in *The Westminster Hymnal,* Burns & Oates Ltd, London, 1965, n. 55, p. 62. Cf. CCC 631–7. John Saward has drawn attention to Balthasar's profound explanation of this apostolic traditional teaching on Christ's descent into hell to liberate humanity by

proclaiming the Word of life (cf. Acts 2:31; 1 Pet. 3:18ff.; 4:6). Cf. *The Mysteries of March*, Collins, 1990, pp. 105ff.; also *Christ is the Answer*, T&T Clark, Edinburgh/Alba House, New York, 1995, p. 51.

23 *En. in Ps. 32, serm. 1*, 7–8; CCL 38.253–4 (ET altered) DO III, Collins, 1974, pp. 411f.

CHAPTER 1

1 In *The Need for Roots*, (ET) Routledge & Kegan Paul Ltd (Ark Paperback), London/New York, 1987, pp. 12, 13, 31.

2 Image Books, Doubleday & Co. Ltd, Garden City, New York, 1958, p. 263.

3 Faber & Faber, London/Boston, 1989, p. 153.

4 The phrase was first used by Cardinal John O'Connor according to Richard A. McCormick; cf. 'The gospel of life' in *America*, Vol. 172, No. 15 (April 1995), p. 11. It appears in Pope John Paul II's Encyclical Letter on the inviolable value of human life; cf. *Evangelium Vitae* (25 March 1995), 12; (ET) Libreria Editrice Vaticana, p. 18, where he states that: 'a kind of "*conspiracy against life*" is unleashed. This conspiracy involves not only individuals in their person, family or group relationships, but goes far beyond, to the point of damaging and distorting, at the international level, relations between peoples and States.' (Italics in text.) The same Pope who wrote these lines was himself on 13 May 1981 the target of an international assassination plot.

5 Cf. DM 2; (ET) Infoform, Catholic Information Office, Abbots Langley Herts. (UK), pp. 8f. (citing GS 9): 'there appears the dichotomy of a world that is at once powerful and weak, capable of doing what is noble and what is base, disposed to freedom and slavery, progress and decline, brotherhood and hatred. Man is growing conscious that the forces he has unleashed are in his own hands and that it is up to him to control them or be enslaved by them.'

6 Cardinal Hume's hope-filled vision of his sermon at Leeds on 1 September 1991 was not lacking in the realistic warning about the danger of nuclear stockpiles falling into the hands of 'new political groupings'; cf. *New Blackfriars*, Vol. 73, No. 856, January 1992, p. 2. His viewpoint, a Western one, however, must be balanced by that expressing the perspective of underprivileged Eastern nations, whose freedom to hope is clouded and curtailed by the economic politics of the dominant Western powers; cf. Jennifer Mourin, *Peace Dividend? The Arms Build-up in the Post-Cold*

War Era, Just World Trust (JUST), Penang, Malaysia, 1994. Cf. also K.R. Panikkar, 'Western domination: the military factor' in *Dominance of the West Over the Rest,* Just World Trust (JUST), Penang, Malaysia, 1995, pp. 61f.

7 Cf. *The Fear of Freedom,* (ET) Routledge, London 1995 (originally published in 1942).

8 Rollo May also speaks of the sense of loss of communication and neuroses of this century; cf. *Love and Will,* Collins, Fountain Paperback, 1977, p. 23.

9 This point is elaborated by Robert Sokolowski in describing the contemporary emphasis placed on relativism and voluntarism; cf., *Eucharistic Presence,* op. cit., pp. 189f.

10 Cf. CCC 2375–9.

11 Cf. Karl Jung, *Modern Man in Search of a Soul,* (ET) Routledge & Kegan Paul, London and Henley, 1978, pp. 235f.: 'Material security, even, has gone by the board, for the modern man begins to see that every step in material "progress" adds just so much force to the threat of a more stupendous catastrophe. The very picture terrorises the imagination.'

12 This dramatic struggle for interiority, which is nothing other than the depths of freedom, is reflected throughout the writings of Pope John Paul II. In his youth he was involved in the world of theatre, both as performer in productions including the poetic works of Cyprian Norwid (1821–83), such as *On the Freedom of the Word,* as well as dramatist; cf. Boleslaw Taborski's introduction to Karol Wojtyla, *The Collected Plays and Writings on the Theater,* (ET) University of California Press, Berkeley, 1987, p. 8. Cf. also Karol Wojtyla, *The Acting Person,* (ET) D. Reidel Publishing Company, Dordrecht: Holland/Boston: USA/London, 1979.

13 Since Vatican II (cf. GS 35) – the danger of this has been repeatedly pointed out: cf. e.g. Paul VI, *Populorum Progressio* (26 March 1967), 15, 19; John Paul II, SRS, 28; 31; EV 98, etc.

14 Cf. *World Within World,* Faber & Faber Paperback, London/Boston, 1991, p. 137.

15 Cf. *The Second Coming.*

16 Cf. e.g. Plato, *The Republic.*

17 Cf. Josef Pieper, *Leisure – the Basis of Culture,* (ET) Random House Inc. (Mentor-Omega Book), New York, 1963, pp. 20f.: 'The word used to designate the place where we educate and teach is derived from a word which means "leisure" [Greek, *skole;* Latin, *scola*]. "School" does not, properly speaking, mean school, but leisure. ... Literally, the Greek says "we are unleisurely in order to have leisure." (*Nicomachean Ethics*). "To be unleisurely" – that is the word

the Greeks used not only for the daily toil and moil of life, but for ordinary everyday work. Greek only has the negative, *a-scolia*, just as Latin has *neg-otium*.'

18 See T.S. Eliot's introductory preface to Pieper's book: ibid., pp. 13f.

19 Cf. Christopher Dawson, *Science and Wisdom*, Geoffrey Bles: The Centenary Press, London, 1940, p. 6.

20 Cf. Mircea Eliade, *The Sacred and the Profane: The Nature of Religion*, (ET) Harper & Row (Torchbooks, The Cloister Library), New York, 1961, pp. 220, 225, 228. Eliade recalls that Aristotle was the first to formulate a theory about the general degeneration of humanity; cf. *Metaphysics*, XII.7. This theory was contended by writers of the Enlightenment in accordance with their overall approach regarding the progress of humanity from a primitive state of natural religious to more sophisticated quality of life.

21 Cf. *Confessions*, III.3.7.

22 Cf. e.g. *Confessions*, VIII.3.6 – 'gaudium sollemnitatis domus tuae'; cf. also IX.4.8–9; IX.7.15; X.33.50. See Dr Mary Berry's article on the Church's use of the ancient melodies of the psalm-tones of the Jewish people: 'The chant at the top of the charts' in *Priests and People*, Vol. 9, No. 7 (July 1995), pp. 270ff.

23 Cf. *Confessions*, I.1.

24 This meaning of the word *confession*, which is the leitmotif of his 'theological autobiography', was already passing out of use, or rather, as St Augustine notes with disappointment it was employed by people more usually for confession of sins – e.g. cf. *Serm.* 29, 2, 2; *En. in Ps.* 117,1. *Confessio* in this sense of praise is the Latin equivalent of the Hebrew *todah*, which was literally translated in the Greek Septuagint as *'eksomologeisthai*, to celebrate with praise and thanksgiving.

25 Cf. e.g. *De vera religione*, 35.65.

26 Cf. Anne-Marie La Bonnardière, *Recherches de Chronologie Augustinienne*, Études Augustiniennes, Paris, 1965, pp. 137ff.

27 Cf. Goulven Madec, 'Connaisance de Dieu et action de grâce: essai sur les citations de l'Ép. aux Romains 1:18–25 dans l'oeuvre de saint Augustin' in *Recherches Augustinienne*, II, Études Augustiniennes, Paris, 1975, pp. 273–309.

28 Cf. Augustine, Discourse 194, 3–4; PL 38, 1016–17. Cf. also Goulven Madec, 'Christus, scientia et sapientia nostra: Le principe de cohérence de la doctrine augustinienne', *Recherches Augustinienne*, X, pp. 77–85.

29 Robert C. Pollock, 'Freedom and History', *Thought*, XXVII (1952), p. 414 cited by Mary T. Clark, *Augustine: Philosopher of Freedom*, Desclée Company, New York/Tournai/Rome/Paris, 1958, p. 5.

30 Cf. ST, III.34.1 ad 1.

31 In St Anselm's famous dictum: '*fides quaerens intellectum*', which is the secondary – perhaps original – title of the *Prologion*.

32 Cf. *Proslogion*, ch. 1; PL 158, 227B: 'Non tento, Domine, penetrare altitudinem tuam, quia nullatenus comparo illi intellectum meum, sed alquatenus desiderio intelligere veritatem tuam quam credit et amat cor meum.'

33 The source for this approach he found in Isaiah 7:9, either in his preferred reading from the old Latin version in use in Africa: *nisi credideritis non intellegetis*; or in the Latin of the Vulgate, which had recently appeared: *si non credideritis non permanebitis*. In *De Doctrina Christiana* (II.12.17) he cites both versions, whereas in many of his sermons he employs the old Latin version.

34 Anthony Kenny drew attention to the recurrence of this problem in the modern, purely secular debate between scientific determinism and a commonsense approach to freedom; cf. Bryan Magee, *The Great Philosophers. An Introduction to Western Philosophy*, BBC Books, 1987, pp. 73f.

35 Cf. *The Social Contract*, ch. VIII; (ET) J.M. Dent, London/E.P. Dutton, New York (Everyman's Library), 1935, pp. 118–20.

36 Christopher Dawson, *Progress and Religion: An Historical Enquiry*, Sheed & Ward (Unicorn Books), London, 1938, pp. 183f. He quotes von Harnack (p. 179): 'Scholasticism is nothing else but scientific thought.' Cf. also Donald J. Keefe SJ, *Covenantal Theology*, op. cit., p. 660.

37 Cf. David Cairns, *The Image of God in Man*, Collins, Fontana Paperback, 1973 (rev. ed.), pp. 116ff. Cairns pays tribute to Augustine, however, as being the first thinker who defined the image in terms of a capacity or power for freedom (cf. p. 101). For a collection of patristic texts on the image and likeness of God; cf. *L'Uomo Immagine Somigliante di Dio*, Edizione Paoline, Milan, 1991. St John Damascene may be taken as representing the common patristic tradition, which links freedom with the capacity to act responsibly in accord with reason: 'The expression "according to the image" indicates rationality and freedom, while the expression "according to the likeness" indicates assimilation to God through virtue.' (Quoted by Timothy Ware, *The Orthodox Church*, Pelican, 1963, p. 224.)

38 Cf. *The Eucharist Makes the Church: Henri de Lubac and John Zizioulas in Dialogue*, T&T Clark, Edinburgh, 1993.

39 Cf. ibid., pp. 43ff. Cf. Zizioulas, *Il Creato Come Eucharistia*, Edizioni Qiqajon, Comunità di Bose, 1994, pp. 16ff. Another Orthodox theologian, Alexander Schmemann, likewise criticises the emphasis

on rational categories in the Middle Ages; cf. *The Eucharist Sacrament of the Kingdom,* (ET) St Vladimir's Seminary Press, Crestwood, New York, 1988, pp. 160f.

40 I am grateful for this point regarding St Bonaventure's approach to Sr Paula Jean Miller of the Franciscan Sisters of the Eucharist; cf. *Marriage: The Sacrament of Divine Human Communion,* Vol. I, 'A Commentary on St Bonaventure's *Breviloquium*', Franciscan Press, Quincy, Il (USA), 1996.

41 *Progress and Religion,* op. cit., p. 179.

42 'An answer to the question: "what is enlightenment?"' in *Kant's Political Writings,* ed. Hans Reiss, tr. H.B. Nisbet, CUP, 1970, p. 54 cited by Professor Nicholas Lash, *Theology on the Way to Emmaus,* SCM Press Ltd, London, 1986, p. 56.

43 Cf. Sir Isaiah Berlin's Introduction to *The Age of Enlightenment: The 18th Century Philosophers,* The New American Library (A Mentor Book), 1961, pp. 14f.

44 Cf. *Pensées,* (ET) loc. cit., n. 200; éd. Brunschvicg, 347.

45 Cf. Stephen Sykes, *The Identity of Christianity: Theologians and the Essence of Christianity from Schleiermacher to Barth,* Fortress Press, Philadelphia/SPCK, London, 1984, pp. 150f., 270.

46 It is interesting to note that, in reaction against the liberal currents of the Enlightenment and the Romantic movement, Coleridge expressed an approach similar to that of Augustine and Anselm as seen above. He rigorously rebutted the Cartesian *cogito ergo sum,* as a betrayal not only of philosophical enquiry into reality, but recognised the distinction of consciousness which Kant and his followers make between the empirical 'I' of and the absolute 'I AM'; cf. *Biographia Literaria,* Dent (Everyman's Library), London and Melbourne, 1987, p. 152.

47 Cf. Don Cupitt, *The Sea of Faith,* BBC, London, 1984, p. 231 *et passim.*

48 Ibid., p. 188.

49 Ibid., p. 190.

50 Cf. Denis de Rougement, 'Religion and the mission of the artist', (International Conference on Christianity and Art, Ecumenical Institute, Château de Bossey, Celigny, Switzerland, May, 1950) in *Spiritual Problems in Contemporary Literature* (ed. Stanley Romain Harper), Harper & Row Publishers (Harper Torchbooks), New York, 1957.

51 Cf. *Surprised by Joy,* ch. 13, where he recounts his story of coming to the Christian faith.

52 *The Screwtape Letters* (first published 1942), No. 25.

53 This essay, which is regarded as one of his 'most valuable pieces of writing'. had originally been published in 1943; cf. Walter Hooper, Preface to *Christian Reflections*, Collins, Fount Paperbacks, 1981, p. 9.

54 Bishop Rowan Williams has described Balthasar as 'a resolutely "unmodern" writer ... seeing with a clinical eye how European rationality from the seventeenth century onwards has more and more tied itself into destructive patterns of self-obsession, alienated from the concrete challenge of the "otherness" of history, art, community and the body itself. Like other contemporary thinkers, he identifies the intellectual "Modernity" of Europe as a sickness of the spirit.' (Foreword to John Saward's most impressive presentation of a synthesis of the Swiss theologian's approach, *The Mysteries of March*, op. cit., pp. viif.)

55 Cf. 'Flight into community' in *New Elucidations*, (ET) Ignatius Press, San Francisco, 1986, pp. 104f.

56 The psychotherapist Rollo May has demonstrated that voluntarism is the terminal stage of becoming fixated by a subjective desire and the power of choice without maintaining any point of reference to reality such as provided by faith, grace or cultural tradition; cf. *Love and Will*, op. cit., pp. 204–13.

57 *The Drama of Atheistic Humanism*, (ET) London, 1949, p. 31 cited by Saward, *The Mysteries of March*, op. cit., p. 175.

58 Cf. *Real Presences*, op. cit., pp. 39ff.

59 Cf. ibid., pp. 44f.

60 'Work and the word', originally in *Esprit*, January 1953, (ET) in *History and Truth*, Northwestern University Press, Evanston, 1965, p. 209.

61 *The Theology of Vatican II*, DLT, London, 1981 (revised and enlarged edition), p. 219; cf. also ibid., pp. 147f.

62 Various new approaches to theology focused on meaning were worked out in the 1960s and 1970s following the lead of the Peruvian theologian, Gustavo Gutiérrez, whose controversial work gave this method and approach its name, 'liberation theology'. Cf. *A Theology of Liberation*, (ET) London, 1974, 1983. For an examination of the origin and presuppositions of the concept of liberation theology and the background to the Church's two declarations on human liberation see Cardinal Joseph Ratzinger's explanation in ch. 12: 'A certain "liberation"', *The Ratzinger Report* (ET) Fowler Wright Books Ltd, Leominster (UK)/Ignatius Press, San Francisco, 1985, pp. 169ff.

63 Sacred Congregation for the Doctrine of the Faith, 22 March 1986, n. 56; (ET) Catholic Media Office, London, p. 30.

64 The literature on these issues, which are particularly focused on
the ordination of women to the ministerial priesthood, is vast. It
would seem that Pope John Paul II's declaration that the Church
has no authority to admit women to the ministerial priesthood
(Apostolic Letter, 22 May 1994) does not meet the theological or
canonical criteria required to make it an infallible statement. Cf.
Ladislaus Orsy, 'The Congregation's "Response": its authority and
meaning' in *America*, December 1995, pp. 4f.; Francis Sullivan,
'Guideposts from Catholic tradition', ibid., pp. 5f. See also Karl
Rahner's assessment of the arguments against women's ordination
to the priesthood in the declaration of Sacred Congregation for
the Doctrine of the Faith, *Inter Insigniores* (15 October 1975):
'Women and the priesthood' in *Theological Investigations*, Vol. 20,
(ET) DLT, London, 1981, pp. 35ff.

65 VS, 34; (ET) Libreria Editrice Vaticana, 1993, p. 103 citing his
Address to those taking part in the International Congress of Moral
Theology (10 April 1986), 1: *Insegnamenti* IX, 1 (1986), 970. Cf.
also Sacred Congregation for the Doctrine of the Faith, *Instruction
on Christian Freedom and Liberation* (22 March 1986), n. 3; (ET)
Catholic Media Office, London, p. 3: 'Truth beginning with the
truth of redemption, which is at the heart of the mystery of faith, is
thus the root and the rule of freedom, the foundation and the
measure of all liberating action.'

66 See Pope John Paul II's Encyclical Letter on Social Concern (30
December 1987), SRS 14. Cf. also Cardinal Ratzinger's statement
in *The Ratzinger Report*, op. cit, p. 172: 'The fundamental
experience of our epoch is precisely the experience of "alienation", that is, the condition which Christianity expresses
traditionally as the *lack of redemption*. It is the experience of a
human existence that has cut itself loose from God, only to find,
not freedom, but slavery.' (Italics in text.)

67 E.g. cf. Pope Gregory XVI's Encyclical *Mirari vos*, 15 August 1832
(DS 2730–2); cf. also Pope Pius IX's *Syllabus of Errors*, 8 December
1864 (DS 2915ff.).

68 *The Theology of Vatican II*, op. cit., p. 184.

69 *Ecclesiam Suam*, 69; (ET slightly revised) CTS DO 354, pp. 41f.

70 His first Encyclical Letter, *Inscrutabili Dei Consilio* (21 April 1878),
outlined his programme to reconcile the Church with modern
civilisation. This was followed by other Encyclical Letters directed
to various social and political questions: e.g. *Arcanum divinae
sapientiae* (10 February 1880); *Diuturnum illud* (29 June 1881);
Immortale Dei (1 November 1885) on the relation between of
spiritual and temporal power; *Libertas Praestantissimum* (20 June
1888) on the freedom of citizens ('civil rights', as we would say
today); *Graves de Communi* (18 January 1901) on Christian
democracy.

71 Cf. his own magistral Encyclical Letter *Centesimus annus* (1 May 1991); also *Laborem Exercens* (14 September 1981); *Sollicitudo Rei Socialis* (30 December 1987); *Evangelium Vitae* (25 March 1995). Cf. Pius XI *Quadragesimo anno* (15 May 1931); John XXIII *Ad Petri Cathedram* (29 June 1959), *Mater et Magistra* (15 May 1961), *Pacem in Terris* (11 April 1963); Paul VI *Ecclesiam Suam* (6 August 1964), *Populorum Progressio* (26 March 1967), *Octogesima Adveniens* (14 May 1971).

72 Cf. TMA 13, where Leo XIII's Encyclical *Rerum Novarum* is again mentioned; cf. also, ibid., 22.

73 Apart from in his Address to Delegates for the 46th IEC (Rome, 16 May 1995), quoted above on p. xxii, the theme of martyrdom significantly recurs in the writings of Pope John Paul II: cf. e.g. RH 12; CA 55; VS 90–4, 107; EV 12; UUS 84; TMA 37.

74 Cf. Pope Paul VI's Apostolic Letter *Alma Parens* on the occasion of the Second Scholastic Congress held at Oxford and Edinburgh, for the seventh centenary of John Duns Scotus' birth, OR 14 July 1966: 'He [Scotus] was indeed one theologian who was constructive because he loved: he showed a concrete love that was *praxis*, as he himself put it: "It has been shown that love is truly practical [*prassi*]".' Cf. Scotus, *Ord.*, prol., n. 303 (Ed. Vat. I, 200).

75 Cf. Mircea Eliade, *The Sacred and the Profane: The Nature of Religion*, (ET) Harper & Row Torchbooks (The Cloister Library), 1961, pp. 215ff.: 'Chronological survey – the "History of Religion" as a branch of knowledge.'

76 Cf. Rudolf Otto's classic study, written in 1917: *The Idea of the Holy*, (ET) Penguin (Pelican), 1959.

77 Cf. 'Theological dimensions of human liberation' in *Communio* 22 (Summer, 1995), pp. 225–41; 'Beyond left and right: a Politics of life', *Communio*, ibid., pp. 381–8.

CHAPTER 2

1 Collins, Fontana Books, 1961, pp. 151f.

2 (ET) DLT, London, 1987, pp. 61, 63.

3 Cf. *Poems*, 'No beauty we could desire' cited in *The Business of Heaven*, (ed. Walter Hooper), Collins, Fount Paperback, 1984, p. 333.

4 In the Gospels, 'to redeem' has the sense of 'to free/loose'. Cf. e.g. Mt 16:19 – whatever you *loose* on earth; Mt 18:18; Lk 1:68 – visited (see Gk) and redeemed (wrought redemption – *lutrōsin*); Lk 2:38 – all who look forward to the deliverance (redemption –

lútrōsin) of Jerusalem; compare Lk 21:28 – your liberation (*hē apolútrōsis*) is near at hand – with 'the kingdom is your midst' (Lk 17:21).

5 To quote the phrase from the Instruction on Christian Freedom and Liberation, *Libertatis Conscientia*, of the Congregation for the Doctrine of the Faith, 22 March 1986, 3; (ET) Catholic Media Office, London, p. 3.

6 Cf. Deut. 4:1–3, 6–8; also 30:11–14 (referred to in Rom. 10:8–10). Cf. especially Deut. 6:4–5, which Jesus quotes in Mt 22:37. Deut. 6:4–5 was the first of the three texts – the other two are Deut. 11:13–21 and Num. 15:37–41 – which pious Jews recited twice daily. This scriptural text, known as the *Shema Israel* (= Hear, O Israel) contains the summary of the law (Torah) which guaranteed Israel's faithful response and freedom. Pope John Paul II comments on Deut. 6:4–6 in relation to Mt 19:16 and points out that the young man's earnest question about the meaning of existence is really a religious question since it concerns the Good, the True and a sense of integrity in life, which are found uniquely in God, the source and fullness of freedom; cf. VS 12f.

7 Cf. 'Redemption' in Xavier Léon-Dufour, *Dictionary of Biblical Theology*, (ET) 2nd. ed., New York, 1973; cf. also, Enrico Mazza, *The Eucharistic Prayers of the Roman Rite*, (ET) Pueblo Publishing Co. Inc., New York, 1996, pp. 102–4.

8 E.g. St Augustine, *Confessions*, X.43.70; *Serm.*, 334.2; St Gaudentius of Brescia, *Tr. II on Exodus*; St Gregory the Great, *Com. on the Book of Job*, Bk. XIII.21–3.

9 DM 2; (ET) Infoform, Catholic Information Office, Abbots Langley, Herts. (UK), p. 8. (Italics in text.)

10 Cf. Pope John Paul II, FC, 6; (ET) CTS S 357, p. 13: 'history is not simply a fixed progression towards what is better, but rather an event of freedom, and even a struggle between freedoms that are in mutual conflict, that is, according to the well-known expression of Saint Augustine, a conflict between two loves: the love of God to the point of disregarding self, and the love of self to the point of disregarding God. (Cf. St Augustine, *De Civitate Dei*, XIV, 28; CSEL 40, II, 56–7)'. Cf. also SRS, 27.

11 Cf. SRS, 31: referring to St Basil the Great, *Regulae fusius tractate, interrogatio* XXXVII, 1–2: PG 31, 1009–12; Theodoret of Cyr, *De Providentia, Oratio*, VII: PG 83, 665–86; St Augustine, *De Civitate Dei*, XIX, 17: CCL 48, 683–5.

12 Gianfranco Ravesi points out the irony of Ernest Renan's 'faith' in the humanity of Jesus (cf. *Life of Jesus*): although he rejects all the miracles of the Gospel and joins the chorus of nineteenth century in debunking anything of the supernatural, Renan, nevertheless, unconsciously became the creator of the constant 'Miracle' that is

Jesus, to whom the last words of his *Life* sound like a profession of lyrical faith; cf. Introduction to *Vita di Gesù*, (Ital. tr.) Biblioteca Universale Rizzoli, Milano, 1992, pp. 18f.

13 Referring to the distinction which became fashionable since Bultmann, Pope John Paul II says (RM 6; [ET] CTS DO 601, p. 6): 'One cannot separate Jesus from Christ or speak of a "Jesus of history" who would differ from the "Christ of faith". The Church acknowledges and confesses Jesus as "the Christ, the Son of the living God" (Mt 16:16): Christ is none other than Jesus of Nazareth; he is the Word of God made man for the salvation of all.' Cf. Xavier Léon-Dufour, *The Gospels and the Jesus of History*, Collins Fontana, 1971. Cf. also Cornelius Ernst's essay, 'A theological critique of experience' in *Multiple Echo*, DLT, London, 1979, p. 56.

14 Sokolowski points out the value of this approach as a useful and corrective tool for entering into dialogue with modernity and for overcoming its excesses; cf. op. cit., pp. 8–10; 129–30; 179–82. This approach is well illustrated in the copious writings of Hans Urs von Balthasar.

15 Pope John Paul II frequently employs this meditative or contemplative approach to the reality of Jesus Christ, to whom he calls all to turn their gaze; cf. RH 10. This is the constant theme of Pope John Paul II's teaching, which John Saward has presented in *Christ is the Answer*, op. cit.

16 Cf. Cornelius Ernst, 'Theological methodology' in *Multiple Echo*, op. cit., p. 77.

17 Cf. *The Rule of St Augustine*, 2 (ET) DLT, London, 1984, p. 11.

18 *Serm. in Ps. 147*, 28 (ET) ibid., p. 45. Cf. also *Serm. in Ps. 132*, 2 and 12.

19 Both the Western and Eastern traditions bear witness to this; e.g. cf. Shakespeare, *Sonnets* 27, 30, etc. or the Sufi mystic Fakhruddin Iraqi, *Divine Flashes*, V.1.

20 *Paedagogus*, I.7.51. Cf. Yves Congar, *The Revelation of God*, (ET) DLT, London/Herder & Herder, New York, 1968, pp. 94ff.

21 Cf. VS 17, where Pope John Paul II brings out very well that freedom is directly related to the divine law of dynamic growth in a deeper quality of human maturity.

22 LG 5; (ET slightly amended) Flannery, pp. 352f.

23 Cf. *The Way of Perfection*, ch. 30, 1–5.

24 As the Second Vatican Council says, citing the teaching of many Fathers of the Church; cf. *Ad Gentes* 7.

25 Cf. Tertullian, *De orat.*, 1; PL 1.1255.

26 *Called to Communion: Understanding the Church Today*, (ET) Ignatius Press, San Francisco, 1996, pp. 22f. The French modernist Loisy's statement referred to here was: 'Jesus proclaimed the Kingdom; what came was the Church.'

27 Cf. Xavier Léon-Dufour, *Sharing the Eucharistic Bread: The Witness of the New Testament*, (ET) Paulist Press, New York, 1987, pp. 77–8 and 336 n. 1. Cf. also, AA, *The Eucharist in the New Testament*, (ET) Geoffrey Chapman, London/Dublin, 1965; Edward J. Kilmartin, *The Eucharist in the Primitive Church*, Prentice-Hall Inc., Englewood Cliffs, NY, 1965.

28 Cf. Dom Gregory Dix, *The Shape of the Liturgy*, Dacre Press, Adam & Charles Black, London, 1970, p. 4: 'By the time the New Testament came to be written the eucharist already illumined everything concerning Jesus for His disciples – His Person, His Messianic office, His miracles, His death [fn. 18: The doctrine of sacrifice (and of atonement) was not read into the Last Supper; it was read out of it] and the redemption that He brought. It was the vehicle of the gift of His Spirit, the means of eternal life, the cause of the unity of His church.'

29 Ratzinger, *Called to Communion*, op. cit., p. 29.

30 LG 3: 'Ecclesia, seu regnum Christi iam praesens in mysterio, ex virtute Dei in mundo visibiliter crescit.' Cf. also GS 39.

31 Cf. SRS 48. Cf. GS 39.

32 Raymond Moloney SJ, *The Eucharist*, Geoffrey Chapman, London, 1995, p. 16.

33 Cf. Ratzinger, *Called to Communion*, op. cit., p. 19, regarding the important principle of tradition for interpreting the scriptures in the light of the Church's liturgical memory. Cf. also Pope John Paul II, *Orientale Lumen* (2 May 1995), 8; (ET) Libreria Editrice Vaticana, p. 15: 'Today we often feel ourselves prisoners of the present. It is as though man had lost his perception of belonging to a history which precedes and follows him. This effort to situate oneself between the past and the future, with a grateful heart for the benefits received and for those expected, is offered by the Eastern Churches in particular, with a clear-cut sense of continuity which takes the name of Tradition and of eschatological expectation. *Tradition is the Heritage of Christ's Church.* This is a living memory of the Risen One met and witnessed to by the Apostles who passed on his living memory to their successors in an uninterrupted line . . .'.

34 Cf. especially C.H. Dodd cited above in note 1. Dodd points out (cf. op. cit., pp. 151f. fn., 3) that the significance of the Eucharist as 'realised eschatology', though not absent from the Western eucharistic prayers, appears most clearly in the divine liturgy of the Eastern Rite.

35 Tillard refers to the vast literature on this point; e.g. O. Cullmann,
   Early Christian Worship, (ET), SCM Press, London, 1953, pp.
   12–26; J. Daniélou, 'Les repas de la Bible et leur signification', *La
   Maison Dieu* [*MD*], 18, 1949, pp. 7–33; C. Perrot, 'Le Repas du
   Seigneur', *MD*, 123, 1975, pp. 29–46; H. Cazelles, 'Eucharistie,
   bénédiction et sacrifice dans l'Ancien Testament', ibid., pp.
   7–28.

36 *The Eucharistic Words of Jesus*, London, 1966, p. 253. (Tillard's note.)

37 J.M.R. Tillard, 'The Eucharist, gift of God', *Ecumenical Perspectives
   on Baptism, Eucharist and Ministry*, ed. Max Thurian, Faith and
   Order Paper 116, World Council of Churches, Geneva, 1983 (third
   printing 1985), p. 109.

38 Cf. *The Outline of History*, quoted in *Words for Worship*, Edward
   Arnold (Publishers) Ltd, London, 1977, n. 618. Wells presents an
   all-too-idealist picture of Jesus, one which may perhaps reflect the
   ideology of Marx, but certainly not the realism of the perspective
   in the Gospels or faith of the Church.

39 In the Synoptic Gospels, 'kingdom of God' is synonymous with
   'kingdom of heaven' and with 'eternal life' in the Fourth Gospel
   cf. Dodd, op. cit., pp. 29ff. This scholar says that to regard the
   parables as presenting 'eminently sound moral and religious
   principles' would produce a flattening effect; cf. ibid., pp. 22f.

40 Cf. John Burnaby, *Amor Dei: A Study of the Religion of St Augustine*,
   (The Hulsean Lectures for 1938), the Canterbury Press, Norwich,
   1991, pp. 228; 238f.

41 Cf. Mazza, op. cit., p. 101; Col. 1:13 in EP II. Cf. the Preface of the
   Solemnity of Christ the King – *Roman Missal*, Pr. 51.

42 Cf. Augustinus Merk SJ (ed.), *Novum Testamentum* (Graece et
   Latine), Pont. Instit. Bibl., Rome, 1957, p. 108 – where reference is
   made to these parallel passages. Cf. also Burton H. Throckmorton,
   Jr (ed.), *Gospel Parallels: A Synopsis of the First Three Gospels*, Thomas
   Nelson Inc., Publishers, Nashville/New York, 1979, pp. 189ff.

43 This christological and ecclesiological dimension of the Blessed
   Virgin Mary's crucial and vital role in the history of salvation was
   brought out in the last chapter of the Second Vatican Council's
   teaching on the Church; cf. LG, ch. 8.

44 Cf. RM, 20.

45 Cf. Pope Paul VI, *Discourse* (21 November 1964): AAS 56 (1964)
   1015 cited by Pope John Paul II in RM 47. Cf. also Paul VI, *Credo of
   the People of God*: 'We believe that the Most Holy Mother of God,
   the new Eve, the Mother of the Church, carries on in heaven her
   maternal role with regard to the members of the Church, co-
   operating in the birth and development of divine life in the souls
   of the redeemed.' Pope Paul VI, *Solemn Profession of Faith* (30 June
   1968), 15; AAS 60 (1968) 438f.

46 St Francis of Assisi cites Mt 28:20 in a eucharistic sense; cf. David Power, *The Eucharistic Mystery*, Gill & Macmillan, Dublin, 1992, p. 201. Later in the same century, in 1264, Pope Urban IV does the same in the Bull *Transiturus* proclaiming the Feast of *Corpus Christi* (cf. DS 846); cf. James T. O'Connor, *The Hidden Manna: A Theology of the Eucharist*, Ignatius Press, San Francisco, 1988, pp. 192–6, where the whole text is translated from Mansi, 28, pp. 484–9. **NB** This may be the first use of the term 'Real Presence' regarding the Eucharist – a use which became common afterwards.

47 Joseph Ratzinger, *In the Beginning: A Catholic Understanding of the Story of Creation and the Fall*, (ET) T&T Clark, Edinburgh, 1995, p. 28.

48 Cf. PDV 1 where Pope John Paul II sees an intrinsic link between the Lord Jesus' command to go to the ends of the earth and make disciples (cf. Mt 28:19) and his instruction at the Last Supper: 'Do this in remembrance of me' (Lk 22:19; cf. 1 Cor. 11:24). Indeed, the mystery of faith requires that basic 'obedience of faith' to which the apostle Paul calls his converts (cf. Rom. 1:5; 15:18; 16:26). This obedience to the mystery of Christ is what St Irenaeus of Lyons in the second century called the essential 'Rule of Faith', which characterises Christ's faithful in the Church.

49 Cf. LG 1, 9, 48, 52; AG 1, 5; PO 22; GS 45.

50 Cf. SC 7; cf. also Pope Paul VI, Encyclical Letter, *Mysterium Fidei* (3 September 1965), AAS 57 (1965), pp. 762ff.; Pope John Paul II, Apostolic Letter on the 25th Anniversary of the Promulgation of the Conciliar Constitution *Sacrosanctum Concilium* (4 December 1988) 7.

51 Cf. *Modern Concordance to the New Testament*, (ET) DLT, London, 1976, p. 163.

52 Cf. Lk 17:21: the kingdom is in your midst/among you/within (the Greek word *entos* can mean any of these). Cf. G.B. Caird, *The Gospel of St Luke*, Penguin (Pelican New Testament Commentaries), 1981, pp. 37; 197.

53 Ibid., p. 35.

54 It is interesting to note that whereas the word used for 'visitation' (*epi-skeptomai*) occurs only a few times in the New Testament, the words for Jesus' coming/entering/going into (*erchomai/eis-erchomai*) are very frequently employed; cf. ibid., pp. 161ff.

55 Cf. *TMA*, 9ff.; (ET) Libreria Editrice Vaticana, pp. 13ff.

56 These words have been emphasised as thematic in the preparations for the Jubilee Year of 2000; cf. TMA 11, 40, cited in the Basic Text of the IEC in Wroclaw, Poland (1997), 3.

57 Cf. Lk 4:20: gazing (*ateinízontes*); 4:22: marvelled / amazed (*ethaūmazon*). Cf. Mk 6:2: astonished / astounded / amazed

(*explēssonto*), where the Greek verb here literally means: were struck by something great and unexpected. The same verb is used to describe the reaction of Mary and Joseph on finding Jesus in the temple – sheer stupefaction (cf. Lk 2:48).

58 Cf. C.M. Martini SJ, *La Gioia del Vangelo: Meditazioni ai giovani*, Edizioni Piemme (Centro Ambrosiano), Milano, 1988, pp. 98f.

59 Cf. Mazza, op. cit., p. 328.

60 Cf. *Modern Concordance to the New Testament*, op. cit., p. 511.

61 Cf. Sermon 74, 2–3. Cf. also *Tractatus* 63 (*De passione Domini* 12), 6; CCL 138/A, 386 – quoted by Pope John Paul II in his post-synodal exhortation, *Reconciliatio et Paenitentia*, n. 8; (ET) in CTS DO 562, p. 28: 'everything that the Son of God did and taught for the reconciliation of the world we know not only from the history of his past actions but we experience it also in the effectiveness of what he accomplishes in the present'.

62 *Apol. Prophetae David*, 12.58.

CHAPTER 3

1 The incident of Jesus' scribbling in the sand when encountering a woman taken in adultery in the Gospel as we have it (Jn 7:53–8:11) is considered as a later interpolation. Some ancient authorities insert it either at the end of the Fourth Gospel or after Lk 21:38; others omit it altogether. [Note in the RSV.]

2 Sonnet 23.

3 *Ethics*, (ET) SCM Press, 1971, p. 14.

4 Cf. J. Daniélou, *The Bible and the Liturgy*, (ET) DLT, London, 1964, pp. 179ff., 183ff.; re. mystical experience rooted in the Eucharist as its effect; cf. ibid., p. 186. The distinction between 'author' and 'compiler' or 'redactor' of this Gospel is an important one. For, while the disciple John is recognised as the author of its overall teaching and approach, which results from his apostolic preaching, it is quite possible and perhaps even probable, that this material was written down and given literary shape by another, that is, by a member of the Johannine community. Although some scholars have continued to debate about the authorship of this Gospel, the weight of evidence favours the tradition which attributes it to the disciple John. Apart from the internal evidence, which points to it being the work of an eye-witness, many indications can be found in the writings of the earliest Fathers (such as Clement of Rome and Ignatius of Antioch at the end of the first century and beginning of the second) to support this claim of Johannine authorship. The first explicit reference is found in

Irenaeus of Lyons (c. 180), *Adv. Haer.*, III.2.2; 3.4: 'Last of all also John himself, the disciple of the Lord who reclined on his breast, brought out a gospel while he was at Ephesus.'

5 This has been argued and shown beyond any doubt in Ignace de la Potterie's magistral study: cf. *La Vérité dans Saint Jean*, 2 Vols, (AnBib 73–4), Biblical Institute, Rome, 1977.

6 Cf. ibid., I, p. 272.

7 Cf. Herman Servotte, *According to John: A Literary Reading of the Fourth Gospel*, (ET) DLT, 1994, p. 89: 'Texts are inexhaustible. Unchanging though they are in the materiality of the printed signs, they keep changing in their meaning. Great religious and secular texts always seem to contain more meanings than their interpreters had imagined; and their interpretations are never final or definitive. They are indeed approached with new questions, related to new issues, framed by a new context and projected against a new horizon of understanding; and that changes them. Moreover, what T.S. Eliot said about the work of art which takes its place among already existing works and thereby changes their relative position, is also valid for texts. And that explains why commentaries continue to be written, even if their writers are aware of their necessarily provisional character.'

8 Cf. *Mysterium Fidei*, 67.

9 The title of 'theologian' or 'divine' was almost accidently bestowed on John. It crept in, as it were, from a marginal gloss a copyist added to the book of Revelation in the fourth century. The appropriateness of this title was readily accepted.

10 Cf. De la Potterie, *The Hour of Jesus: The Passion and the Resurrection of Jesus According to John: Text and Spirit*, (ET) St Paul Publications, Slough (England), 1989, p. 11; cf. ibid., p. 74. Cf. also, *La Vérité dans Saint Jean*, t.I, op. cit., pp. 2ff. Cf. also John Saward who comments on Balthasar's teaching, *The Mysteries of March*, op. cit., pp. 34f.: '"No one has ever seen God", says St John, "the only Son, who is in the bosom of the Father, he has made him known" (John 1:18). The Greek word here translated as "to make known" means "to expound, to explain, to reveal". It is the verb from which the noun "exegesis" is derived. So what St John is saying here, in Balthasar's view, is that the Only-Begotten has become man to reveal his Father, to be his *Exegete*. ... The paradoxical eloquence of the silent Word particularly haunts Balthasar's imagination. Like the Fathers before him, he is stunned by the Christmas mystery of a *Verbum infans*, the divine Word who has become *in-fans*, a baby who cannot speak. The Word is made flesh at the moment of his conception in the Virgin's womb, and so his revealing work begins in the hiddenness and silence of his Mother's body.'

11 Eugene H. Peterson, *Reversed Thunder: The Revelation of John and the Praying Imagination*, Harper Paperback, San Francisco, 1991, p. 3.

12 Cf. D. Mollat, 'The sixth chapter of Saint John' in *The Eucharist in the New Testament*, op. cit., p. 152.

13 Cf. Raymond E. Brown, *The Community of the Beloved Disciple*, Geoffrey Chapman, London, 1979.

14 The classic treatment of this is by O. Cullmann, *Early Christian Worship*, (ET) SCM, London, 1953. Tad Guzie in *Jesus and the Eucharist*, Gracewing/Fowler Wright Books, Herts., 1995 (rev. ed.), p. 159 fn. 2 states that though Cullmann has been criticised for pushing Johannine 'sacramental' symbolism too hard, his study nonetheless calls attention to symbolic elements that cannot be overlooked in the Gospel as it stands.

15 Cf. John Paul II's comment on the importance of this 'as' – VS 20.

16 Cf. *The Paradise Tree*, pp. 34ff. (note in text).

17 *The Eagle's Word*, Collins, London, 1961, pp. 90f. (Italics in text.)

18 Cf. Pope John Paul II, RM 20; 21, 28.

19 *In Joh. Ev.*, Tr. 17.8; (ET) DO I, op. cit., p. 274.

20 'The socius and the neighbour' in *History and Truth*, (ET) Northwestern University Press, Evanston, 1965, p. 99.

21 Cf. ibid., p. 109.

22 This translation follows the Latin of Jerome's Vulgate: *Verbum erat apud Deum*, rather than the Greek text.

23 Joseph Ratzinger, 'On the theological basis of prayer and liturgy' in *The Feast of Faith*, (ET) Ignatius Press, San Francisco, 1986, p. 25.

24 In Matthew's version it is not the 'sons of Zebedee' but their mother who makes the audacious request.

25 Cf. St John Chrysostom, *Hom.* 50, 3–4; (ET) DO, III, op. cit., pp. 480f.: 'Would you honour the body of Christ? Do not despise his nakedness; do not honour him here in church clothed in silk vestments and then pass him by unclothed and frozen outside. Remember that he who said, "This is my body", and made good his words, also said, "You saw me hungry and gave me no food", and, "in so far as you did it not to one of these, you did it not to me". In the first sense the body of Christ does not need clothing but worship from a pure heart. In the second sense it does need clothing and all the care we can give it.'

26 Cf. Tertullian, *Apol.*, 15.8; CCL 1.114. This description goes back to Irenaeus and the *Ep. to Diog.*, which is cited by de la Potterie, *La Vérité dans Saint Jean*, t.II, op. cit., p. 1026–36. Later, Gregory the Great also uses this expression; cf. ibid., p. 1035. Disciples were characterised as living according to 'the rule of [the] truth'; cf.

Irenaeus (ibid., p. 1028); Tertullian (ibid., p. 1030); and Gregory the Great, taking up a theme so dear to John, speaks of interiorising this 'rule of truth' (ibid., p. 1035).

27 Cf. Antonio Donghi, 'Il discepolo è memoria vivente di Cristo' in *La Nuova Alleanza*, Aprile 1995, n. 3, pp. 132–7.

28 This section presents a summary of de la Potterie's exegesis: cf. *La Vérité dans Saint Jean*, t.II, op. cit., pp. 789ff.; 816ff.; 857f.

29 Though Søren Kierkegaard would in no way deny this, the approach he takes would seem to be predominantly psychological; cf. e.g. *The Concept of Anxiety: A Simple Psychologically Orienting Deliberation on the Dogmatic Issue of Hereditary Sin*, (ET) Princeton University Press, Princeton, New Jersey, 1980, pp. 138f.

30 This annual agricultural festival took on the significance of being a solemn commemoration of the period of dwelling in tents in anticipation of the messianic and eschatological time of being liberated in the final kingdom of God. The festival therefore was both an evocation of the past and a promise of the future.

31 Mollat points out that the last part of the discourse on 'the Bread of Life' is more and more accepted by scholars as referring to the eucharistic sacrament, even by those who, like Bultmann, question or deny that it was spoken by Jesus; cf. 'The sixth chapter of Saint John' in *The Eucharist in the New Testament*, op. cit., pp. 143ff.

32 The formula 'Amen, amen I say to you' occurs no less than twenty-five times in John; cf. Jn 1:51; 3:3, 5, 11; 5:19, 24, 25; 6:26, 32, 47–53; 8:34, 51, 58; 10:1, 7; 12:24; 13:16, 20, 21, 38; 14:12; 16:20, 23; 21:18. The Synoptics have the single 'amen' emphasising Jesus' important utterances – in Matthew, no less than thirty-one times. It is unique to this Gospel with the repeated 'amen'. It is always employed only by Jesus and has the solemn tone that is almost prophetic, giving his words an emphatic quality challenging those who hear him to pay strict attention and change their attitudes. According to Francis Moloney, *A Body Broken for a Broken People*, Collins, Dove, Melbourne, Australia, 1990, p. 84: 'It appears in 13:1–38 more times (four uses) than in any other chapter of the whole Gospel, and it appears only three more times in the Last Discourse (14:12; 16:20, 23).'

33 Cf. Mollat, l.c., pp. 151f.

34 Cf. Mollat, l.c., p. 146. The Second Vatican Council, following Fathers of the Church, refers to the rich symbolism of this 'sign' of the Christian sacraments of baptism and Eucharist; cf. SC 5; LG 3; cf. Augustine, *Enarr. in Ps*, 138, 2. Cf. also, John Chrysostom, *Catecheses* 3.13–19; S.C. 50, 174–7; Office of Readings for Good Friday, DO II, op. cit., pp. 297f.

35 Cf. Virgil, *Eclogues*, 2.65: 'trahit sua quemque voluptas'.

36 *In Joh. Ev.*, Tr.26.4.(ET) DO III, op. cit., pp. 649f. (revised).

37 The occurrence of this statement here is found in 8:12, 18, 23, 24, 28, 58; 10:7, 9, 11, 14. It is absent from chapters 1–3; six times in chapters 4–6; six times in chapters 11–15; and three times in chapter 18. 'Christ' (excluding mention in the Prologue and conclusion, 1:17 and 20:31) occurs seventeen times in the Fourth Gospel, of which eight are in this section: 7:26, 27, 31, 41 (twice), 42; 9:22; 10:24.

38 JBC, op. cit., #78:58; p. 777. Cf. C.H. Dodd, *The Interpretation of the Fourth Gospel*, CUP, Cambridge, 1968, pp. 93ff., 417; also Gerald Vann, *The Eagle's Word*, op. cit., pp. 33f.

39 Cf. *La Vérité dans Saint Jean*, op. cit., t.II, pp. 820f.

40 **NB** 'from sin' later addition of the tradition of the Fathers, who thus interprets the blindness of people which is illumined by Christ, the true light (cf. 9:39–41).

41 Cf. St Augustine: *Sermo. de Symbolo*, 1; *Serm. 144*, 2.2; *In Joh. Ev.*, Trs. 25.12; 29.7.6; *Enarr. in Ps. 77*, 8; *En. in Ps. 130*, 1, etc. Cf. Christine Mohrmann, *Études sur le Latin des Chrétiens*, t.I, Edizioni di Storia e Letteratura, Roma, 1961, pp. 195ff.: 'Credere in Deum. Sur l'interpretation théologique d'un fait de langue'.

42 Cf. *Cat. 5*, 10–11; PG 33.518–19.

43 Cf. Paul McPartlan, *The Eucharist Makes the Church*, op. cit., pp. 244f.; reference given to de Lubac on the trinitarian aspect of faith in Augustine in *Christian Faith* (Geoffrey Chapman, London, 1986, pp. 67, 70, 189).

44 Walter J. Ong SJ, 'Voice as summons for belief: literature, faith, and the divided self' in *Literature & Religion*, (ed. Giles B. Gunn), SCM Ltd, London, 1971, p. 75. Ong's analysis of faith from a literary point of view borrows from the phenomenological approach of Gabriel Marcel's *The Mystery of Being*.

45 Cf. RH 10; (ET) CTS DO 506 (revised): 'Man cannot live without love. He remains a being that is incomprehensible to himself, his life is senseless, if love is not revealed to him, if he does not encounter love, if he does not experience it and make it his own, if he does not participate intimately in it.'

46 Cf. John Saward, *The Mysteries of March*, op. cit., pp. 3–17.

47 'The Samaritan Woman' in *The Place Within*, op. cit., p. 35.

CHAPTER 4

1 See the excellent treatment of Christians' relation to the State by Jaroslav Pelikan, *Jesus through the Centuries: His Place in the History of Culture*, Yale University Press, New Haven and London, 1985, esp. Chapter 4: 'The King of Kings', pp. 46–56. Cf. also W.H.C. Frend in *Martyrdom and Persecution in the Early Church: A Study of a Conflict from the Maccabees to Donatus*, Blackwell, Oxford, 1965.

2 Cf. Justin, *Apol. I*, 5–6, and 16. In another place he extols the peace-loving quality of life that followed conversion to Christianity; cf. *Dial. with Trypho the Jew*, 110, 3–4. The philosopher Galen was the first pagan to recognise the value of Justin and his school in bearing positive fruit, unlike the priests of the traditional mystery religions and inane ritual cults; cf. J. Stevenson, *A New Eusebius: Documents Illustrating the History of the Church to AD 337*, SPCK, London, 1993, pp. 136f.

3 Cf. Rom. 13:1–2; 1 Tim. 2:2; referred to in CCC 2238, 2240 on the duties of citizens.

4 Cf. *Ad Diogn.*, 5–6; Funk 397–401 given as the second reading for Wednesday of Week 5 in Eastertide, DO II, op. cit., pp. 590f. as a spiritual commentary on Rev. 21:1–8 regarding the vision of the new Jerusalem.

5 *On Idolatry*, 15; cf. Mt 22:21.

6 Cf. Tacitus *Annals*, XV.44.2–8. Tacitus, as governor of the Asia (c. 112), had many dealings with denounced Christians, whom he regarded as 'scum' for their apparent disinterest in this world and its affairs. His opinion is an important witness regarding Nero's scape-goating of Christians to avert the report circulated about his own burning of Rome. Cf. Stevenson, *A New Eusebius*, op. cit., pp. 2–3.

7 Cf. Pliny, *Ep. X.* 96. This letter bears witness to the separation by this time of the more social gathering of Christians for an *agapē* meal in the evening from the Eucharist as such, which was celebrated in the early morning (before dawn) – because Christians had to go to work! Cf. Stevenson, op. cit., pp. 18f.

8 Cf. Vat. II, Declaration on the Relationship of the Church to Non-Christian Religions, *Nostra Aetate* (28 October 1965), 4. Professor Pelikan regards this declaration as more significant than the report published in 1932 by the Commission representing seven American Protestant denominations, *Re-thinking Missions: A Layman's Inquiry After One Hundred Years*. Cf. Pelikan, *Jesus through the Centuries*, Yale University Press, New Haven/London, 1985, pp. 228ff.

9 This accusation against the Jews of 'deicide' became taken up as part of the standard Christian apologetic – as in Stephen's lengthy defence reported in Acts 7:51ff. In the light of this apologetic we must regard Paul's use of this argument; cf. 1 Thess. 2:14f.

10 *The Crucifixion and the Jews,* read on 20 March 1966 at Our Lady of Sion, London, published by the Centre for Biblical and Jewish Studies, London, pp. 22f.

11 Cf. C.H. Dodd, *The Epistle of Paul to the Romans,* Collins/Fontana, 1960, pp. 25–8.

12 Cf. Gal. 1:11–24; Acts 7:58—8:1; 9:1–30.

13 Cf. A.D. Nock, *Conversion,* OUP Paperback, 1969 (rev. ed.).

14 Jesus' criticism of the Pharisees is thought to be strictly speaking an anachronism of the redactors of the original oral tradition, which is better represented in the passion narratives. The real opponents to Jesus were the chief priests and Sadducees. Cf. Hubert Richards' paper, referred to above in Note 10. Cf. also, M. Kelly and C. Klein, *The Primitive Church and its Break with the Synagogue,* The Study Centre for Christian Jewish Relations, London, 1974.

15 Cf. Max Scheler, *On Feeling, Knowing, and Valuing,* The University of Chicago Press, Chicago and London, 1992, pp. 156f.: 'The beginning as well as the end of all religious knowledge and healing processes lie, therefore, in God. The Indian–Greek notion of self-salvation through knowledge is replaced by the idea of *becoming* redeemed through divine love.'

16 Cf. Raymond Brown, *The Semitic Background of the Term 'Mystery' in the New Testament,* Facet Books, Fortress Press, Philadelphia, 1968, pp. 38f.

17 CCC 385.

18 Cf. *Confessions,* VII.xxi.27, where the great Doctor of divine grace says that even the highest sources of human wisdom, such as the writings of the Platonists, do not offer relief or consolation such as found in the scriptures, which reveal the remedy of Christ's sacrifice shared in 'the cup of our redemption'. At the end of the tenth book of the *Confessions* he says (X.xliii.70; [ET] Chadwick, *Confessions,* OUP Paperback, 1992, p. 220): 'I think upon the price of my redemption, and I eat and drink it, and distribute it. In my poverty I desire to be satisfied from it together with those who "eat and are satisfied" (Ps. 61:5). "And they shall praise the Lord who seek him" (Ps. 21:27).'

19 Cf. Anthony Storr's chapter on this theme in *Solitude,* Flamingo/Fontana Paperback, London, 1989, pp. 145ff.

20 'The Poison of Subjectivism' in *Christian Reflections,* op. cit., p. 106. Cf. also Sebastian Moore's interpretation of this much discussed dilemma at the depths of our awareness: *The Inner Loneliness,* The Crossroad Publishing Co., New York, 1982, p. 48.

21 Quite possibly Augustine's reading of Paul was guided and influenced by St Ambrose, who himself seems to have owed much to

Origen, with whose writing he was acquainted. Cf. Origen, *De principiis*, Praef., 5; I.5, 2; II.5–6.

22 Cf. *Confessions* VII.21.27. Cf. GS 13 (cited in CCC 1707). A great deal may be learnt by the perceptive insights of psychologists about the dividedness of human personality in behavioural disorganisation, disintegration, etc. which are rooted in fear.

23 E.G., cf. *Confessions*, X.30.

24 *Jesus through the Centuries*, op. cit., p. 80.

25 Cf. Augustine's commentary on Jesus' freedom *In Joh. Ev.*, Tr.47.11–13; *En. in Ps. 89.* 37.

26 Cf. David Jones, 'An introduction to *The Rime of the Ancient Mariner*' in *The Dying Gaul and Other Writings* (ed. Harman Grisewood), Faber & Faber, 1978, p. 197 fn. 5. Cf. also Gerald Vann's superb Aquinas Paper, 'The Sorrow of God', published with six Lenten sermons preached at Westminster Cathedral in 1947 in *The Pain of Christ and the Sorrow of God*, Blackfriars, London, 1954 (4th ed.).

27 'Qui fecit te sine te, non te iustificat sine te.' *Serm. 169, 13*, cited by John Burnaby in his fine treatment of Augustine's doctrine on grace and freedom: *Amor Dei*, op. cit., p. 228.

28 *Confessions*, X.29 (40). Since a similar idea is expressed in other places of his writings and preaching there can be little doubt that this prayer characterises Augustine's spirituality; cf. e.g. *Enarr. in Ps. 118*, 41; Serm. XII.5. The influence of this famous line is evident in Pascal; cf. *Pensées*, 767 [Brunschvicg 522]; (ET) Everyman: J.M. Dent, London/E.P. Dutton, New York, 1960, p. 215: 'The Law required what it did not give. Grace gives what it requires.'

29 *Confessions*, OUP (Word Classics Pb.), Oxford/New York, 1992, p. 202 fn.27.

30 Dr Eamon Duffy severely castigates the ICEL translators for playing down or omitting references to grace; cf. 'The stripping of the liturgy', *The Tablet*, 6 July 1996, pp. 882f.

31 Cf. *On the Creed*, 9; also, *In Joh. Tr.* 26.13.

32 Cf. *Augustine of Hippo: A Biography*, Faber, London, 1969, pp. 373f.

33 Cf. C.F.D. Moule, *Worship in the New Testament* (Part II), Grove Books (n. 13), Bramcote, Notts., pp. 62ff. Cf. also Rudolf Schnackenburg, *The Moral Teaching of the New Testament*, (ET) Burns & Oates, London, 1975, p. 229.

34 'The word "grace" (*charis*) as it is used here emphasises not so much the interior gift that makes a human being holy, as the gratuitousness of God's favour and the way he manifests his glory, cf. Ex. 24:16f. These are the two themes that run through this account of God's blessings: their *source* is God's liberality, and their

purpose is to make his glory appreciated by creatures. Everything comes from him, and everything should lead to him.' (Note in JB.) Cf. also Rom. 3:24; 8:28ff.

35 Whether by Paul or one of his close followers; cf. Carol L. Stockhausen, *Letters in the Pauline Tradition*, Michael Glazier, Wilmington, Delaware, 1989, pp. 20ff.

36 The phrase in italics is given in some ancient manuscripts.

37 This is expressed by the Greek aorist verbal form: 'have been created'. For the patristic interpretation of this text see the note-worthy study by Raniero Cantalamessa, 'Cristo immagine di Dio: le tradizioni patristiche su Colossesi 1, 15' in *Rivista di storia e letteratura religiosa*, 16 (1980), pp. 181–92.

38 Indeed, so far as I can trace it, it occurs only twice in the New Testament as referring to God properly speaking. Both occurrences are in the corpus of the Pauline letters: Col. 1:15: 'He [the beloved Son] is the image of the invisible [*tou aorátou*] God . . .'; and 1 Tim. 1:17: 'To the King of the ages, immortal, invisible [*aoratōi*], the only God, be honour . . .'. In this latter case the adjective strictly speaking applies to Christ.

39 Cf. e.g. Plato, *Parmenides* 132d.

40 Cf. Paul Ricoeur, 'The image of God and the epic of man' in *History and Truth*, Northwestern University Press, Evanston, Illinois, 1965, pp. 110–28.

41 Ibid., p. 121.

42 In exploring the situation of humanity in terms of having (*avoir*), power (*pouvoir*) and value (*valoir*), Ricoeur (l.c., p. 114) sought to recover, or rather, to reinterpret the Fathers' understanding of the work of redemption as 'the divine pedagogy working within the economic, political, and cultural spheres, strengthening individual attitudes and the life of groups with their structures and institutions'.

43 *The Epistle of Paul to the Romans*, op. cit., p. 196.

44 *Paidagōgos*, II.4.43.

45 Cf. *Paidagōgos*, II.2.29. This passage is recognised as textually difficult from the point of view of syntax, etc. Clement seems to be trying to combine many images about the lukewarmness of the old law and fervour of the new word being mixed in the blood of the vine, who is Christ.

46 St Ignatius of Antioch also seems to cite verses which may have formed part of hymns either addressed to or about Christ, e.g. cf. *Eph.*, 7; (ET) *Early Christian Writings*, Penguin, 1968, pp. 77f.: 'Very Flesh, yet Spirit too; / Uncreated, and yet born; / God-and-Man in One agreed, / Very-Life-in-Death indeed, / Fruit of God and Mary's seed; / At once impassible and torn / By pain and suffering here below:/ Jesus Christ, whom as our Lord we know.'

47 Cf. Joseph Jungmann, *The Place of Christ in Liturgical Prayer* (ET) Geoffrey Chapman, London, 1965.

48 Cf. Gawronski, op. cit., p. 149.

49 *Worship in the New Testament*, op. cit., p. 66.

50 Ibid., p. 71.

51 Cf. Thomas Lane CM, *A Priesthood in Tune: Theological Reflections on Ministry*, The Columba Press, Dublin, 1993, pp. 58ff.

52 *The Feast of Faith*, op. cit., pp. 26f.

53 Cf. Ernest Lussier SSS, *Jesus Christ is Lord: Adoration Viewed through the New Testament*, Alba House, Staten Island, New York, 1979, p. 148.

54 Cf. Hans Urs von Balthasar, Preface to *Heart of the World*, op. cit., pp. 13f.

55 Cf. CCC nn 1741–2.

56 Cf. David Jones, l.c., p. 190: 'What is pleaded in the Mass is precisely the argosy or voyage of the Redeemer, his entire sufferings, death, resurrection and ascension. It is this that is offered on behalf of us argonauts and the whole argosy of mankind and indeed in some sense of all earthly creation, which, as Paul says, suffers a common travail.' In this splendid essay, Jones points to Coleridge's faultless theology in so far as in his poem 'The rime of the ancient mariner' appreciates that 'the prayer of praise far excels that of petition' (ibid., p. 193).

57 Cf. *Adv. Haer.*, I.10.1; III.16.6. Cf. Henry Bettensen, *The Early Christian Fathers*, OUP Paperback, 1969, p. 81 n. 2: the Greek verb *anakephalaioō* occurs twice in the New Testament.

58 CCC 1327 citing *Adv. Haer.*, IV.18.5; PG 7/1, 1028. Cf. BT II.3.15.

59 Cf. G. Theissen, 'Social integration and sacramental activity: an analysis of 1 Cor. 11:17–34' in *The Social Setting of Pauline Christianity: Essays on Corinth*, Fortress Press, Philadelphia, 1982, pp. 145–74. Cf. also Dale B. Martin, *The Corinthian Body*, Yale University Press, 1995. This book tends to distort the Christian message by reducing it to a sociological interpretation of ideological attitudes pertaining to the ancient Graeco-Roman world.

60 Cf. Austin Farrer, 'The eucharist in 1 Corinthians' in *Eucharistic Theology Then and Now*, SPCK, London, 1968, pp. 15–33.

61 Cf. e.g. A. Piolanti, *The Holy Eucharist*, Desclée, New York, 1961, pp. 45f.; also, P. Benoit, 'The accounts of the institution and what they imply' in *The Eucharist in the New Testament*, op. cit., pp. 130f. J. Murphy-O'Connor suggests that this traditional Catholic position stems from preoccupation with the doctrine of the real presence, which was not Paul's; cf. *1 Corinthians*, New Testament Message 10, Michael Glazier, Wilmington, 1979, p. 114.

62 Cf. C.K. Barrett, *The First Epistle to the Corinthians*, Black's New Testament Commentaries, A & C Black, London, 1971, pp. 273ff.; also G. Bornkamm, 'Lord's Supper and Church in Paul' in *Early Christian Experience*, SCM Press, London, 1969, pp. 148ff.

63 Moloney, *A Body Broken for a Broken People*, op. cit., pp. 116f.

64 This has been also pointed out by Père M.E. Boismard OP, cf. 'The Eucharist according to Saint Paul' in *The Eucharist in the New Testament*, op. cit., pp. 137f.

65 It is interesting to note that the echo of this pair of verbs is heard in those employed in the Synoptics' institution narrative of the Eucharist at the Lord's Last Supper: Mt 26:26–8; Mk 14:22–4; Lk 22:17–19: *lábete . . . 'édoken* (take . . . he gave).

66 Cf. CT 6 fn. 14 referring to Pope Paul VI's Apostolic Exhortation, *Evangelii Nuntiandi*, 4, 15, 78, 79.

67 *The Theology of Vatican II*, op. cit., p. 218.

68 Cf. CT 5.

69 BT 7. Cf. Pope John Paul II, Encyclical Letter, VS 84.

70 On the seminal contribution of Courtney Murray SJ, one of the great architects of this Declaration, cf. Donald Pelotte SSS, *John Courtney Murray: Theologian in Conflict*, Paulist Press, New York, 1975. See also David L. Schindler's treatment of the contribution of John Courtney Murray: *Heart of the World, Center of the Church: Communio Ecclesiology, Liberalism and Liberation*, William B. Eerdmans, Grand Rapids, Michigan/T&T Clark, Edinburgh, 1996, pp. 43–88.

71 In interpreting history in the light of Christ, Eusebius states something like Karl Rahner's notion of the 'anonymous Christian', viz. that human experience from its very beginnings teaches us of the existence of Christians 'in fact if not in name'; cf. *Hist. Eccl.*, I.4.6. Cf. also Tertullian, *Apol.*, 17: 'O testimonium *animae naturaliter Christianae*'.

72 Apropos the first commandment of the Decalogue, the Declaration is quoted in the *Catechism of the Catholic Church*, 2104–6, regarding the social duty of religion and the right to religious freedom.

73 *Faith and Freedom*, op. cit., p. 296.

74 However, Pelikan soberly reminds us (*Jesus through the Centuries*, op. cit., p. 222) that it would be 'an oversimplification to dismiss the missions as nothing more than a cloak for white imperialism'.

75 CCC 854.

76 Walter J. Ong SJ, 'Do we live in a post-Christian age?' in *America*, 3 February 1996, p. 17.

77 As Bishop Stephen Sykes clarifies in *The Identity of Christianity*, Fortress Press, Philadelphia, 1984, p. 214. He refers to the first known usage of the word by Ignatius of Antioch: cf. *Ep. to the*

Magn., 10. He quotes Gregory of Nyssa's succinct definition: '*Christianismos* is imitation (*mimesis*) of the divine nature'; cf. *De Profess. Christi*; (ET) *St Gregory of Nyssa Ascetical Works*, FC, Washington DC, 1967, Vol. 58, p. 85.

CHAPTER 5

1 Chapters 60 and 61 (tr. into modern English), Penguin, 1985, pp. 170, 171.

2 BT Introduction, 2: words in italics refer to Eucharistic Prayer IV.

3 'On the structure of the liturgical celebration' in *The Feast of Faith: Approaches to a Theology of the Liturgy*, (ET) Ignatius Press, San Francisco, 1986, pp. 63ff.

4 *Tractatus Logicus-Philosophicus*, 5.6 cited by Cornelius Ernst, 'Words, facts and God' in *Multiple Echo*, op. cit., p. 15.

5 *In Search of the Sacred*, Ignatius Press, San Francisco, 1991, pp. 125, 127.

6 Cf. SC 7: '*actio sacra praecellenter*'.

7 Cf. SC 10; LG 11; cf. also 17, 26; PO 5, 6, 14; UR 15. The liturgy is the *culmen et fons* not only when the Eucharist is celebrated, but also in other ways, especially during the liturgy of hours; cf. Gen. Instruction on the Liturgy of Hours, n.13; DO I, op. cit., p. xxvii.

8 This twofold sense is most clearly seen in PO 5.

9 Cf. CCC 1328–32. Cf. C.F.D. Moule, *Worship in the New Testament*, Grove Books, Bramcote, Notts., 1977, pp. 22f.; cf. also Michael Evans, 'Perspectives of the catechism on the Eucharist' in *Adoremus*, LXXV No. 1 (1995), pp. 6–15.

10 Cf. PO 5. The Council refers here to St Thomas Aquinas' teaching on this: ST III, q.73, a.3c: 'The Eucharist is indeed as if the consummation of the spiritual life, and the goal (*finis*) of all the sacraments' (cf. also ST III, q.65, a.3); ST III, q.65, a.3 ad 1; q.79, a.1c and ad 1.

11 SC 10.

12 *Roman Missal*, postcommunion of the Easter Vigil Mass.

13 Cf. ibid., opening prayer of Easter Tuesday.

14 LG 26; cf. *Serm.* 53, 7; PL 54 357 C. St Gregory the Great summed up the approach of the Fathers regarding the closest connection between liturgy and life: 'If the mystery of the Lord's passion is to

be effectual in us, we must imitate what we receive and proclaim to others what we venerate.' (*Com. in Job*, Bk 13, 21–3; PL 75, 1028–9; [ET] DO II, op. cit., p. 167.) Earlier St Augustine said that our 'Amen' to Christ's sacramental body of Christ implies acknowledging his presence also in one another, for the eucharistic sacrifice of the altar expresses our mystery (cf. *Serm.* 272). A similar idea is echoed in the admonition to the newly ordained priests to become what they handle; cf. *Pontificale Romanum. De Ordinatione Diaconi, Presbyteri et Episcopi*, ed. typica, 1968, p. 93; cited by Pope John Paul II, Letter on the Mystery and Worship of the Holy Eucharist *Dominicae Cenae* (24 February 1980), 11.

15 *Serm. 2 de Ascensione* 74, 3.

16 Cf. A. Hamman (ed.), *The Paschal Mystery: Ancient Liturgies and Patristic Texts* (tr. Thomas Halton), Alba House, Staten Island, NY, 1969, pp. 25ff. Cf. J.M. Tillard's excellent study: *The Eucharist Pasch of God's People*, (ET) Alba House, New York, 1967.

17 Apart from various sermons, clearly the most famous of Augustine's texts on this is his letter to Januarius: *Ep. 55.2*; PL 33, 205. Cf. Christine Mohrmann, *Études sur le Latin des Chrétiens*, op. cit., t. I, pp. 205–22. Raniero Cantalamessa has usefully described the somewhat complicated history in the Western approach to the meaning of *pascha*; cf. *Easter in the Early Church*, (ET) The Liturgical Press, Collegeville, Minnesota, 1993.

18 *Ep. 54.1*; PL 35.215.

19 *Sermo* 219; PL 38.1088.

20 *Sermo Guelferbytan.*, 5.4; PLS 2.552 cited in the Letter of the Congregation for Divine Worship on Celebrating Easter (16 January 1988): (ET) in CTS DO 580, p. 31.

21 Thus, for example, Paul Bernier SSS describes the pastoral task today by considering the implications of what he identifies as the five main rhythms in celebrating the eucharistic mystery: gathering, storytelling, prophesying, nurturing and missioning. Cf. *Eucharist: Celebrating its Rhythms in Our Lives*, Ave Maria, 1993.

22 Cf. Joseph Gelineau SJ, 'Le mouvement interne de la Prière Eucharistique' in *La Maison-Dieu*, 94 (1968), pp. 114–24. Cf. also Robert Sokolowski, 'Praying the Canon of the Mass' in *Homiletic and Pastoral Review*, July 1995, pp. 8–15. See also my attempt at providing a deepened catechesis of the Eucharistic Prayers in *Heart in Pilgrimage: Christian Spirituality in the Light of the Eucharistic Prayer*, Alba House, New York, 1994.

23 'On the structure of the liturgical celebration' in *The Feast of Faith*, op. cit., p. 65.

24 On the First Sunday of Advent (30 November 1969) following the promulgation of Pope Paul VI's Apostolic Constitution of 3 April 1969.

25 Cf. SC 21: 'both texts and rites should be drawn up so that they express more clearly the holy things they signify'. Cf. also ibid., 50, 51, 58.

26 Cf. GS 1 and 38–9.

27 'On the structure of the liturgical celebration' in *The Feast of Faith*, op. cit., pp. 69f.

28 EM 12 referring to SC 55.

29 Pope John Paul II reminds us that there are many among the 'unnumbered generations of the faithful, who were often heroic witnesses to Christ, educated in the school of the Cross (Redemption) and of the Eucharist'; cf. *Dominicae Cenae*, 11; (ET) CTS DO 529 p. 38.

30 Cf. ST III, qq.73–83; *Summa Contra Gentiles*, IV, cc. 61–9; *Libri Sententiarum*, IV; also commentary on 1 Cor. 11. Aquinas also quotes the words *opus nostrae redemptionis* (cf. ST III, q.83, a.1, c.), but in the context of the prayer from the Missal: 'Quoties huius hostiae commemoratio celebratur, opus nostrae redemptionis exercetur.' Power notes that he identifies the enactment of the work of redemption with the fruits of the Mass, rather than with the actual ritual celebration of the Mass; cf. *The Eucharistic Mystery*, op. cit., p. 228 (fn.).

31 Cf. *De Sacramento Altaris*, II.1; S.C. n. 93 (critical edition of the Latin text by J. Morson OCSO of Mt St Bernard's Monastery, Leics.), p. 180. Cf. *Poesie latine chrétienne du Moyen Age* (tr./ed. H. Spitzmuller), 'Bibliothèque européene', Desclée de Brouwer, Bruges, 1971, p. 188.

32 *De Sacramento Altaris*, III.2.1; op. cit., n.94, p. 530. Cf. St Augustine, *In Joh. Ev.*, Tr. 41.1: 'The truth is bread which refreshes our minds.'

33 In the *Catechism of the Catholic Church* the treatment of the sacraments is presented within – not as separate from – the context of the paschal mystery celebrated in liturgical worship; cf. CCC Part II, 1066ff.; 1075.

34 Cf. SC 5, 6, 47, 61, 81, 102–11, etc.

35 *Opus nostrae redemptionis exercetur.* Cf. SC 2, 5, 6, 102, 107 and 109; LG 3, 8; PO 13, 18. Cf. also the Decree on the Apostolate of the Laity (*Apostolicam Actuositatem*) 2; the Decree on Religious Freedom (*Dignitatis humanae*) 11; and also in the Proemium of GIRM 2 (most accurately quoted; ref. to Sacramentarium Veronese); Ch. 1, note 1 (ref. to SC 102).

36 SC 5b citing an Easter Preface.

37 Cf. Jordi Pinell OSB, 'I testi liturgici, voci di autorità, nella constituzione "sacrosanctum Concilium"' (Studia) in *Notitiae*, 1979, pp. 77–108. Cf. also E. Denys Rutledge OSB, 'Thoughts on

an ancient "Secret" Prayer' in *Priests & People* (February 1988), Vol. 2 No. 1, pp. 34f.

38 According to Pinell, the verb *exercetur* should be linked with *exeritur*, the verb which is given not in the text of the Roman Missal quoted or referred to by the Council, but in the so-called Leonianum Sacramentary, that is, the *Sacramentarium Veronese*; cf. *Notitiae*, art. cit., pp. 93, 95ff., 97; re the textual history and correction.

39 Cf. Dom Anscar Vonier OSB, *A Key to the Doctrine of the Eucharist*, Burns Oates & Washbourne Ltd., London, 1925, p. 76. In this classic work the author returns to the teaching of St Thomas Aquinas (cf. ST III q.79, a.5), whose explanation is based largely on the insights of St Augustine (cf. *De Civitate Dei*, X.6).

40 Cf. Mazza, *The Eucharistic Prayers of the Roman Rite*, op. cit., pp. 69ff.

41 According to Joachim Jeremias, this better translates St Paul's phrase [*eis ten emen anamnesin*] than 'Do this *in* memory of me'.

42 This is in complete accord with the Jewish idea of memorial, which was expressed by the word *zikkaron* as different scholars have brought out: cf. Max Thurian, *L'Eucharistie*, op. cit. Ch. 1; Louis Bouyer, *Eucharist: Theology and Spirituality of the Eucharistic Prayer*, University of Notre Dame Press, Notre Dame/London, 1968, Ch. 4 on the 'Berakah'; B.S. Childs, *Memory and Tradition in Israel*, Naperville, Illinois (USA), 1962.

43 Cf. Rom. 10:8, 17 (cf. Deut. 30:14): 'The word is near you, on your lips and in your heart (that is, the word of faith which we preach) . . . So faith comes from what is heard, and what is heard comes by the preaching of Christ.'

44 Cf. Peter J. Elliott, *Ceremonies of the Modern Roman Rite*, Ignatius Press, San Francisco, 1995, p. 118 (n. 321): 'Because the words of this prayer are addressed to Jesus Christ, it would seem appropriate for him (the celebrant) to direct his eyes towards the Host.'

45 Mazza puts it this way (op. cit., p. 75): 'In the anamnesis, the Church tells God what it is doing, why it does it, and what the object is of its commemorative action. And in telling him all this, the Church itself becomes conscious of it. The anamnesis is the moment in which the Mass defines itself, and it does so through the text of the celebration.'

46 Pope John Paul II's presentation of Christian morality based on the truth of Christ's redemptive sacrifice; cf. VS 84–105.

47 Cf. VS 103 citing an *Address* to those taking part in a course on 'responsible parenthood' (1 March 1984), 4: *Insegnamenti* VII, 1 (1984), 583.

48 Especially when commenting on this text; cf. e.g. St Cyril of Jerusalem, *Mystagogical Catecheses*, II, v. Participation means sacramental *imitation* of Christ. This *imitation* is not a matter of external observance, but of inner assimilation of Christ's attitude and spirit. Thanksgiving/praise was characteristic of Christ – see below where 'thanksgiving/praise' is treated.

49 Cf. Dom Odo Casel OSB, *La Fête de Pâques dans l'Église des Pères* (French tr. by J.C. Didier in the Lex Orandi series 37), Éd. du Cerf, Paris 1963, p. 98.

50 *Dominicae Cenae* 9; (ET) l.c., pp. 31f. (Italics in text.)

51 Cf. Everett A. Diederich, 'The unfolding presence of Christ in the celebration of Mass' in *Communio* 5/4 (1978), pp. 326–43.

52 Cf. Klaus Gamber, 'Celebrating the Mass *Versus Populum*: liturgical and sociological aspects' in *The Reform of the Roman Liturgy: Its Problems and Background*, (ET) Una Voce Press, San Juan Capistrano, California and the Foundation for Catholic Reform, Harrison, New York, 1993, pp. 77–89. The related topics of the eastward facing altar and celebrating 'towards the altar' are a matter of debate by serious liturgical theologians. Among those who advocated the eastward facing altar are: Josef Jungmann, Erik Peterson, Louis Bouyer. In the preface to the French edition of Monsignor Gamber's book, Cardinal Ratzinger considers that Mass 'facing the people' runs the risk of introducing a serious theological mistake: 'We risk seeing the assembly turning itself into a closed circle, in the name of community life. Liturgical education will have to work most vigorously against the concept of an autonomous, self-sufficient assembly. The assembly does not converse with itself, but sets out unanimously towards the coming Lord.' (Cited in the Preface to the English edition of Gamber's book, p. ix.) Cf. also, Ratzinger, 'Eastward- or westward-facing position? a correction' in *The Feast of Faith*, op. cit., pp. 144f. Elliott notes that the new *Ordo Missae* 'assumes that Mass can be celebrated either facing the people or facing the altar' (op. cit., p. 23, no. 61).

53 Christian 'conversion' fulfils what was intuitively seen and perhaps prophetically taught by Plato in his famous passage on the nature of true education consisting in turning from fascination with shadows to the full-brightness of reality; cf. *Republic* VII.518ff. The significance of 'conversion' is closely linked with 'conversation', both words sharing the same Latin double-rooted word *con-versio*, which literally means a turning over together. Indeed, there can hardly be any conversion without conversation: 'Faith comes from hearing' (Rom. 10:17). This is the greatest of all revolutions! For a general treatment of the notion of conversion; cf. Nock, *Conversion*, op. cit.; cf. also John S. Dunne, *A Search for God in Time and Memory*, Sheldon Press, London, 1975.

54 Cf. 'Priest and poet' in *Theological Investigations*, vol. 3, op. cit., pp. 306f.: 'Which is *the word* of the priest, of which all others are mere explanations and variations? It is the word which the priest speaks when, quietly, completely absorbed into the person of the incarnate *Word* of the Father, he says: "This is my Body . . . this is the chalice of my Blood . . .". Here only the word of God is spoken.'

55 Agreed Statement, Munich, 1982; (ET) in McPartlan (ed.), *One in 2000?*, op. cit., pp. 41f.

56 Cf. Power. *The Eucharistic Mystery*, op. cit., pp. 43f.

57 Consecration is not effected essentially in our offering, but by God's Spirit who consecrates by accepting Christ's sacrifice – that sacrifice to which his Supper points. Again, in communion also the initiative is God's; not our sharing in Christ's sacrificial meal so much as God eating with us. Cf. Austin Farrer, 'The Eucharist in 1 Corinthians' in *Eucharistic Theology Then and Now*, op. cit., p. 22. Cf. also Jeremias, *The Eucharistic Words of Jesus*, London, 1955, pp. 161ff; Max Thurian, 'The eucharistic memorial, sacrifice of praise and supplication' in *Ecumenical Perspectives on Baptism, Eucharist and Ministry*, op. cit., pp. 91ff.

58 Power, op. cit., p. 51.

59 C.S. Lewis, *Of This and Other Worlds*, Collins, Fount Paperbacks, 1982, pp. 120f.

60 Cf. Dom Illtyd Trethowan's lucid discussion of these viewpoints in *The Absolute and the Atonement*, George Allen & Unwin Ltd, New York: Humanities Press Inc., 1971, p. 195ff. Cf. also Eugène Masure, *The Christian Sacrifice*, (ET) Burns Oates & Washbourne, London, 1944.

61 'Form and content in the Eucharist' in *The Feast of Faith*, op. cit., p. 45.

62 Cf. Ratzinger, ibid., p. 37: 'Luther's use of the word "Supper" [*Abendmahl*] was a complete innovation. After 1 Corinthians 11:20 the designation of the Eucharist as a "meal" does not occur again until the sixteenth century, apart from direct quotations of 1 Corinthians 11:20 and references to the satisfaction of hunger (in deliberate contrast to the Eucharist).'

63 OL (2 May 1995), 11; (ET) Libreria Editrice Vaticana, pp. 22ff.

64 *In Act. Apost. Homil.*, 11, 3; PG 60, 97–8.

65 Cf. Basic Text of the 46th International Eucharistic Congress, Wroclaw, Poland, 1997, 30.

66 Cf. St Bernard's Sermon on the inner drama of acceptance of the angelic message at the Annunciation; *Hom. 4, 8–9 in Laudibus Virginis Matris; Edit. Cisterc. 4 [1966], 53–4*; DO I, op. cit., pp. 141f. (20 December).

67 OL 8.

68 Cited in the section of the Constitution on the Sacred Liturgy on the sacred mystery of the Eucharist: SC 47; cf. CCC 1323; 1139.

69 Cf. OL 8; loc. cit., pp. 16–17.

70 *Dominicae Cenae*, 12; (ET slightly revised) l.c., p. 44. (Italics in text.)

71 This in no way is meant to favour the idea popularised today, namely, that the eucharistic celebration is only a *meal* so that its sacred character as communion in Christ's sacrifice becomes obscured or even denied. This popularised attitude is the root of a diminution in reverence and the spirit of religious worship due to the holy presence of God in this sacrament; cf. *Dominicae Cenae*, 11.

72 Cf. SC 48, 51; DV 21. Cf. *Dominicae Cenae*, 10.

73 Biblical scholars (e.g. Jeremias, *The Eucharistic Words of Jesus*, op. cit., p. 253), maintain that the messianic hope implied in 1 Cor. 11:26 means that believers both wait and actively reach out for the Lord's coming in their eucharistic celebrations.

74 Cf. CCC 760; 775 referring to LG 1; cf. also CCC 1045. Cf. McPartlan, *Sacrament of Salvation*, op. cit., pp. 3ff.; 36; 64; 95f.

75 SC 8; (ET) *The Documents of Vatican II*, ed. Walter M. Abbott, Geoffrey Chapman, London/Dublin, 1966, pp. 141f. (italics mine) referred to in CCC 1090.

76 Cf. Power, *The Eucharistic Mystery*, op. cit., pp. 74ff.

77 Cf. *Ep. ad Mag.*, 9.1–2. Cf. also Justin Martyr, *Apologia I*, 65; 67; 3–5. Cf. the splendid recent study of the historical origins, theological meaning and pastoral significance of Sunday by Enzo Bianchi: *Giorno del Signore Giorno dell'Uomo* (Day of the Lord: Day of Humanity), Edizione Piemme, 1994. It is hoped that this work will be translated and made available to the English-speaking world.

78 McPartlan, *Sacrament of Salvation*, op. cit., pp. 12f., 23f. reference given to Zizioulas, 'The mystery of the Church in Orthodox tradition' *One in Christ* 24 (1988), p. 301. Cf. also the Orthodox theologian's major work in English: *Being as Communion: Studies in Personhood and the Church*, DLT, London, 1985.

79 Cf. BT III.5.28.

80 Cf. *In Ev. Joh. Tr.*, 104.2. Cf. La Bonnardière, *Recherches de Chronologie Augustinienne*, op. cit., pp. 152ff. This scholar also lists the following references where Augustine employs this *catena* of scriptural texts: *Ad Cath. contra Don.*, 7.16; *Enarr. in Ps. 117*, 19; *Enarr. in Ps. 118*, serm. 26.7.

81 Cf. Dom Maria Bernard De Soos, *Le Mystère Liturgique d'après Saint Léon le Grand*, Aschendorffsche Verlagsbuchhandlung, Münster, Westfalen, 1958.

82 CCC 1165 citing Ps.-Hippolytus, *De Pasch.* 1–2: S.C. 27, 117.

83 In the five volumes of his most celebrated work, *De Consolatione Philosophiae*, Boethius deals with the spiritual progress through philosophy to knowledge of the vision of God. This treatise, though lacking specifically Christian teaching, claimed wide interest in mediaeval times; King Alfred is reputed to have translated it into Anglo-Saxon.

84 *Four Quartets: Little Gidding*, V. The reference here is clearly to Julian of Norwich's teaching; cf. *Revelations of Divine Love*, 63 (Penguin, 1985, p. 176): 'I understood that there is no higher state in this life than that of childhood . . . And then the true meaning of those lovely words will be made known to us, "It is all going to be all right. You will see for yourself that everything is going to be all right."'

85 William Johnston sees this well exemplified in Gandhi's seemingly meaningless death; cf. *The Inner Eye of Love*, Collins, Fount Paperback, 1981, pp. 170f.

86 'God has spoken in human language' in *The Liturgy and the Word of God*, The Liturgical Press, Collegeville, Minnesota, 1959, p. 36.

87 Ibid., p. 37.

88 Ratzinger, *The Feast of Faith*, op. cit., p. 130 (italics in text). Cf. SC 6, where most significantly the Fathers of Vatican II apply a phrase from the Council of Trent regarding processions and public manifestations of eucharistic worship to the celebration of the Mass (cf. DACE 1644, Sees XIII C.5: 11 October 1551, Decr. de Ss Eucharistia): 'celebrating the Eucharist in which "the victory and triumph of his death are actualised [*repraesentantur*]".'

89 See the quotation from Ratzinger at the beginning of this chapter and note 3.

90 Cf. Gerald Vann's fine essay on 'The sorrow of God', op. cit.

91 Cf. Francesca Murphy, *Christ the Form of Beauty*, T&T Clark, Edinburgh, 1995, p. 180.

CHAPTER 6

1 Cf. e.g. EM 50: 'When the faithful adore Christ present in the Sacrament, they should indeed remember that this presence derives from the Sacrifice and leads [*tendere*] to sacramental and at the same time spiritual communion. Therefore the devotion which moves the faithful to visit the Holy Eucharist draws them to participate more deeply in the Paschal mystery and to

respond with grateful hearts to the gift of him, who through his humanity constantly pours divine life into the members of his Body.'

2 EM 3(g).

3 Cf. Pope John Paul II's Address (18 May 1995) to the National Delegates, who met in Rome to prepare the 46th IEC in Wroclaw (1997): *L'Osservatore Romano*, 19 May 1995, p. 5.

4 Cf. Pope Paul VI, *Mysterium Fidei*, 67.

5 EM 60. Cf. St Pius X, Decr. *Sacra Tridentina Synodus*, 20 December 1905: Denz. 1981 (3375). This paragraph is included in the *Ritual for Holy Communion and Worship of the Eucharist Outside Mass* (1973) 82.

6 Cf. CCC 1325 citing EM 6; cf. LG 11; UR 2, 15; SC 10; 2.

7 CCC 1323.

8 CCC 1337.

9 CCC 1380.

10 Ibid. citing *Dominicae Cenae*, 3.

11 CCC 1379. Perhaps one of the contributing causes for decline in devotion to the Blessed Sacrament was because this distinction was not sufficiently made in the Instruction *Eucharisticum Mysterium* (1967) and in the Roman Ritual [RR] of 1973, which followed it. Cf. EM 3f., 49, 60; RR 3, 5, 82.

12 Cf. O'Connor, *The Hidden Manna*, op. cit.; cf. also my anthology, *The Real Presence through the Ages*, op. cit.

13 Encyclical Letter *Mysterium Fidei*, 67.

14 Cf. SC 7.

15 'Eucharistic Presence and the Christian Vision', translated from *Nouvelle Revue Théologique*, 85 (1963), pp. 19–39, published in *The Eucharist Today* (ed. Raymond Tartre), P.J. Kenedy & Sons, New York, 1967, p. 93.

16 Cf. ibid., pp. 102ff. regarding the divine manifestation and presence in the 'tent', 'temple' and 'visitation', which reach their full significance in the revelation of presence of God in Jesus Christ.

17 Cf. Karl Rahner, 'On Visiting the Blessed Sacrament', in *The Eucharist Today*, op. cit., p. 195: 'Theologically . . . it is the sentence "Take and *eat*, this is my body" that is the first and basic proposition of Eucharistic theology, and not the sentence: Christ is here present . . . the tripartite division of the tractate on this sacrament, beginning with the Real Presence and only then going on to deal with Communion and sacrifice, is unsatisfactory and misleading. "*Institutum est ut sumatur*" (Denzinger 878).'

18 Ibid., p. 89. In a similar vein Giuseppe Crocetti says: 'Christ does not say: "take and eat my body"; but he says: "take and eat; this is my body". The statement: "this is my body" is distinct from the command to take and eat; this suggests that the presence has a value in itself, even if it is essentially ordained to the spiritual banquet. Christ, who becomes present in the Eucharistic celebration, does not withdraw this presence once the liturgical action is completed, but remains in the consecrated bread as food and sacrificial offering.' (Tr. from the article: 'L'adorazione eucaristica "per estendere la grazia del sacrificio"' in *La Nuova Alleanza*, 1973, p. 466.)

19 *The Eucharistic Heart*, Veritas, Dublin, 1990, p. 31.

20 Ibid., pp. 127f.

21 'The Admonitions', in *Francis and Clare: Complete Works*, Paulist Press, New York, 1982, pp. 26f.

22 *The Eucharistic Mystery: Revitalizing the Tradition*, Gill & Macmillan, 1992, pp. 201f.

23 For the translation of the full text of Urban IV's Bull. Cf. O'Connor, *The Hidden Manna*, op. cit., pp. 192ff.

24 VS 87. Cf. EV 29–30 et 50–1 where the Pope again insists on the importance of fixing our gaze on Christ; cf. also his first Encyclical, *Redemptor Hominis*, 10: 'adoration of God . . . deep wonderment of humanity's worth'; also, the apostolic letter on human suffering, *Salvifici Doloris*, 23: 'Those who share in Christ's sufferings have before their eyes the Paschal Mystery of the Cross and Resurrection, in which Christ descends, in a first phase, to the ultimate limits of human weakness and impotence: indeed, he dies nailed to the Cross. But if at the same time in this *weakness* there is accomplished his *lifting up*, confirmed by the power of the Resurrection, then this means that the weaknesses of all human sufferings are capable of being infused with the same power of God manifested in Christ's Cross.'

25 Cf. VS 85.

26 Cf. de la Potterie, *La Vérité dans Saint Jean*, op. cit., t. I., p. 67. Cf. also CCC 2716.

27 CCC 2559 – cf. *Manuscrits autobiographiques*, C 251.

28 CCC 2715.

29 It is interesting to recall that George Steiner likewise speaks of 'courtesy' in regard to the moment of encountering the numinous aspect of art; cf. *Real Presences*, op. cit., pp. 137, 139, 143, 155.

30 Cf. Ritamary Bradley, 'Patristic background of the motherhood similitude in Julian of Norwich', *Christian Scholar's Review* 8 (1978), pp. 101–13; cf. also, Caroline Walker Bynum, *Jesus as Mother:*

Studies in the Spirituality of the High Middle Ages, University of California Press, Berkeley, Los Angeles/London, 1982; Grace Jantzen, *Julian of Norwich: Mystic and Theologian,* SPCK, London, 1987, pp. 115–24.

31 Courtesy leads to and expresses freedom and real liberation; cf. Jantzen, *Julian of Norwich,* op. cit., 1987, pp. 134; 158.

32 *Revelations,* c.41; (ET) loc. cit., p. 125.

33 Cf. the concluding section of my book on Christian spirituality drawn from the Eucharistic Prayers, *Heart in Pilgrimage,* op. cit., pp. 230ff.

34 Cf. Cardinal Ratzinger, *The Feast of Faith,* op. cit., p. 32: 'Put in the briefest possible form, we can say something like this: in Jesus God participates in time. Through this participation he operates in time in the form of love. His love purifies men; through purification (and not otherwise) men are identified and united with him. Or we could say this: as a result of God's participation in time in Jesus, love becomes the causality operating in the world to transform it; in any place, at any time, it can exercise its influence. As a cause, love does not vitiate the world's mechanical causality but uses and adopts it. To pray is to put oneself on the side of the love-causality, this causality of freedom, in opposition to the power of necessity. As Christians, as those who pray, this is our very highest task.'

35 Cf. Julian, *Revelations,* 43; (ET) loc. cit., pp. 128f.: 'when our Lord in his courtesy and grace shows himself to our soul we have what we desire. Then we care no longer about praying for any thing, for our whole strength and aim is set on beholding. This is prayer, high and ineffable, in my eyes. The whole reason why we pray is summed up in the sight and vision of him to whom we pray. Wondering, enjoying, worshipping, fearing . . . and all with such sweetness and delight that during that time we can only pray in such ways as he leads us. . . . I saw that he is at work unceasingly in every conceivable thing, and that it is all done so well, so wisely, and so powerfully that it is far greater than anything we can imagine, guess, or think. Then we can do no more than gaze in delight with a tremendous desire to be wholly united to him, to live where he lives, to enjoy his love, and to delight in his goodness.'

36 The classic work on this is by C.S. Lewis, *The Allegory of Love,* OUP, London/Oxford/New York (first publ. 1936), paperback 1970. Humility and courtesy are two of the four features of the art of courtly love, which quite suddenly sprang up among the Troubadour poets of Languedoc about the end of the eleventh century – the other two being adultery and the 'religion of love', which amounted to a refinement of the pagan cult of the

love-god Cupid. The first two characteristics obviously presented no difficulty in being 'converted' to religious writing such as in Julian – or indeed, in that masterpiece from the same period, *The Pearl.*

37 This word refers to the profound sense of cultic act of prostration in worship – even more than genuflection. In modern Greek the verb *proskunō* means: to worship; pay respects to; submit to; and the noun *proskunēma* means: an act of worship; respect or submission; (place of) pilgrimage; *proskunēmata* (pl.) respects; cf. *The Oxford Dictionary of Modern Greek* (J.T. Pring), Clarendon Press, Oxford, 1983, p. 162.

38 Zoltàn Alszeghy SJ, 'L'Eucaristia Parola Fondamentale della Chiesa' in *Studi Eucaristici*, VII Centenario of the Bull '*Transiturus*' (1264–1964), Comitato Esecutivo Centrale, Orvieto, 1966, pp. 127f.

39 'What Corpus Christi means to us' in *Seek that which is Above*, (ET) Ignatius Press, San Francisco, 1986, pp. 92f.

40 Cf. 'On the structure of the liturgical celebration' in *The Feast of Faith*, op. cit., pp. 74f.

41 Ratzinger, 'Theological basis of prayer and liturgy', *The Feast of Faith*, op. cit., pp. 29f.

42 *Meditations on a Theme*, London, 1951 cited by Robert Llewelyn in 'Woman of consolation and strength' in *Julian Woman of Our Day*, DLT, London, 1986, p. 130.

43 Cf. C.S. Lewis' splendid explanation: 'Of forgiveness' in *Fern Seeds and Elephants*, Fontana/Collins, 1976, pp. 39ff.

44 Cf. McPartlan, *Sacrament of Salvation*, op. cit., p. 120, where reference is made to Jean Daniélou's comparison of the Platonist and biblical approaches to forgetfulness. Cf. Introduction to Herbert Musurillo (ed.), *From Glory to Glory: Texts from Gregory of Nyssa's Mystical Writings*, St Vladimir's Seminary, Crestwood, 1979, p. 61.

45 *La Presence Réelle*, I, Librairie Eucharistique, Paris/Montréal/Bruxelles, pp. 260f.

46 Cf. ibid., pp. 13ff.

47 *Le Très Saint Sacrement*, Juin 1864, pp. 5–13. This article is cited in *The Real Presence through the Ages*, op. cit., pp. 146f.

48 *La Presence Réelle*, I, op. cit., pp. 27f.

49 Cf. *Annunciation.*

50 Cf. St Ambrose, *Comm. in Lk.*, II.22–3; CCL 14.39–42 – (ET) DO I, op. cit., p. 149 (Office of readings for December 21): 'Where could she who was filled with God hasten to, except to the heights? There is no such thing as delay in the working of the Holy Spirit. The

arrival of Mary and the blessings of the Lord's presence are also speedily declared. "As soon as Elizabeth heard the greeting of Mary, the babe leaped in her womb; and she was filled with the Holy Spirit."'

51 Cf. *The Revelation of God*, (ET) DLT, London/Herder and Herder, New York, 1968, p. 196. (It was originally published in *Bible et Terre Sainte*, no.12, June 1958, pp. 2–4.)

52 Cf. ibid., p. 196.

53 This imagery is similarly employed at the end of the film *The Mission*, in which the priest is holding a monstrance, in the radiance of which the world is ultimately transformed.

54 *Lord of the World*, Communion and Liberation, Cambridge, 1988, p. 221.

CHAPTER 7

1 On the final transformation of human life, St Augustine quotes this verse and goes on to comment: 'Obviously, then, some kind of beatific vision is reserved for us. If at present only a partial glimpse may be caught *in a mirror dimly* [1 Cor.13:12], the radiant beauty of that beatitude which God keeps in store for those who hold him in awe . . . completely transcends the capacity of language to express. For this our hearts have been schooled through all the rigours and trials of this life. So do not be surprised at being exercised through toil; you are being prepared for a marvellous destiny.' Cf. *En. in Ps. 36*, 2.7.

2 'The creative vow as essence of fatherhood' in *Homo Viator*. An Introduction to a Metaphysic of Hope, (ET) Victor Gollancz Ltd, London, 1951, p. 101.

3 *Prayer in Practice*, (ET) Burns & Oates, London, 1957, pp. 113f.

4 Cf. Rubin, *Corpus Christi: The Eucharist in Late Medieval Culture*, CUP, 1991.

5 Cf. *The Stripping of the Altars: Traditional Religion in England c.1400– c.1580*, Yale University Press, New Haven and London, 1992, pp. 92f. More recently Duffy has ventured to argue the case in favour of Shakespeare's possible or even probable Catholic faith as contributing to the bard's complex and profound portrayal of a Christian humanism. Cf. his article 'Was Shakespeare a Catholic?' in *The Tablet*, 27 April 1996, pp. 536ff.

6 Cf. *A Precocious Autobiography;* passage cited in *Words for Worship*, Edward Arnold (Publishers) Ltd., London, 1977, n. 676.

7 Cf. Monsignor Ronald Knox's classic study: *Enthusiasm: A Chapter in the History of Religion,* OUP, 1950.

8 See John Saward's summary of modern forms of Gnosticism and Pelagianism, *Christ is the Answer,* op. cit., pp. xivf.

9 Cf. John Navone SJ, *The Dynamic of the Question in Narrative Theology,* Pontificia Università Gregoriana, Rome, 1986, pp. 107f.

10 Cf. *Choruses from 'The Rock',* III.

11 TMA 7; (ET) Libreria Editrice Vaticana, 1994, pp. 10f. Cf. also CCC 2560ff., 2566–7.

12 CT 60; (ET) *Catechesis in Our Time,* St Paul Publications, Slough, p. 55 citing Blaise Pascal, *Le Mystère de Jésus,* 553.

13 See Yves Congar's 'Additional note – forgetting the Holy Spirit' on the tendency of Catholic theology from the Counter-Reformation until recent times to substitute 'three white things', the Host, the Immaculate Virgin Mary, and the Pope, for the third Person of the blessed Trinity: *I Believe in the Holy Spirit,* I, (ET) The Seabury Press, New York/Geoffrey Chapman, London, 1983, pp. 159ff.

14 As Congar states in the conclusion of his study, *I Believe in the Holy Spirit,* III, op. cit., pp. 267ff.

15 Cf. Pope John Paul II, OL 8; (ET) Libreria Editrice Vaticana, pp. 15ff.

16 Cf. *The Go-Between God: The Holy Spirit and the Christian Mission,* SCM Press Ltd, London, 1972 (twelfth impression 1987), pp. 16f.

17 *The Go-Between God,* op. cit., p. 17. (Italics in text.) It is interesting to recall Yves Congar's observation (*I Believe in the Holy Spirit,* I, op. cit., pp. viif.): to reveal himself, the Holy Spirit does not use 'I', unlike Yahweh in the OT or Jesus in the NT, 'but through what he brings about in us'.

18 Cf. Congar, *I Believe in the Holy Spirit,* II, op. cit., p. 29: 'The "anointing" of faith, which comes of the "Holy One", in other words, the Holy Spirit, takes place in history. A very common practice among the Fathers of the Church, which continued until the period of the Council of Trent and even later, was to describe the effectiveness of the Spirit in the Church by the words *revelatio (revelare), inspiratio (inspirare), illuminare, suggestio (suggerere)* and related terms. I have provided a documentation on this subject which could be extended almost indefinitely.' Congar is referring to his meticulous research in *Tradition and Traditions* (ET) London and New York, 1966, Part One, pp. 119–37.

19 Cf. DVi 12 Pope John Paul II's profoundly beautiful Encyclical Letter on the Holy Spirit (18 May 1986).

20 Cf. EV 19; also Paul VI's Encyclical Letter Ecclesiam Suam (6 August 1964), pp. 70f.

21 Cf. the Sacred Congregation for Doctrine and the Faith, *Letter to the Bishops on Christian Meditation* (15 October 1989), n. 3 and 14; (ET) Vatican City, pp. 4f.

22 The expression 'anonymous Christian' was used by Karl Rahner SJ to refer to those who implicitly believe as Christians do in the same life-values such as committed members of the great non-Christian religious; cf. 'Christianity and the non-Christian religions', *Theological Investigations*, V, (ET) DLT, London, and Helicon, Baltimore, 1966, Ch. 6.

23 Cf. E. Yarnold SJ, *The Second Gift*, St Paul Publications, Slough, England, 1974 pp. 70f.

24 Cf. GS 38–9.

25 Cf. LG 3.

26 Cf. VS 13.

27 UUS 35; (ET) Libreria Editrice Vaticana, p. 41. Cf. Paul VI, *Ecclesiam Suam*, III: AAS 56 (1964), 642.

28 TMA, 37; (ET) l.c., pp. 45f.

29 *The Westminster Hymnal*, Burns & Oates Ltd., London, 1965, Nos. 246, 264. English translation by Monsignor Ronald Knox.

30 Cf. Bamber Gascoigne, *The Christians*, Jonathan Cape Ltd., London, 1977, esp. ch. 9 'In search of tolerance', pp. 199–217.

31 Cf. TMA, 35; (ET) l.c., p. 41 (italics in text). Cf. also GS 19, where the Council points to the defects of Christians themselves (either through their false presentation of the Church's teaching or lack of moral and social example, etc.) as being partly responsible for modern atheism.

32 From the Message *Urbi et Orbi*, Easter Sunday, 15 April 1990 cited by John Saward, op. cit., p. xxviii.

Bibliography

AA, *The Eucharist in the New Testament*, (ET) Geoffrey Chapman, London/Dublin, 1965.

Alszeghy, Zoltàn, 'L'Eucaristia Parola Fondamentale della Chiesa' in *Studi Eucaristici*, Comitato Esecutivo Centrale, Orvieto, 1966.

Balthasar, Hans Urs von, 'God has spoken in human language' in *The Liturgy and the Word of God*, The Liturgical Press, Collegeville, Minnesota, 1959.

——, *The Heart of the World*, (ET) Ignatius Press, San Francisco, 1979.

——, *The Glory of the Lord: A Theological Aesthetics*, (ET) T&T Clark, Edinburgh/Ignatius Press, San Francisco, 1982.

——, *Does Jesus Know Us – Do We Know Him?*, (ET) Ignatius Press, San Francisco, 1983.

——, *New Elucidations*, (ET) Ignatius Press, San Francisco, 1986.

——, *Mysterium Paschale: The Mystery of Easter*, (ET) T&T Clark, Edinburgh, 1993 (1990).

Barrett, C. K., *The First Epistle to the Corinthians*, A. & C. Black, London, 1971.

Basic Text of the Forty-sixth International Eucharistic Congress, (ET) Pontifical Committee for IEC, Vatican City, 1995.

Bernier, Paul, *Eucharist: Celebrating its Rhythms in Our Lives*, Ave Maria, 1993.

Bianchi, Enzo, *Giorno del Signore Giorno dell'uomo*, Edizione Piemme, Casale Monferrato (AL), 1994.

Bonhoeffer, D., *Ethics*, (ET), SCM Press, London, 1971.

Bornkamm, G., *Early Christian Experience*, SCM Press, London, 1969.

Bouyer, Louis, *The Paschal Mystery: Meditations on the Last Three Days of Holy Week*, (ET) George Allen & Unwin Ltd, London, 1951.

——, *Life and Liturgy*, (ET) Sheed & Ward, London, 1956.

——, *Christian Initiation*, (ET) Collier Books, New York, 1962.

——, *Eucharist*, (ET) Notre Dame, 1968.

Brown, Peter, *Augustine of Hippo: A Biography*, Faber Paperback, London, 1969.

Brown, Raymond, *The Semitic Background of the Term 'Mystery' in the New Testament*, Fortress Press (Facet Books), Philadelphia, 1968.

——, *The Community of the Beloved Disciple*, Geoffrey Chapman, London, 1979.

Burnaby, John, *Amor Dei: A Study of the Religion of St Augustine*, (The Hulsean Lectures for 1938), The Canterbury Press, Norwich, 1991.

Butler, Christopher, *The Theology of Vatican II*, DLT, London, 1981.

Bynum, Caroline Walker, *Jesus as Mother: Studies in the Spirituality of the High Middle Ages*, University of California Press, Berkeley, Los Angeles/London, 1982.

Cairns, David, *The Image of God in Man*, Collins, Fontana, 1973.

Cantalamessa, Raniero, *Easter in the Early Church*, (ET) The Liturgical Press, Collegeville, Minnesota, 1993.

——, *The Eucharist: Our Sanctification*, (ET) The Liturgical Press, Collegeville, Minnesota, 1993.

Casel, O., *The Mystery of Christian Worship*, (ET) DLT, 1962.

——, *La Fête de Pâques dans l'Église des Pères*, Lex Orandi 37, ed. du Cerf, Paris, 1963.

Chesterton, G.K., *Orthodoxy*, Unicorn Books, London, 1939.

Childs, B. S., *Memory and Tradition in Israel*, Naperville, Illinois, 1962.

Clark, Mary T., *Augustine Philosopher of Freedom*, Desclée Company, New York/Tournai/Rome/Paris, 1958.

Coleridge, S.T., *Biographia Literaria*, Dent (Everyman's Library Paperback), London and Melbourne, 1987.

Congar, Yves, *The Revelation of God*, (ET) DLT, London/Herder & Herder, New York, 1968.

——, *I Believe in the Holy Spirit* (Vols 1–3), (ET) The Seabury Press, New York/Geoffrey Chapman, London, 1983.

Corpus Christi: An Encyclopedia of the Eucharist, (Michael O'Carroll, ed.), Michael Glazier, Inc., Wilmington, DE, 1988.

Cullmann, O., *Early Christian Worship*, (ET) SCM Press, London, 1953.

Cupitt, Don, *The Sea of Faith*, BBC, London, 1984.

Daly, Robert J., *Christian Sacrifice: The Judaeo-Christian Background Before Origen*, Studies in Christian Antiquity 18; Washington: The Catholic University of America Press, 1978.

——, *The Origins of the Christian Doctrine of Sacrifice*, DLT, London, 1978.

Daniélou, J., *The Bible and the Liturgy*, (ET) DLT, 1964.

Dawson, Christopher, *Progress and Religion: An Historical Enquiry*, Sheed & Ward (Unicorn Books), London, 1938.

——, *Science and Wisdom*, Geoffrey Bles: The Centenary Press, London, 1940.

De la Potterie, I., *La Vérité dans Saint Jean*, Vols 1 & 2, Biblical Institute Press (Analecta Biblica 73 & 74), Rome, 1977.

——, *The Hour of Jesus: The Passion and the Resurrection of Jesus According to John: Text and Spirit*, (ET) St Paul Publications, Slough, 1989.

De Lubac, H., *Corpus Mysticum*, 2nd ed., Aubier, Montaigne, Paris, 1949.

——, *Catholicism: Christ and the Common Destiny of Man*, (ET) Burns & Oates (Universe Edition), London, 1962 (1950).

——, *The Splendour of the Church*, (ET) Sheed & Ward, London, 1986 (1956).

——, *Paradoxes of Faith*, (ET) Ignatius Press, San Francisco, 1987.

De Soos, M. Bernard, *Le Mystère Liturgique d'après Saint Léon le Grand*, Munster, Westfalen, 1958.

Dix, G., *The Shape of the Liturgy*, A. & C. Black, London, 1970.

Dodd, C.H., *The Epistle of Paul to the Romans*, Collins/Fontana Paperback, 1960.

Dodd, C.H., *The Parables of the Kingdom*, Collins, Fontana Books, 1961.

——, *The Interpretation of the Fourth Gospel*, CUP, 1968.

Duffy, Eamon, *The Stripping of the Altars: Traditional Religion in England c.1400–c.1580*, Yale University Press, New Haven/London, 1992.

Dunne, John S., *A Search for God in Time and Memory*, Sheldon Press, London, 1975.

Eliade, Mircea, *The Sacred and the Profane: The Nature of Religion*, (ET) Harper & Row (Torchbooks, The Cloister Library), New York, 1961.

Elliott, Peter J., *Ceremonies of the Modern Roman Rite*, Ignatius Press, San Francisco, 1995.

Ernst, Cornelius, *Multiple Echo: Explorations in Theology*, DLT, London, 1979.

Farrer, Austin, 'The Eucharist in 1 Corinthians' in *Eucharistic Theology Then and Now*, SPCK, London 1968, pp. 15–33.

FitzPatrick, P.J., *In Breaking of Bread: The Eucharist and Ritual*, CUP, 1993.

Flannery, A. (ed.), *Vatican Council II: The Conciliar and Post-Conciliar Documents*, Dominican Publications, Dublin, 1975.

——, *Vatican Council II: More Post-Conciliar Documents*, Fowler Wright Books Ltd, Leominster, Hereford, 1982.

Frend, W.H.C., *Martyrdom and Persecution in the Early Church*, Blackwell, Oxford, 1965.

Fromm, Erich, *The Fear of Freedom*, Routledge, London/New York, 1995 (originally in 1942).

Galot, Jean, *Jesus our Liberator: A Theology of Redemption*, (ET) Gregorian University Press, Rome/Franciscan Herald Press, Chicago, 1982.

——, *The Eucharistic Heart*, (ET) Veritas, Dublin, 1990.

Gamber, Klaus, *The Reform of the Roman Liturgy: Its Problems and Background*, (ET) Una Voce Press, San Juan Capistrano, California/The Foundation for Catholic Reform, Harrison, New York, 1993.

Gascoigne, Bamber, *The Christians*, Jonathan Cape Ltd, London, 1977.

Gaudoin-Parker, M.L., 'St Ignatius' sacrifice for unity' in *Adoremus*, Vol. LXI, No. 1 1981, pp. 60–73.

Gaudoin-Parker, M.L., 'The glory of God, man fully alive in the Eucharist: the eucharistic teaching of St Irenaeus' in *Adoremus*, Vol. LXII, No. 2 1982, pp. 14–21.

——, 'The mystery of the Passover: the catechesis of Melito of Sardis' in *Adoremus*, Vol. LXII, No. 1 1982, pp. 33–42.

——, 'Hymn of the Word's creation: the Alexandrians' spiritual understanding of the Eucharist' in Adoremus, Vol. LXIII, No. 2 1983, pp. 28–37.

——, 'The flesh, the pivot of salvation: Tertullian's insight into the Eucharist' in *Adoremus*, Vol. LXIII, No. 1 1983, pp. 20–34.

——, 'Cyprian's cup of delight' in *Adoremus*, Vol. LXIV, No. 1 1984, pp. 33–8.

——, 'Augustine's "Conversion" considered in the light of the eucharistic imagery in his hymn of beauty' in *Adoremus*, Vol. LXVI, No. 2 1986, pp. 19–29.

——, 'The beauty of the Eucharist – St Augustine's experience of the mystery of faith', *The Clergy Review*, Vol. LXXI, No. 12 (December 1986), pp. 438–44.

——, *The Real Presence through the Ages: Jesus Adored in the Sacrament of the Altar*, Alba House, Staten Island, NY, 1993.

——, *Heart in Pilgrimage: Mediating Christian Spirituality in the Light of the Eucharistic Prayer*, Alba House, Staten Island, NY, 1994.

Gawronski, Raymond, *Word and Silence: Hans Urs von Balthasar and the Spiritual Encounter Between East and West*, T&T Clark, Edinburgh, 1995.

Gutiérrez, Gustavo, *A Theology of Liberation*, (ET) London, 1983.

Guzie, T., *Jesus and the Eucharist*, Paulist Press, New York, 1974.

Harmless, William, *Augustine and the Catechumenate*, Liturgical Press, Collegeville, Minnesota, 1995.

Jantzen, Grace, *Julian of Norwich, Mystic and Theologian*, SPCK, London, 1987.

Jeremias, J., *The Eucharistic Words of Jesus*, (ET) London, 1966.

Johanny, Raymond, *L'Eucharistie Chemin de Résurrection*, Desclée, Paris, 1974.

Johnson, C. and Ward, A., 'The sources of the Roman Missal . . .' in *Notitiae*, Vol. 22 (1986), pp. 445–747; and, ibid., Vol. 24 (1987), pp. 413–1009.

Johnston, William, *Silent Music: The Science of Meditation*, Collins, Fount Paperback, 1981 (6th impression), first publ. 1974.

——, *The Inner Eye of Love*, Collins, Fount Paperback, 1981.

Jones, David, *The Dying Gaul and other Writings*, Faber & Faber, 1978.

Jung, Karl, *Modern Man in Search of a Soul*, (ET) Routledge & Kegan Paul, London and Henley, 1978.

Jungmann, J., *The Mass of the Roman Rite* (2 Vols), (ET) Benzinger Bros., New York, 1955.

——, *The Early Liturgy*, (ET) DLT, 1963.

——, *The Place of Christ in Liturgical Prayer*, (ET) Geoffrey Chapman, London, 1965.

——, *The Mass: An Historical, Theological, and Pastoral Survey*, (ET) The Liturgical Press, Collegeville, Minnesota, 1976.

——, *The Eucharistic Prayer* (revd), (ET) Anthony Clark, 1978.

Keefe, Donald J., *Covenantal Theology: The Eucharistic Order of History*, 2 Vols, University of America Press Inc., Lanham, New York/London, 1991.

Kierkegaard, Søren, *The Concept of Anxiety: A Simple Psychologically Orienting Deliberation on the Dogmatic Issue of Hereditary Sin*, (ET) Princeton University Press, Princeton, New Jersey, 1980.

Kilmartin, E.J., *The Eucharist in the Primitive Church*, Prentice-Hall Inc., Englewood Cliffs, NY, 1965.

Kirk, K.E., *The Vision of God: The Christian Doctrine of the Summum Bonum* (The Bampton Lectures for 1928), Longmans, Green & Co., London/New York/Toronto, 1931.

Knox, Rolald, *Enthusiasm: A Chapter in the History of Religion*, OUP, 1950.

Lane, Thomas, *A Priesthood in Tune: Theological Reflections on Ministry*, The Columba Press, Dublin, 1993.

Lash, N., *His Presence in the World*, Sheed & Ward, London, 1968.

——, *Theology on the Way to Emmaus*, SCM Press, London, 1986.

Léon-Dufour, X., *The Gospels and the Jesus of History*, Collins, Fontana, 1971.

——, *Dictionary of Biblical Theology*, (ET) 2nd ed., New York, 1973.

——, *Sharing the Eucharistic Bread: The Witness of the New Testament*, (ET), Paulist Press, Mahwah, New Jersey, 1987.

Lonergan, Bernard, *Method in Theology*, DLT, London, 1972.

Lussier, Ernest, *Jesus Christ is Lord: Adoration Viewed through the New Testament*, Alba House, Staten Island, New York, 1979.

McPartlan, P., *The Eucharist Makes the Church: Henri de Lubac and John Zizioulas in Dialogue*, T&T Clark, Edinburgh, 1993.

——, *One in 2000? Towards Catholic-Orthodox Unity*, St Pauls, London, 1993.

——, *Sacrament of Salvation: An Introduction to Eucharistic Ecclesiology*, T&T Clark, Edinburgh, 1995.

Magee, Bryan, *The Great Philosophers: An Introduction to Western Philosophy*, BBC Books, 1987.

Martelet, G., *The Risen Christ and the Eucharistic World*, Collins, 1976.

Martin, Dale B., *The Corinthian Body*, Yale University Press, 1995.

Martini, C.M., *La Gioia del Vangelo: Meditazioni ai giovani*, Edizioni Piemme, Milano, 1988.

Masure, E., *The Christian Sacrifice: The Sacrifice of Christ Our Head*, (ET) Burns Oates and Washbourne, London, 1944.

May, Rollo, *Love and Will*, Collins, Fountain Paperback, 1977.

Mazza, E., *The Eucharistic Prayers of the Roman Rite*, (ET) Pueblo Publ. Co., NY, 1986.

——, *Mystagogy*, (ET) Pueblo Publ. Co., NY, 1989.

Miller, Paula Jean, *Marriage: The Sacrament of Divine Human Communion*, Vol. I, Franciscan Press, Quincy, IL, 1996.

Moloney, Francis J., *A Body Broken for a Broken People*, Collins, Dove, Melbourne, Australia, 1990.

Moloney, Raymond, *The Eucharist*, Geoffrey Chapman, London, 1995.

Moore, Sebastian, *The Inner Loneliness*, The Crossroad Publishing Co., New York, 1982.

Moule, C.F.D., *Worship in the New Testament*, Vols 1 and 2, Grove Books, Bramcote, Notts., 1977/78.

Hymn of Freedom

Mourin, Jennifer, *Peace Dividend? The Arms Build-up in the Post-Cold War Era*, Just World Trust (JUST), Penang, Malaysia, 1994.

Murphy, Francesca Aran, *Christ the Form of Beauty: A Study in Theology and Literature*, T&T Clark, Edinburgh, 1995.

Murphy-O'Connor, J., *1 Corinthians*, New Testament Message, 10, Michael Glazier, Wilmington, DE, 1979.

Muzaffar, Chandra, 'Human rights and hypocrisy in the international order' in *Dominance of the West Over the Rest*, Just World Trust (JUST), Penang, Malaysia, 1995.

Navone, John, *The Dynamic of the Question in Narrative Theology*, Pontificia Università Gregoriana, Rome, 1986.

Nichols, A., *The Holy Eucharist from the New Testament to Pope John Paul II*, Oscott 6, Veritas, Dublin, 1991.

Nichols, A., *Scribe of the Kingdom: Essays on Theology and Culture*, Vol. I, Sheed & Ward, London 1994.

Nock, A.D., *Conversion*, OUP Paperback, 1969 (rev. ed.).

O'Connor, J.T., *The Hidden Manna: A Theology of the Eucharist*, Ignatius Press, San Francisco. 1988.

Otto, Rudolf, *The Idea of the Holy*, (ET) Penguin (Pelican), 1959.

Panikkar, K.R., 'Western domination: the military factor' in *Dominance of the West Over the Rest*, Just World Trust (JUST), Penang, Malaysia, 1995.

Pascal, Blaise, *Pensées*, (ET) Penguin, 1970 (1966).

Pelikan, Jaroslav, *Jesus through the Centuries: His Place in the History of Culture*, Yale University Press, New Haven/London, 1985.

Pelotte, Donald, *John Courtney Murray: Theologian in Conflict*, Paulist Press, New York, 1975.

Pieper, Josef, *Leisure: The Basis of Culture*, (ET) Random House Inc. (Mentor-Omega Book), New York, 1963.

——, *In Search of the Sacred: Contributions to an Answer*, (ET) Ignatius Press, San Francisco, 1991.

Piolanti, A., *The Holy Eucharist*, (ET) Desclée, New York, 1961.

Power, David, *The Eucharistic Mystery*, Gill & Macmillan, Dublin, 1992.

Rahner, Karl, *Theological Investigations*, Vol. 4, (ET) Helicon Press, Baltimore, 1966.

——, *Theological Investigations*, Vol. 6, (ET) DLT, London/Helicon Press, Baltimore, 1969.

Rahner, Karl, *Theological Investigations*, Vol. 20, (ET) DLT, London, 1981.

Ratzinger, Joseph, *Introduction to Christianity*, (ET) Burns & Oates, London, 1969.

——, *Popolo e Casa di Dio in sant'Agostino*, (Ital. tr.) Jaca, Milan, 1971.

——, *The Ratzinger Report*, (ET) Fowler Wright, Leominster (Herts.)/Ignatius Press, San Francisco, 1985.

——, *Seek that which is Above: Meditations through the Year*, (ET) Ignatius Press, San Francisco, 1985.

——, *Feast of Faith: Approaches to a Theology of the Liturgy*, (ET) Ignatius Press, San Francisco, 1986.

——, *In the Beginning: A Catholic Understanding of the Story of Creation and the Fall*, (ET) T&T Clark, Edinburgh, 1995.

——, *Called to Communion: Understanding the Church Today*, (ET) Ignatius Press, San Francisco, 1996.

Ricoeur, Paul, *History and Truth*, Northwestern University Press, Evanston, Illinois, 1965.

Rubin, Miri, *Corpus Christi: The Eucharist in Late Medieval Culture*, CUP, 1991.

Saward, John, *The Mysteries of March: Hans Urs von Balthasar on the Incarnation and Easter*, Collins, London, 1990.

——, *Christ is the Answer: The Christ-Centred Teaching of Pope John Paul II*, T&T Clark, Edinburgh, 1995.

Sayers, Dorothy L., *The Mind of the Maker*, Mowbray, London/New York, 1994.

Scheler, Max, *On Feeling, Knowing, and Valuing*, The University of Chicago Press, Chicago/London, 1992.

Schillebeeckx, E., *Christ the Sacrament*, (ET) Sheed & Ward, London, 1963.

——, *The Eucharist*, (ET) Sheed & Ward, London, 1968.

Schindler, David L., *Heart of the World, Center of the Church: Communio Ecclesiology, Liberalism and Liberation*, William B. Eerdmans, Grand Rapids, Michigan/T&T Clark, Edinburgh, 1996.

Schmemann, Alexander, *The Eucharist: Sacrament of the Kingdom*, (ET) St Vladimir's Seminary Press, Crestwood, New York, 1988.

Schnackenburg, Rudolf, *The Moral Teaching of the New Testament*, (ET) Burns & Oates, London, 1975.

Servotte, Herman, *According to John: A Literary Reading of the Fourth Gospel*, (ET) DLT, 1994.

Sokolowski, Robert, *Eucharistic Presence: A Study in the Theology of Disclosure*, CUA, Washington, DC, 1994.

Steiner, George, *Real Presences*, Faber & Faber, London/Boston, 1989.

Stevenson, J., *A New Eusebius: Documents Illustrating the History of the Church to AD 337*, SPCK, London, 1993.

Stockhausen, Carol L., *Letters in the Pauline Tradition*, Michael Glazier, Wilmington, DE, 1989.

Storr, Anthony, *Solitude*, Flamingo/Fontana Paperback, London, 1989.

Sykes, Stephen, *The Identity of Christianity: Theologians and the Essence of Christianity from Schleiermacher to Barth*, Fortress Press, Philadelphia/SPCK, London, 1984.

Tatre, R. (ed.), *The Eucharist Today*, P.J. Kenedy & Sons, New York, 1967.

Taylor, John V., *The Go-Between God: The Holy Spirit and the Christian Mission*, SCM Press Ltd, London, 1972.

Theissen, G., *The Social Setting of Pauline Christianity: Essays on Corinth*, Fortress Press, Philadelphia, 1982.

Thurian, Max (ed.), *Ecumenical Perspectives on Baptism, Eucharist and Ministry*, Faith and Order Paper 116, World Council of Churches, Geneva, 1985[3].

Tillard, J.M.R., *The Eucharist Pasch of God's People*, (ET) Alba House, Staten Island, NY, 1967.

Trethowan, Illtyd, *The Absolute and the Atonement*, George Allen & Unwin Ltd., London/Humanities Press Inc., NY, 1971.

Vann, Gerald, *The Wisdom of Boethius*, Blackfriars Publications, London, 1952.

——, *The Pain of Christ and the Sorrow of God*, Blackfriars, London, 1954.

——, *The Eagle's Word*, Collins, London, 1961.

Vonier, A., *Key to the Doctrine of the Eucharist*, Burns, Oates & Washbourne, London, 1925.

Ward, Barbara, *Faith and Freedom*, Image Books, Doubleday & Co. Ltd., Garden City, New York, 1958.

Ward, Heather, *The Gift of Self*, DLT, London, 1990.

Weil, Simone, *The Need for Roots*, (ET) Routledge & Kegan Paul (Ark Paperback), London/New York, 1987.

Wojtyla, Karol, *The Acting Person*, (ET) D. Reidel Publishing Company, Dordrecht: Holland/Boston/London, 1979.

Wojtyla, Karol, *The Collected Plays and Writings on the Theater*, (ET) University of California Press, Berkeley/Los Angeles/London, 1987.

——, *The Place Within: The Poetry of Pope John Paul II*, (ET) Hutchison, London, 1995.

Yarnold, E., *The Awe-Inspiring Rites of Christian Initiation*, St Paul Publications, Slough (UK), 1973.

——, *The Second Gift*, St Paul Publications, Slough, 1974.

Young, F., *Sacrifice and the Death of Christ*, SCM, London, 1983.

Zizioulas, John, *Being as Communion: Studies in Personhood and the Church*, DLT, London, 1985.

——, *Il Creato Come Eucharistia*, (ET) Edizioni Qiqajon, Comunità di Bose, Magnano (VC – Italy), 1994.

Zundel, Maurice, *The Splendour of the Liturgy*, (ET) Sheed & Ward, London, 1941.

Index of Names

Alszeghy, Zoltàn 153, 218n, 223
Ambrose 57, 202n, 218n
Anselm 12, 17, 186f.nn
Aquinas, Thomas 11, 14, 21, 116,
 207n, 209f.nn
Aristotle 9, 185n
Augustine xxiv, 10ff., 17, 39f., 47,
 66, 74, 76, 89ff., 112f., 134,
 170, 185ff.nn, 191f.nn, 194n,
 199f.nn, 202f.nn, 208ff.nn,
 213n, 219n

Baldwin of Ford 116
Balthasar, Hans Urs von xxi, 19,
 79, 137, 182n, 188n, 192n,
 197n, 205n, 223
Barrett, C.K. 206n, 223
Barth, K. 187n
Basil the Great 191n
Benoît, P. 205n
Benson, R.H. 159
Berlin, Isaac 187n
Bernard 212n
Bernier, Paul 208n, 223
Berry, Mary 185n
Bettensen, Henry 205n
Bianchi, Enzo 213n, 223
Blondel, Maurice 158
Bloom, Anthony 154
Boethius 14, 135, 214n

Boismard, M.E. 206n
Bonaventure 14, 187n
Bonhoeffer, Dietrich 28, 59, 223
Bornkamm, G. 206n, 224
Bouyer, Louis 210f.nn, 224
Bradley, Ritamary 216n
Brown, Peter 92, 224
Brown, Raymond 198n, 202n,
 224
Bultmann, R. 199n
Burnaby, John 194n, 203n, 224
Butler, Christopher 22, 25, 101,
 224
Bynum, Caroline Walker 216n,
 224

Caird, G.B. 195nn
Cairns, David 186n, 224
Caldecott, Stratford xxiii, 29
Camus, Albert 19, 115
Cantalamessa, Raniero 204n,
 208n, 224
Carretto, Carlo 33
Casel, Odo 211n, 224
Cazelles, Henri 194n
Chadwick, Henry 91, 202n
Chesterton, G.K. xx, 224
Childs, B.S. 210n, 224
Cicero 10
Clark, Mary T. 185n, 224

Clement of Alexandria 40, 61, 96
Clement of Rome, Pope 196n
Coleridge, Samuel Taylor 91,
    187n, 224
Congar, Yves 158f., 192n, 220n,
    225
Crocetti, Giuseppe 215n
Cullmann, Oscar 194n, 198n,
    225
Cupitt, Don 16f., 187n, 225
Cyril of Jerusalem 76, 211n

Daly, Robert J. 225
Damascene, John 186n
Daniélou, Jean 194n, 196n,
    218n, 225
Dawson, Christopher 14f., 185n,
    225
De Beauvoir, Simone 115
De la Potterie, Ignace 71, 75,
    197ff.nn, 216n, 225
De Lubac, Henri 20, 186n, 200n,
    225
De Rougement, Denis 187n
De Soos, Maria Bernard 213n,
    225
Descartes, René 15f., 18
Didier, J.C. 211n
Diederich, Everrett A. 211n
Diognetus, Epistle to 81, 198n, 201n
Dix, Gregory 44, 193n, 225
Dodd, C.H. 33, 95, 193fn, 200n,
    202n, 225f.
Donatist/Donatus 92, 201n
Donghi, Antonio 199n
Donne, John 152, 156
Duffy, Eamon 167, 203n, 219n,
    226
Dunne, John S. 211n, 226

Eliade, Mircea 185n, 190n, 226
Eliot, T.S. xx, 84, 135, 169, 182n,
    185n, 197n

Elliott, Peter J. 210n, 226
Ernst, Cornelius 192n, 207n, 226
Eusebius 206n, 232
Evans, Michael 207n
Eymard, Peter Julian 156

Fakruddin Iraqi 192n
Farrer, Austin 205n, 212n, 226
FitzPatrick, P.J. 226
Francis of Assisi 149f., 195n, 216n
Frank, Anne 40
Frend, W.H.C. 201n, 226
Freud, Sigmund 90, 136
Fromm, Erich 7, 71, 226

Galot, Jean 146ff., 226
Gamber, Klaus 211n, 226
Gandhi, Mohandas 28, 214n
Gascoigne, Bamber 221n, 226
Gaudentius of Brescia 191n
Gaudoin-Parker, M.L. 226f.
Gawronski, Raymond 182n,
    205n, 227
Gelineau, Joseph 208n
Green, Julien 7
Gregory the Great, Pope 191n,
    198f.nn, 207n
Gregory of Nyssa 207n, 218n
Gregory XVI, Pope 189n
Guardini, Romano 163
Gutiérrez, Gustavo 188n, 227
Guzie, Tad 198n, 227

Hamman, A. 208n
Harmless, William 227
Harnack, Adolf von 186n
Hitler, Adolf 20, 83
Hooper, Walter 188n, 190n
Hopkins, Gerard Manley 14
Hume, Cardinal Basil 183n

Ignatius of Antioch 133, 196n,
    204n, 206n

Irenaeus of Lyons 70, 99, 195n, 197ff.nn

Jantzen, Grace 217f.nn, 227
Jeremias, Joachim 46, 210n, 212n, 227
Jerome 198n
Johanny, Raymond 227
John Chrysostom 129, 198ff.nn
John XXIII, Pope 25, 190n
John Paul II, Pope i, ix, x, xi, xiii, xviii, xxi, xxii, 17, 23, 27, 29, 36, 44, 79f., 122, 128, 130, 145, 150, 169, 175, 177f., 181n, 183f.nn, 189ff.nn, 195f.nn, 198n, 200n, 206n, 209f.nn, 210n, 215n, 220n
Johnson, C. 228
Johnston, William 214n, 228
Jones, David 91, 203n, 205n, 228
Julian of Norwich 107, 137, 151ff., 214n, 216ff.nn
Jung, Karl Gustav 184n, 228
Jungmann, Joseph 205n, 211n, 228
Justin 81, 201n, 213n

Kafka, Franz 7
Kant, Immanuel 15, 187n
Keefe, Donald J. 181n, 186n, 228
Kenny, Anthony 186n
Kierkegaard, Soren 199n, 228
Kilmartin, Edward 193n, 228
King, Martin Luther 28
Kirk, K.E. 228
Knox, Ronald A. 182n, 220n, 221n, 228

La Bonnardière, Anne-Marie 185n, 213n
Laing, Ronald D. 89
Lane, Thomas 205n, 228
Langton, Stephen 176

Lash, Nicholas 187n, 228
Leo the Great, Pope 56, 111, 118, 134, 213n
Leo XIII, Pope 25, 27, 190n
Léon-Dufour, Xavier 191ff.nn, 229
Lewis, C.S. 18f., 35, 90, 126, 212n, 217f.nn
Llewelyn, Robert 218n
Loisy, Alfred Firmin 193n
Lonergan, Bernard 229
Lussier, Ernest 205n, 229
Luther, Martin 212n

McCormick, Richard A. 183n
McPartlan, Paul 14, 133, 182n, 200n, 212n, 213n, 218n, 229
Madec, Goulven 185n
Magee, Bryan 186n, 229
Marcel, Gabriel 163, 200n
Martelet, G. 229
Martin, Dale B. 205n, 229
Martini, Cardinal Carlo-Maria 196n, 229
Marx, Karl 194n
Masure, Eugène 212n, 229
May, Rollo 184n, 188n, 229
Mazza, Enrico 191n, 194n, 196n, 210n, 229
Melito of Sardis 112f.
Michelangelo 13
Mill, J.S. 19
Miller, Paula Jean 187n, 229
Mohrmann, Christine 200n, 208n
Mollat, D. 198f.nn
Moloney, Francis J. 100, 199n, 206n, 229
Moloney, Raymond 193n, 229
Moore, Sebastian 202n, 229
Morson, J. 209n
Moule, C.F.D. 97, 203n, 207n, 229

Mourin, Jennifer 183n, 230
Murphy, Francesca 214n, 230
Murphy-O'Connor, J. 205n, 230
Murray, John Courtney 206n
Mussolini, Benito 20
Musurillo, Herbert 218n
Muzaffar, Chandra 181n, 230

Navone, John 220n, 230
Nero 201n
Newman, John Henry 182n
Nichols, Aidan 230
Nock, A.D. 202n, 211n, 230
Norwid, Cyprian 184n

O'Connor, James T. 195n,
    215f.nn, 230
O'Connor, Cardinal John 183n
Orwell, George 8
Ong, Walter J. 200n, 206n
Origen 203n
Orsy, Ladislas 189n
Otto, Rudolf 190n, 230

Panikkar, K.R. 184n, 230
Pascal, Blaise xxi, 16, 170, 203n,
    220n, 230
Paul VI, Pope x, 25f., 30, 49, 62,
    141, 146, 175, 181n, 184n,
    190n, 194f.nn, 206n, 208n,
    215n, 220n
Pelagius 91f.
Pelikan, Jaroslav 90, 201n, 206n,
    230
Pelotte, Donald 206n, 230
Penn, William 178
Perrot, C. 194n
Peterson, Erik 211n
Peterson, Eugene H. 198n
Pieper, Josef 109, 184f.nn, 230
Pinell, Jordi 209n
Piolenti, A. 205n, 230
Pius IX, Pope 189n

Pius X, Pope 215n
Pius XI, Pope 190n
Plato 9, 184n, 204n, 211n
Pliny 201n
Pollock, Robert C. 185n
Power, David 125f., 149f., 195n,
    212f.nn, 230

Rahner, Karl 124, 189n, 206n,
    215n, 221n, 230f.
Raphael 166
Ratzinger, Cardinal Joseph 42f.,
    51, 68, 98, 107, 114f., 128, 138,
    153, 188f.nn, 193n, 195n,
    198n, 211f.nn, 214n, 217f.nn,
    231
Ravesi, Gianfranco 191n
Renan, Ernest 191n
Richards, Hubert 84, 202n
Ricoeur, Paul 21, 66f., 95, 204n,
    231
Robinson, John A.T. 16
Romero, Oscar 28
Rousseau, Jean-Jacques 13
Rubin, Miri 166f., 219n, 231
Rutledge, E.Denys 209n

Sartre, Jean-Paul 7, 19, 115
Saward, John 182n, 188n, 192n,
    197n, 200n, 220n, 221n, 231
Sayers, Dorothy L. 231
Scheler, Max 202n, 231
Schillebeeckx, E. 231
Schindler, David L. 206n, 231
Schleiermacher, F. 187n
Schmemann, Alexander 186n,
    231
Schnackenburg, Rudolf 203n,
    232
Scotus, Duns 14, 190n
Servotte, Herman 197n, 232
Shakespeare, William 59, 192n,
    219n

Shaw, George Bernard 182n
Sokolowski, Robert 181n, 184n, 192n, 208n, 232
Spender, Stephen 8
Stalin, Josef 167
Steiner, George 3, 20, 216n, 232
Stevenson, J. 201n, 232
Stockhausen, Carol L. 204n, 232
Storr, Anthony 202n, 232
Sullivan, Francis A. 189n
Sutherland, Graham xx, 182n
Sykes, Stephen 187n, 206n, 232

Taborski, Boleslaw 184n
Tacitus 201n
Tartre, Raymond 215n, 232
Taylor, John V. 171, 232
Teresa of Avila 43, 152
Teresa, Mother 6
Tertullian 70, 82, 192n, 198f.nn, 206n
Theissen, G. 205n, 232
Theodoret of Cyr 191n
Thérèse of the Child Jesus 151
Thompson, Francis 169
Thurian, Max 194n, 210n, 212n, 232
Tillard, Jean-Marie 45, 194nn, 208n, 232
Tolkien, J.R.R. 126

Trethowan, Illtyd 212n, 232

Urban IV, Pope 150, 195n, 216n

Vann, Gerald 65, 200n, 203n, 214n, 232
Vasari 166
Venantius Fortunatus 116
Virgil 200n
Vonier, Anscar 210n, 232

Ward, Barbara 3, 102, 232
Ward, Heather 233
Ware, Timothy 186n
Weil, Simone 3, 233
Wells, H.G. 46
Wesley, Charles 17
Williams, Rowan 188n
Wittgenstein, L. 109
Wojtyla, Karol 178f., 181n, 184n, 233
Also see: John Paul II

Yarnold, Edward 221n, 233
Yeats, William Butler 9
Yevtushenko, Yevgeny 168
Young, F. 233

Zizioulas, John 14, 133, 186n, 200n, 213n, 233
Zundel, Maurice 233